Narrator and Character in *Finnegans Wake*

Michael H. Begnal *and* Grace Eckley

Lewisburg
Bucknell University Press
London: Associated University Presses

© 1975 by Associated University Presses, Inc.
Associated University Presses, Inc.
Cranbury, New Jersey 08512

Associated University Presses
108 New Bond Street
London W1Y OQX, England

Library of Congress Cataloging in Publication Data

Begnal, Michael H
    Narrator and character in Finnegans wake.

    Includes bibliographies.
    1.   Joyce, James, 1882–1941. Finnegans wake.
I. Eckley, Grace. II. Title.
PR6019.09F554   1974   823'.9'12   73–4957
ISBN 0–8387–1337–8

Extracts from FINNEGANS WAKE by James Joyce, Copyright
1939 by James Joyce, © 1967 by George Joyce and Lucia Joyce,
are reprinted by permission of The Viking Press, Inc., with world
rights excluding the U.S.A. granted by The Society of Authors as
the literary representative of the Estate of James Joyce.

PRINTED IN THE UNITED STATES OF AMERICA

_24088_

Contents

Foreword

Wakeschrift, the confounding art of confronting *Finnegans Wake,* has not become a booming business. Despite the productivity of the James Joyce Industry in general, and the commendable industriousness of many capable Joyceans, the *Wake* is still far from being overworked. A new era in *Wake* scholarship became apparent toward the end of the 1950s, and for a while it was assumed that an increasing degree of concentration on *Finnegans Wake* would continue, but it seems to have lasted less than a decade. The boom years produced many basic tools for the enterprising Wakean: a concordance, two censuses, German and Gaelic lexicons, studies of motifs, literary allusions, Irish, Catholic, and Scandinavian elements, songs and nursery rhymes, and examinations of notebooks, drafts, and manuscripts by Fred Higginson, Walton Litz, David Hayman, and Thomas Connolly. *A Wake Newslitter* began publication in 1962 and the *James Joyce Quarterly* followed suit a year later; both have maintained healthy productivity. *Wake* studies had come a long way since the pioneer days of the *Skeleton Key.*

It was generally assumed that with so much work being done on *Finnegans Wake* the trend would continue, and the strategies for future investigations were feverishly being planned. Yet an apparent recession has set in: only two books in the last five years have been published on *Finnegans Wake,* and articles in periodicals are equally scarce. A glance through the contents of the *James Joyce Quarterly* since its 1965 *Wake* issue will indicate how disproportionately minimal are the treatments lately of Joyce's final masterpiece. With so much yet to be accomplished in *Wake* explication, and especially with so many useful apparatuses available for the exegete's assistance, far less is being published now than ten years ago, which makes this brace of solid monographs by Grace Eckley and Michael Begnal all the more welcome. Rather than having to apologize for still another book on James Joyce's *Finnegans Wake*, the writer of its Foreword can instead introduce it not only for its own merits but for its unique contribution.

It is almost inevitable that, given any two scholars writing on the works of James Joyce, both sides of the polarity will be represented: the critical overview of the work as a whole and a close concentration on the text. While Dr. Eckley demonstrates firm control of the *Wake* as an entity, her approach functions in terms of the individual word or phrase, and although Dr. Begnal is sensitive to the fluctuations within Joyce's night-language, he works toward encompassing the *Wake* as a novel. And each employs his own critical tools. For the author of "Queer Mrs Quickenough and Odd Miss Doddpebble," *Finnegans Wake* is a document in folk literature; its antecedents are to be found in the wealth of Irish folklore and throughout world mythology. Her view of the book is centered upon its thematic development, with tree-and-stone utilized as guidelines (touchstones and touchtrees) through the complex jungle of words, and so unfolds layer upon layer of themes and motifs deriving from the basic interaction and contrast between the living tree and the dead stone. She marshals Graves and Frazer, Ovid and Homer, the *Eddas* and the *Book of Kells*, Christ and Christians and the druidy druids, P. W. Joyce and J. A. Joyce, Rees and Rees, and by indirection Jung and Freud, and they serve to underscore the *Wake* as a cosmic novel.

For the author of "The Dream Voices of *Finnegans Wake*," Joyce's book is an exercise in narrative fiction, in addition to whatever else it contains within its epic scope. It is a novel with a plotline and characters, and is organized along artistic lines of development toward the depiction of its events for interpretive perception by the astute reader. It has its roots in the development of the modern novel in the 20th century, specifically in the innovations in literary style, coupled with Joyce's amused interest in the "experiments" of Lewis Carroll. The method of its presentation is contained in its narration, in the succession and diversity of the narrative voices that undertake the piecemeal unfolding of the cumulative dream.

Despite the basic differences in their scholarly approaches to the *Wake*, both authors share many essential virtues in their monographs, not least of which is an appreciation of Joyce's seriousness, humor, and ambitious scheme. They avoid the extremes too often evidenced in attempts to deal with Joyce's impossible book—timidity and hysteria. Neither falters in facing the difficulties or is hesitant in making definite statements about what things mean and how the parts function. Nor do they indulge in grandiose overstatements, idiosyncratic readings, or hobbyhorse theories (neither tries to prove by algebra that Earwicker's grandson is Joyce's grandfather and that he himself is the ghost of his own father). Unafraid to commit themselves to interpreting, they are nonetheless careful to weigh and measure the extent of an interpretation and to document specifically from the text. Perhaps they usher in a new generation of Wakeans. Several decades removed from the 1944 *Skeleton Key*, they neither lean heavily upon it as gospel nor self-consciously feel compelled to refute it at every turn. In fact, both writers maintain a balanced attitude toward the body of secondary material that has grown up around *Finnegans Wake*. They pick and choose selectively for substantiation but treat no previous explication as sacrosanct. Each goes his own way, accepting the text of the *Wake* as the essential source of all verification and insisting that all questions regarding it remain open.

The greatest value of these two essays to the experienced Wakean lies in the fresh approaches offered. Basic aspects of interpretation are reexamined with new insight, and if they do not vote themselves in by unanimous acclaim as final answers, they will hopefully reengender important controversy. Who dreams in *Finnegans Wake*? And how many dreamers are there in it? Who are Shem and Shaun the living sons and daughters of? And who are they when they are somebody else? Who's he when he's at home? What's this here, guv'ner? Does "Joyce says what he means" mean the same as "Joyce means what he says"? What was thaas? Fog was whass? By examining the leaves and the branches, by chipping away at the bark and counting the rings round the trunk, by sifting pebbles and rocks and leaving no stone unturned, Grace Eckley discerns a consistency in the placement and positioning of the opposing elements of Shem/Shaun. By tuning in to the *Wake* stereophonically and putting his ear to the text, Michael Begnal hears distinct voices with changes in pitch and timbre, peculiarities in phraseology and pet expressions, telltale signs of the individual nightspeech of a decade of characters. This sort of scholarship has the ultimate advantage of sending many a Joycean back to the primary text for his own elucidation.

For Grace Eckley the "Anna Livia Plurabelle" chapter stands at the center (not only structurally but thematically) of *Finnegans Wake*. Like Joyce she is willing "to stake everything" on its importance: she treats it as a barometer of the book, beginning her examination of "The Tree and the Stone in *Finnegans Wake*" by offering a studied reading of chapter 8, and then applies what she has gleaned from it and its components to the work as a whole. As she notes, "the washerwomen, in their combined functions of telling the story of Anna Livia and transforming into the brothers Shem and Shaun (the tree and the stone), represent Joyce's view of artistic and material creation and establish characteristics for determining Shem and Shaun identities throughout the novel." This is certainly not an audacious consideration of the basics of the *Wake*, but it does provide the author with a coherent and direct avenue through the maze. From this opening gambit she works with consistency through its ramifications in the work, toward the eventual dissection of that enigmatic "treestone," separating Shem from Shaun with a scalpel, so that in her conclusion she can assert: "I believe that common associations on which Joyce based this novel include items as familiar as the first Psalm's description of the godlike man: 'And he shall be like a tree planted by the rivers of water.' In tree and stone Joyce could embody the philosophy of the young Stephen of the *Portrait* ('The past is consumed in the present and the present is living only because it brings forth the future'—*AP* 251) and thereby present a view of imminent creation."

For Michael Begnal a careful isolation of the separate speakers in *Finnegans Wake* acts as an operative instrument in explicating numerous difficulties. He is intent on proving that "the book is perhaps not quite as complicated as has been made out . . . through an examination of narration and point-of-view " In setting about to achieve his contention, Begnal maintains that

> the single dreamer theory, which names Humphrey Chimpden Earwicker as the sole narrator, overlooks the use of multiple point of view that is almost standard in Joyce's work and creates more critical problems than it overcomes. When one realizes that several people are dreaming together, it becomes much easier to individualize them and to redefine them in greater depth. Though, on the thematic level, all the voices and characters rep-

resent various aspects of the character of HCE, on the primary, narrative level they should and must be seen as separate and distinct. Also, one of the central voices in the novel, that of a faceless and nameless omniscient narrator has escaped a great deal of critical recognition. It is he who provides the framework for the other voices. With his role and purpose in the drama more clearly spelled out, the movements of the Earwickers and those associated with them become more structured and discernible.

And as he uncovers and distinguishes these voices, Begnal systematically provides a reading of *Finnegans Wake* that is coherent and sustained. Both he and Dr. Eckley, coincidentally, spend much of their time listening to voices in the *Wake:* both are conscious of what has too easily and too often been overlooked, that every opinion and pronouncement uttered in *Finnegans Wake* must be analyzed in regard to its source. Pompous Polonius, not Prince Hamlet, cautions against borrowing and lending; evil Iago, not Othello, is the origin of the lecture on reputation. With Shakespeare and Joyce busy paring their fingernails, it is crucial for the reader to discern the actual speaker.

An even odder coincidence in this volume is the demotion of Humphrey Chimpden Earwicker in the estimation of both Grace Eckley and Michael Begnal. So casually accepted as the center of *Finnegans Wake* and even as the composite totality of the *Wake,* HCE now finds himself with second fiddle in hand and relegated to a back seat in the punt. This may be a necessary corrective to both a cycloptic vision and a male-chauvinist misperception, or it may only be an inadvertent adjunct to the particular approaches of these two essays. Dr. Eckley elevates Anna Livia to a kind of primacy in the Wakean scheme of things, and finds it important that from the two washerwomen along the banks of the Liffey the basic contentions of sons Shem and Shaun evolve. Begnal democratizes the book to an even greater extent, finding many more voices—and consequently alternative dreamers—than just Earwicker, especially noting that the unreliable and hypocritical Shaun ironically proves to be the most frequent of the narrative voices. Even so, Begnal goes an important step further. As he discloses the numerous instances at which Shaun destroys the efficacy of his own arguments and reveals himself as a pathetic voice, Begnal also rescues Shem from his role of lesser significance, reminding us that despite Joyce's commendable balance of the two antagonists and fairness to both brothers, it is penman Shem who is the creative artist at the center of Joyce's values—and of the *Wake*.

In this pairing of two assertive and reasonably balanced monographs there may well be an indication of the direction and tone of a new wave of *Wakeschrift* activity. Many of those who had been so energetic in explicating *Finnegans Wake* only a few years ago seem to have run out of steam, and can be discovered of late concentrating their energies on certainly worthwhile but less challenging areas like *Ulysses* and *A Portrait* and *Dubliners*. All Wakeans are painfully aware of what still needs to be done. The necessity for precise explication remains paramount, the word-by-word multiple analysis that is essential for anyone attempting to arrive at a primary level of meaning. This kind of exegesis is often lost when a commentator realizes that he must make a single selection while arguing a specific thesis. The Joycean uses of languages persist as a mystery. Why Nippon English for Saint Patrick? Why lapses into American Negro dialect on occasion and into esoteric and obscure tongues at others? What relationship exists between a historic setting or context and the languages employed at the time? And surely the nature of Joyce's use of language is as important as his use of languages: in an era when the study of linguistics is developing so rapidly, it is appropriate that the new science be brought to bear upon the old practitioner.

Joyce's own metaphor for his creative productivity involved the burrowing into the sides of a mountain with the hope that such tunneling parties will eventually link up. Considering how massive that mountain remains, there is certainly an employable need for more hands at this time. In "Queer Mrs Quickenough and Odd Miss Doddpebble: The Tree and the Stone in *Finnegans Wake*" and "The Dream Voices of *Finnegans Wake:* An Orchestration," Eckley and Begnal have burrowed well and tunneled deep—and seem to have met in mid-mountain. Since every *Wake* telling must by its very nature have its own taling, here in tandem are one pair of "the he and the she of it."

Bernard Benstock
Kent State University

Narrator and Character
in *Finnegans Wake*

PART ONE

The Dreamers at the Wake:
A View of Narration and Point of View
Michael H. Begnal

Once again,
for Cynthia,

The silver apples of the moon,
The golden apples of the sun.

Introduction

The period of the composition of *Finnegans Wake*, the second and third decades of the twentieth century, was a time of radical experimentation in all of the arts. Joyce's final, and possibly greatest, work is still described by many as the farthest any writer has yet attempted to stretch or extend the conventions of the novel, and the furor over its success or failure continues unabated to this day. To Max Eastman in 1932, "reading Joyce's *Work in Progress* is a good deal like chewing gum—it has flavor at the start but you soon taste only the motion of your jaws,"[1] and to David Daiches thirty years later the novel is simply "a purely verbal structure in which the enormous reverberation of meaning is but reverberation of meaning."[2] Joyce himself wrote to his brother Stanislaus, asking jokingly that he quell the rumor "that I founded in Zurich the dadaist movement that is now exciting Paris (report of the Irish press last week)."[3] Whether for or against, readers of *Finnegans Wake* seem unable to speak about the novel in anything but passionate and often shrill tones.

In a time of extreme deviation from the accepted norms of

1. *The Literary Mind* (New York: Viking Press, 1932), p. 66.
2. *The Novel and the Modern World* (Chicago: University of Chicago Press, 1960), p. 122.
3. *Letters of James Joyce*, ed. Richard Ellmann, vol. 2 (New York: Viking Press, 1966), p. 22.

fictional or any other art, however, it should be remembered that Joyce accepts experimental techniques as a means of enhancing his presentation, but remains a classicist, perhaps even a conservative, in his conception of the role of the artist. To him, as to T. S. Eliot, structural unity in a work of art is essential; it should contain nothing that is without meaning. Though such a claim may at first seem a bit flimsy in regard to *Finnegans Wake,* it does not really seem that hard to justify when one carefully examines any given section of the novel in relation to the whole. As Vivian Mercier expresses it, Joyce possessed "a traditional sense of the professional, almost sacred prestige of poetry and learning; a traditional sense of the supreme importance of technique to a writer, coupled with the realization that technique must be learned by imitation, study, and practice."[4] Joyce's mentors are Homer and Vico, rather than Gertrude Stein or Ezra Pound.

The purpose of this study of some of the narrative techniques in *Finnegans Wake* will be to show that the book is perhaps not quite so complicated as has been made out, initially through an examination of narration and point of view. (No claim, however, will be made to "simplification" of the text itself, à la Anthony Burgess.[5]) Recently John Gross complains that: "as crucial a question as the identity of the Dreamer still remains unresolved,"[6] and this problem will be at the center of my discussion. The single-dreamer theory, which names Humphrey Chimpden Earwicker as the sole narrator, overlooks the use of multiple point of view, which is almost standard in Joyce's work and creates more critical problems than it overcomes. When one realizes that several people are dreaming together, it becomes much easier to individualize them and to redefine them in greater depth. We can only

4. *The Irish Comic Tradition* (Oxford: Oxford University Press, 1962), p. 242.
5. *ReJoyce* (New York: W. W. Norton, 1965).
6. *James Joyce* (New York: Viking Press, 1970), p. 81.

agree in small part that: "the chief way of telling a story in *Finnegans Wake* proves to be the metamorphic manner in which identity of narrator or characters is unspecifiable by exclusion."[7] Though on one thematic level all the voices and characters may represent various aspects of the character of HCE, on the primary, narrative level they should and must be seen as separate and distinct. Also, one of the central voices in the novel, that of a faceless and nameless omniscient narrator, has escaped a great deal of critical recognition. It is he who provides the framework for the other voices. With his role and purpose in the drama more clearly spelled out, the movements of the Earwickers and those associated with them become more structured and discernible.

Viewing Joyce's techniques of narration from a different perspective, there are several sequences of narrative action whose resemblances have long been noted, but no one has yet managed to explain what it is they share in common and what Joyce's purpose is in linkage of this kind. The several interpolated tales or fables comprise such a group, and I will attempt to show how one builds upon and grows out of another, and how Joyce uses them both to particularize his characters and to place them in a more general historical setting. Furthermore, it should become clear that the tales are not interpolations at all, in the sense that they interrupt or divert one's attention from the central narrative, for they prove crucial to an understanding of the primary level of action in Chapelizod.

In much the same way, riddles and letters are scattered throughout *Finnegans Wake*, and, by tracing and exploring several of the most important, I would hope to explain how they too confirm the overlying dictum that nothing impinges on the narrative line of the book merely for the sake of

7. John B. Vickery, "*Finnegans Wake* and Sexual Metamorphosis," *Contemporary Literature* 13 (Spring 1972): 215.

amusement or decoration. (Even the hundreds of river names that dot the ALP chapter serve their own thematic function.) The elements of play and puzzlement loom on almost every page of *Finnegans Wake,* as they do on the pages of Sterne, Swift, and Beckett, but never do they join forces with frivolity. As Adaline Glasheen warns: "No question, Joyce is out to trick the reader, play jokes, pose puzzlers, lead up garden paths; but only that queer little band that has always hated Joyce could suppose he had no reason for his tricks."[8]

The *Wake* is more and more becoming the province of the specialist, who bags his limit of Serbo-Croatian words or references to obscure Irish poets and retires self-satisfied from the field, and this is a situation that Joyce himself would have abhorred. In his own strange way, he believed that *Finnegans Wake* has something to offer to everyone. Perhaps he overestimated his own work, as well as overestimating the public's interest in things rich and strange, but it does seem that critical perspectives of the work have in a few instances gone somewhat askew. There *is* a story being told here, and the reader must proceed through the text horizontally, with less emphasis on the vertical, if he is to see what is going on. The critical standards and assumptions that we bring to the conventional novel (plot, character, point of view, purpose, etc.) should be the tools used for this novel too. This may be something of an unusual tale, but it is still a tale as we know one and it has its own specific group of tellers.

Little changed since the publication in the *New Republic* in 1939 of Edmund Wilson's groundbreaking review of *Finnegans Wake,*[9] the critical consensus has been that James Joyce's

8. *A Second Census of Finnegans Wake* (Evanston: Northwestern University Press, 1963), p. xvi.
9. "The Dream of H. C. Earwicker," *The Wound and the Bow* (New York: Galaxy Books, 1965), pp. 198–222. Agreement ranges from Campbell and Robinson's *A Skeleton Key to Finnegans Wake* (New York: Harcourt, Brace, 1944) to Bernard Benstock's *Joyce again's Wake* (Seattle: University of Washington Press, 1965).

novel is the dream of a single character, the pubkeeper Humphrey Chimpden Earwicker. Though alternate theories have been proposed, such as Ruth von Phul's that the son Shem is the dreamer,[10] or Clive Hart's that the mythic giant Finn MacCool is doing the dreaming,[11] almost every commentator has agreed that the narrative is the product of a single, sleep-ridden consciousness. Though Hart himself agrees that due to the HCE-dreamer idea "structural criticism of *Finnegans Wake* has been befogged for over twenty years,"[12] and J.S. Atherton feels that the theory "that Joyce is the dreamer has a great deal to recommend it,"[13] virtually nothing has been written on the subject. Hugh Kenner accounts for the many voices in the novel by seeing all of them as various "disintegrated portions of the dreaming mind"[14] of Earwicker.

Though the last theory is attractive, it fails to explain the multiplicity of styles in the book and makes of Joyce's bourgeois publican a deeply complicated schizophrenic, a characterization that does not seem justified by this narrative. Troubles he certainly has, and those in plenty, and overwhelming guilt as well, but he is more in need of comfort than the psychiatrist's couch. None of the single-dreamer theories explains the sudden jumps from style to style, subject to subject, and voice to voice. J. Mitchell Morse is perhaps closer to the truth when he says: "in *Finnegans Wake* every change of style indicates that another person, awake or half-awake or asleep as they sit up with the body, is dreaming or being

10. "Who Sleeps at *Finnegans Wake?*" *James Joyce Review* 1 (June 1957): 27–38. This view is shared by Francis Thompson in his "Portrait of the Artist Asleep," *Western Review* 14 (Summer 1950): 245–53.

11. *Structure and Motif in Finnegans Wake* (Evanston: Northwestern University Press, 1962), pp. 81–83.

12. *Structure and Motif*, p. 78.

13. *The Books at the Wake* (New York: Viking Press, 1960), p. 12.

14. *Dublin's Joyce* (Bloomington: Indiana University Press, 1956), p. 285.

dreamed about."[15] Morse has not substantiated or pursued this line of reasoning, but he has certainly pointed the way to the solution of one of the book's most complicated problems. In a letter to J.S. Atherton, Harriet Shaw Weaver, Joyce's friend and patron, has provided an important clue:

> The ascription of the whole thing to a dream of HCE seems to me nonsensical. My view is that Mr. Joyce did not intend the book to be looked upon as the dream of any one character, but that he regarded the dream form with its shiftings and changes and chances as a convenient device, allowing the freest scope to introduce any material he wished—and suited to a night-piece.[16]

Despite the fact that most of Joyce's own explication of the content and structure of the *Wake* was divulged in personal letters to Miss Weaver, strangely enough virtually everyone has chosen to discount her statement.

To begin with, we might suspect that Joyce is doing something different here, since each of his books is an additional experimentation, and each goes a step beyond the previous one. As a precedent for the use of several narrators in Joyce's work, of course, one has only to look to *Ulysses*, where the action is seen primarily through the eyes of three narrators—Stephen, Bloom, and Molly—and even Gerty MacDowell and the nameless narrator of the "Cyclops" chapter are allowed their views. It should come as no suprise, then, that Joyce would use the same device again, in an even more complicated way, to increase the fullness of his presentation by comment from several different perspectives. It is only if one realizes and acknowledges the presence of these multiple points of view that the many difficulties involved with shifts of style and

---

15. "On Teaching *Finnegans Wake*," *Twelve and a Tilly* (London: Faber and Faber, 1966), p. 69.
16. Quoted in Atherton, *Books at the Wake*, p. 17.

subject matter can be overcome. Bernard Benstock notes that "a change in the poetic style of a paragraph indicates the introduction of a new motif or a new variant on the theme under consideration,"[17] but this change also indicates a new speaker.

Rather than being the dream of a single character (though the thoughts of HCE are of primary importance), the narrative of *Finnegans Wake* is composed of multiple layers of consciousness or dream that shift back and forth as one is called upon to speak by the narrator, or as one intrudes upon another. Individual characters are brought to the front of the dream-stage and afforded their share of comment and limelight until it is the turn of another. Each character, as we shall see, has certain specific topics and special ways of discussing them. *Finnegans Wake* is a web of dreams, each connected to, and quivering at, the vibrations of the others. The answer to the ninth query of the "Questions" chapter, which has to do with the dream structure itself, is: "A collideorscape!" (143.28), with its connotations of kaleidoscope and colliding or conflicting points of view. Later, in the stage directions to the Mime, we learn that the production is to be staged with "nightly redistribution of parts and players by the puppetry producer and daily dubbing of ghosters" (219.7). Perhaps this is what Frank Budgen, probably Joyce's closest confidante, hints at when he says: "All the characters in the book seem to have read, marked, learned and inwardly digested universal history; that is to say, read it at a glance, marked it with their thumbmarks, learned it from back to front and digested it while sleeping. When they have it properly in their bloomstream they play it."[18]

17. *Joyce-again's Wake,* p. 158.
18. *James Joyce and the Making of Ulysses* (New York: Smith and Haas, 1934), p. 307.

The narrative structure of *Finnegans Wake* might be seen as several different streams of consciousness, each superimposed upon the other—in other words, an extension or complication of the basic technique of *Ulysses*. Each of the ten central voices or consciousnesses (HCE, ALP, Shem, Shaun, Issy, Mamalujo, and the fairly objective narrator— even Kate and Joe are occasionally allowed equal time) is tuned in to the wave-lengths of the others, and is free to break in with his own comments at any time he can. Hans Castorp's revelation in *The Magic Mountain* might also be applied to Joyce's novel: "Now I know that it is not out of our single souls we dream. We dream anonymously and communally, if each after his fashion."[19] And as a variation, Proust has his Marcel discover:

> Once the novelist has brought us to that state, in which, as in all purely mental states, every emotion is multiplied ten-fold, into which his book comes to disturb us as might a dream, but a dream more lucid, and of a more lasting impression, than those which come to us in sleep; why, then, for the space of an hour he sets free within us all the joys and sorrows in the world.[20]

Within the text are constant allusions to a wireless or short-wave radio as a central symbol or unifying device, and the basic problem in an understanding of the action is the recognition on the part of the reader of the individual voices of the characters. For an objectification of this we might turn to the description of the set in Earwicker's pub. It is a

> tolvtubular high fidelity daildialler, as modern as tomorrow and in appearance up to the minute . . . equipped with supershielded umbrella antennas for distance getting and connected by the magnetic links of a Bellini-Tosti coupling system with a vitaltone

19. Thomas Mann, *The Magic Mountain* (New York: Alfred Knopf, 1921), p. 495.
20. Marcel Proust, *Swann's Way* (New York: Modern Library, 1956), p. 119.

speaker, capable of capturing skybuddies, harbour craft eminences, key clickings, vaticum cleaners, due to woman formed mobile or man made static and bawling the whowle hamshack and wobble down in an eliminium sounds pound so as to serve him up a melegoturny marygoraumd filtered for allirish earths and ohmes. (309.15 ff.)

Another parallel is the situation in the "Lessons" chapter, where the three youngsters comment upon the main text with side and footnotes whenever they so desire, as the narrative moves along its way. Or we might listen in on the short-wave communication typical of the Four Old Men:

(hello, Hibernia!)—from sea to sea (Matt speaking!) . . . /to/ (Marcus Lyons speaking!) . . . /to/ (Lucas calling, hold the line!) . . . /to/ (Johnny MacDougall speaking, give me trunks, miss!). (388.30 ff.)

Examples of this kind abound throughout the pages of the *Wake*, and we may remember as yet another situation in Book III, chapter three where the sleeping body of Shaun, now Yawn, serves as a radio receiver for the Four: "His dream monologue was over, of cause, but his drama parapolylogic had yet to be, affact" (476.4). All the characters in the novel speak through this sleeper, but he serves only as a medium through which they may be heard and is not able to control them.

Finally, as another item on the list of possible models or analogues is Lewis Carroll's *Sylvie and Bruno*, which Joyce admits to having read while in the process of putting *Finnegans Wake* together. Both Atherton and Kenner have mentioned this,[21]

21. Atherton says that: "it may even be time to say that from the Viconian standpoint Joyce regarded Carroll as another incarnation of himself," *The Books at the Wake*, p. 135.

but neither illustrates many of the definite parallels. Carroll felt that *Sylvie* had to be something different from *Alice* and *Through the Looking Glass*: "The path I timidly explored—believing myself to be 'the first that ever burst into that silent sea'—is now a beaten highroad: all the wayside flowers have long ago been trampled into the dust: and it would be courting disaster for me to attempt that style again."[22] As for the problem of Joyce's having considered the children's book seriously, we might compare this speech of Carroll's Chancellor:

> Your true friend is the *Sub-Warden*! Day and night he is brooding on your wrongs—I should say your *rights*—that is to say your *wrongs*—no, I mean your *rights*—" ('Don't talk no more!' growled the man under the window. 'You're making a mess of it!'). (Carroll, *Works*, p. 388),

with Shaun's: "It's more important than air—I mean eats—air (Oops, I never open momouth but I pack mefood in it)" (437.19).

Shem and Shaun, as Atherton suggests, could easily be put up against Carroll's Uggug and Bruno, while Issy is actually quite close in character to Sylvie. Also, Joyce would have been sure to capitalize on such linguistic situations as this:

> "So the Mouse gave the Man his Shoe. And the Man were welly glad, 'cause he hadn't got but one Shoe, and he were hopping to get the other."
> Here I ventured on a question. "Do you mean 'hopping' or 'hoping'?"
> "Bofe," said Bruno. (Carroll, *Works*, p. 526)

The ending of *Sylvie and Bruno*, with its rising sun and prayer to the day, is almost a direct parallel with the concluding chapter of the *Wake*. Carroll places his hope in the cyclical coming of the new day:

22. *The Works of Lewis Carroll*, ed. Roger L. Green (London: Paul Hamlyn, 1965), p. 381.

Fading with the Night, the chilly mists, and the noxious vapours, and the heavy shadows, and the wailing gusts, and the owl's melancholy hootings: rising, with the Day, the darting shafts of light, and the wholesome morning breeze, and the warmth of a dawning life, and the mad music of the lark! Look Eastward! (Carroll, *Works*, p. 538)

Most important, perhaps, is Carroll's own description of his technique in his Preface: "I have supposed a human being to be capable of various psychical states, with varying degrees of consciousness, as follows: . . . (C) a form of trance, in which, while *un*conscious of actual surroundings, and apparently asleep, he (i.e., his immaterial essence) migrates to other scenes, in the actual world, or in Fairyland, and is conscious of the presence of Fairies" (Carroll, *Works*, p. 539). Here is something of an approximate description of what is going on in the *Wake*, as one character or speech blends into another and scenes change with each speaker.

1
The Voices of the Parents

The dreamers of the drama have their own peculiar and particular modes of speech and matters of concern, and on these terms we can tell them apart and assign identification to any part of the novel. Since it is the voice of HCE that is heard quite frequently and at extended length, its characteristics, both stylistic and thematic, should fittingly be treated at the beginning of this investigation. Following the shooting of the Russian General, in a play on the pub's television set, after an evening in which the drinkers have torn his reputation to shreds, HCE, before collapsing from drunkenness, takes the stand in his own defense:

—Guilty but fellows culpows! It was felt by me sindeade, that submerged doughdoughty doubleface told waterside labourers. But since we for athome's health have chanced all that, the wild whips, the wind ships, the wonderlost for world hips, unto their foursquare trust prayed in aid its plumptylump piteousness which, when it turtled around seeking a thud of surf, spake to approach from inherdoff trisspass through minxmingled hair. Though I may have hawked it, said, and selled my how hot peas after theactrisscalls from my imprecurious position and though achance I could have emptied a pan of backslop down drain by whiles of dodging a rere from the middenprivet appurtenant thereof, salving the presents of the board of wumps and pumps, I am ever incalpable, where release of prisonals properly is concerned, of unlifting upfallen girls wherein dangered from them in thereopen out of unadulteratous bowery, with those hintering influences from an angelsexonism. It was merely my barely till their oh offs. Missaunderstaid. (363.20–36)

Immediately apparent in this brief excerpt is one of the main stylistic pointers to HCE: a tendency toward long, involved, disjointed sentences that seem to jump freely from one association to another. As he makes one statement, he quickly qualifies it, adds whatever associated information occurs to him as he goes along, and wanders farther and farther from where he began. There is usually little discernible rhythm to his constructions (despite the "whips-ships-hips" in this excerpt), as there will be in the statements of the other characters. His tone always borders on the pompous, and he is fond of clichés ("athome's health"; "unlifting upfallen girls"), though he often confuses them (as in the last example and in "may the duvlin rape the handsomst" [364.25]). Perhaps the easiest way to recognize HCE is through his stutter, which becomes more noticeable as he becomes more nervous and involved in what he is saying ("doughdoughty doubleface"). In the next few lines we will stumble over "twingty to twangty too" and "peace peace perfectpeace." As the narrator informs us, he "stoatters some; but quite a big bug after the dahlias" (596.27).

As Earwicker warms to his subject and passes on to a specific denial of the charge that young girls are his main sexual interest, the *double entendres* or Freudian slips increase proportionately with the vehemence of his denial. Both "wonderlost" and "dodging" point to the suspicious role of Lewis Carroll. His first few sentences are relatively free of such inadvertant punning, but as they progress they show a marked lack of control ("my imprecurious position" for "my impecunious position"; "salving the presents" for "saving the presence"). The last long sentence of the section has lapsed into chaos as HCE's unconscious sexual desires break to the surface: "unlifting upfallen girls"; "unadulteratous bowery," and the final, scintillating "angelsexonism" with its multiple associations of holy and unholy intercourse, onanism, and Anglo-Saxonism. Characteristically, he incriminates himself once again through the force of his lusts, but an important distinction can be drawn between Earwicker's linguistic missteps and those of his son Shaun. While the former's sexual tastes may not be those of the ordinary man, they are always presented in a forthright manner, never with the snicker and the leer that seem omnipresent in Shaun's lecture to the girls of St. Bride's:

> Whalebones and buskbutts may hurt you (thwackaway thwuck!) but never lay bare your breast secret (dickette's place!) to joy a Jonas in the Dolphin's Barncar with your meetual fan, Doveyed Covetfilles, comepulsing paynattention spasms between the averthisment for Ulikah's wine and a pair of pulldoors of the old cupiosity shape. (434.25–30)

Earwicker is, as he says, "missaunderstaid." The sexual punning in Shaun's speeches almost always has an air of intention and self-knowledge about it, but Earwicker's slips usually seem just that—mistakes in word or syllable choice that his conscious mind is not strong enough to resist. Like Bloom, HCE transgresses against accepted morality, but, again like Bloom, he is basically a good person who has nothing to do with smallness and nastiness. His essential nature is reflected in his speech. As Campbell and Robinson say: "he is a man who has won his place in society, a place not of high distinction but of decent repute."[1]

In a different light, here is Earwicker, boastful, loving, and fond, describing his first sexual encounter with his bride:

1. *A Skeleton Key to Finnegans Wake* (New York: Harcourt, Brace, 1944), p. 7.

But I was firm with her. And I did take the reached of my delights, my jealousy, ymashkt, beyashmakt, earswathed, snoutsnooded, and did raft her flumingworthily and did leftlead her overland the pace, from lacksleap up to liffsloup, tiding down, as portreeve should, whimpering by Kevin's creek and Hurdlesford and Gardener's Mall, long riverside drive, embankment large, to Ringsend Flott and Ferry, where she began to bump a little bit, my dart to throw . . . and I abridged with domfine norsemanship till I had done abate her maidan race, my baresark bride, and knew her fleshly when with all my bawdy did I her whorship, min bryllupswibe. (547. 14–29)

He demonstrates his masculinity and his strength in quite graphic terms, yet he shows his love too in the doubleness of "with all my bawdy did I her whorship," (the "worship" is self evident), and closes the statement with "so streng we were in one." He is, for the public, the Henry Millerish dominant male, but he is also the lover who participates in a shared experience. He can be sexual and spiritual at once, as Anna Livia plays Galatea to his Pygmalion. Humphrey Chimpden Earwicker encompasses the oneness and the disparity of all love's parts, something for which his sons can only strive. He is Leopold Bloom raised to an even more cosmic fulfillment.

Earwicker's statements in *Finnegans Wake* are integrally wrapped up with the sin of uncertain nature that he did, or did not, commit sometime in the recent past in Phoenix Park. As is well known, the sin involved Earwicker's encounter with two girls and three soldiers, is sexual in nature, and runs a gamut of possibility from voyeurism to seduction.[2] "Which moral turpitude would you select of the two, for choice, if you had your way? Playing bull before shebears or the hindlegs off a clotheshorse" (522. 14). (It is interesting to recall that Cissy

2. J. Mitchell Morse, however, in "HCE's Chaste Agony," *Yale Review* 56 (March 1967): 397–405, feels the sin may be essentially religious.

Caffrey in *Ulysses* accuses Stephen: "I was in company with
the soldiers and they left me to do—you know and the young
man ran up behind me."[3]) Consequently, almost without
exception, each of the statements of HCE is concerned with
self-justification, with an avowal of innocence and denial of
every possible charge he can imagine. He is at pains to point
out his respectable status in the community as a businessman,
husband, and father, and often he says he is hurt that such
terrible things might be believed of him: "I protest there is
luttrelly not one teaspoonspill of evidence at bottomlie"
(534.9); "Pity poor Haveth Childers Everywhere" (535.34).
He even goes so far as to call himself "respectable" nineteen
times in a little more than two pages (543.28–545.12). Along
with this, he must continually uphold his sexual purity: "I
am ever incalpable [like Gladstone], where release of prisonals
properly is concerned, of unlifting upfallen girls" (363.32);
"I would not know to contact such gretched youngsteys"
(538.24). He brings the subject up so often and discusses it at
such great length that any listener is bound to become suspicious. These, then, are HCE's two central topics each time
his voice is heard: his worthiness and his accomplishments
in society, and his freedom from sins of the flesh. That he
manages in the course of his avowals to destroy his own fic-
tions is a consequence of his guilt and uncertainty.

One of the major keys to an understanding of Earwicker's
character, and a book that Joyce is almost sure to have read,
is Sigmund Freud's *Totem and Taboo* (first published in 1913).
It is well known that Joyce detested Freud and Jung ("Jung-
fraud's Messongebook" [460.20]), but he was certainly not
above using them for all they were worth. He probably refers
to Freud's study in: "the cubs are after me, it zeebs, the whole

---

3. James Joyce, *Ulysses* (New York: Modern Library, 1961), p. 587. Further
references will be included in the text.

totem pack" (480.30). Discussing the relationship between the psychic lives of savages and neurotics, Freud offers an almost perfect description of HCE: "a compulsion neurotic may be oppressed by a sense of guilt which is appropriate to a wholesale murderer, while at the same time he acts toward his fellow beings in a most considerate and scrupulous manner, a behaviour which he evinced since his childhood."⁴ The work contains a lengthy discussion of exogamy, the incest prohibition, one of HCE's major concerns in his relationship with Issy, as well as continuing with a treatment of the innate desire of the sons to overthrow the father. As Edmund L.. Epstein says, Earwicker "is sure that the children are plotting to overthrow him, and he keeps trying to destroy them or, at least, to render them impotent."⁵ Freud's following comment might explain as well the strife between Shem and Shaun: "Sexual need does not unite men; it separates them. Though the brothers had joined forces in order to overcome the father, each was the other's rival among the women. Each one wanted to have them all to himself like the father."⁶

As a final tie, we might examine Earwicker's name which, we are told, is derived from the earwig, a pestiferous insect. The first of our Dubliner's line, named Humphrey or Harold, was a caretaker of the king's roads who spent most of his time sleeping and drinking in his cottage, so that the sudden appearance of the royal party resulted in a great deal of consternation. His majesty demanded to know what "had caused yon causeway to be thus potholed" (31.5), to which his trusty retainer, with great quickness of mind, replied that he had been busy ridding the area of bothersome pests: "Naw, yer maggers, aw war jist a cotchin on thon bluggy earwuggers"

4. Sigmund Freud, *Totem and Taboo* (New York: Vintage Books, 1946), p. 113.
5. *The Ordeal of Stephen Dedalus* (Carbondale: S. Illinois University Press, 1971), p. 13.
6. Freud, *Totem and Taboo*, pp. 185–86.

(31.10). From that day forward the family name was Earwicker, and Freud would explain it thus:

> a name is not indifferent and conventional as it seems to us, but is something important and essential. A man's name is one of the main constituents of his person and perhaps a part of his psyche. . . . The practical need of differentiation compelled the individual tribes to assume names, and therefore they tolerated the names which every tribe ascribed to the other. . . . The fact that the names which thus originated were borrowed from animals is not further remarkable and need not have been felt by primitive man as abuse or derision. . . . names given from without that were first meant to be derisive were accepted by those nicknamed and voluntarily borne.[7]

For Joyce, who constantly experimented with the possibilities of his own name, here was the rationale for Earwicker.[8]

Since, as befits the head of the household, Earwicker's consciousness is the strongest, and it is he who breaks in most upon the others, we might attempt to enumerate the causes of these breakthroughs. As the characters sleep, it seems that each, besides having his own thoughts, is tuned in to those of the others, and each can be stirred into action by an outside thought that he finds emotionally threatening or alarming. In such an instance the character affected will attempt to interpose his side of the story or even, if he proves strong enough, censor the offending statement entirely. Shaun, as Jaun, perhaps sums up the situation best as he speaks of his family: "I feel spirts of itchery outching out from all over me and only for the sludgehummer's force in my hand to hold them the darkens alone knows what'll who'll be saying of next" (439.22). As has already been noted, HCE is most sen-

---

7. *Ibid.,* pp. 145–46.
8. John B. Vickery sees the technique of naming as derivative from Frazer's *Golden Bough* in "*Finnegans Wake* and Sexual Metamorphosis," *Contemporary Literature* 13 (Spring 1972): 213–42.

sitive about the events in Phoenix Park, and so becomes involved momentarily in Book III, chapter 3 as Anna Livia strives to justify his actions to the Four Old Men who are questioning every available witness. She has just begun to describe his patriotism (491.26), and Luke asks: "And for that he was allaughed? And then baited? The whole gammat?" (492.3). Unable to contain himself, Earwicker breaks in with a string of almost incomprehensible excuses and justifications: "Loonacied! Marterdyed!! Madwakemiherculossed!!! Judascessed!!!! Pairaskivvymenassed!!!!! Luredogged!!!!!! And, needatellye, faulscrescendied!!!!!!!" (492.5). Understandably, Luke is stunned by the outburst and can make nothing of it, while Anna Livia continues with her calm defense of "my dodear devere revered mainhirr" (492.16).

In another instance in the same section, the Four are confused by several different voices that all speak at once. Again sounding like a shortwave radio operator, Matt says: "Now we're gettin it. Tune in and pick up the forain counties! Hello!" (500.35). They are finally able to contact the daughter Issy, but unfortunately she first asks for the time, and all action is momentarily suspended:

> Tit! What is the ti. . ?
>
> SILENCE. (501.5)

The reason for this seemingly irrational interruption is again to be found in Earwicker's guilt. While walking through the Park on the day after those shadowy occurrences, HCE was accosted by the Cad, Magrath, who asked him for the time: "could he tell him how much a clock it was" (35.18). Mistaking this request for an inquiry about the two girls and three soldiers, Earwicker begins the first of his many self-justifications: "there is not one tittle of truth, allow me to tell you, in that purest of fiffib fabrications" (36.33), and gives himself away.

From this point on, the asking of the time or the mention of a clock is to Earwicker an attempt to indict him, and he is immediately put on his guard. So it is that, when he hears once again the fateful question, he silences the speaker at once, and the narrative halts for a moment until it can be begun again on another track with Shaun as substitute speaker. Issy, scared away, reprimands her mirror personality a little later for causing the uproar: "you are a viry vikid girl to go in the dreemplace and at that time of the draym and it was a very wrong thing to do, even under the dark flush of night, dare all grand passia [HCE]" (527.5).

HCE even seems able to influence another character's speeches, especially those of Shaun, to whom he is closest. As Shaun is quizzed by the Four on the sins of his father, his statements are punctuated by derisive laughs, which he says he had not intended: "I didn't say it aloud, sir. I have something inside of me talking to myself" (522.25). This "something" is diagnosed by the old men as "homosexual cathexis of empathy" (522.30), and the initial letters of the term point clearly to the influence of the father, HCE. Thus Earwicker, whenever he feels threatened about the goings on in Phoenix Park, will interrupt or take over the narrative line, or will shape the replies of the other characters to his own ends. There do seem to be definite explanations for what Campbell and Robinson call "incoherent shifts of scene and character."[9]

There is one other type of situation that can induce the publican to intrude, and that is a welling up of sexual desire for his daughter, Issy, or any young girl in general. Whether the attitude of the girl be innocent or enticing, there are certain occasions in *Finnegans Wake* where Earwicker cannot resist an impulse to make his presence known. Such an instance occurs in the "Mime of Mick, Nick, and the Maggies"

9. *A Skeleton Key to Finnegans Wake*, p. 65.

(219 ff.), as Issy imagines herself with her ideal lover "Stainusless," or Shaun, or Stanislaus Joyce. The tone of her reverie waxes quite lush and becomes too much for the eavesdropping HCE:

> Next to our shrinking selves we love sensitivas best. For they are the Angeles. Brick, fauve, jonquil, sprig, fleet, nocturne, smiling bruise. For they are an Angele's garment. We will be constant (what a word!) and bless the day, for whole hours too, yes, for sold long syne as we shall be heing in our created being of ours elvishness, the day you befell, you dreadful temptation! (238.8)

He throws all caution to the wind, answering her "Will bee all buzzy one another minnies for the mere effect that you are so fuld of pollen yourself. Teomeo!" (238.34), with a cry of "Daurdour," or "daughter," from the depths of his sleep. The interruption is overlooked, as such breaks always seem to be, and the speech is concluded by a dance of the Maggies: "ringing hands in hands in gyrogyrorondo" (239.26). Later, Issy will again feel his presence: "somebody's coming, I feel for a fect" (248.25), but he seems to restrain himself and does not intrude.

In contrast to Matthew, Mark, Luke, and John, or Mamalujo, whose stances are passive and voyeuristic when confronted with a sexual scene in *Finnegans Wake* (they observe the lovemaking of Tristan and Isolde as hovering seagulls and that of HCE and ALP as the four posts of the bed), Earwicker always becomes excited and involved, and his consciousness cannot help breaking in upon the situation. We must examine carefully each section of the novel in which the two above-mentioned thematic lines are primary, since it is likely that Earwicker's voice can be heard above or through the others. As the narrator assures us in Book I, chapter 3: "if you are looking for the bilder [HCE] deep your ear on the movietone!" (62.8). Earwicker can be separated from the others, both by an awareness of his style and tone and awareness of the instances in which he is most likely to speak.[10] If we are attuned to his voice's peculiarities and placed on guard by the unfolding of certain events that are closest to Earwicker, we can separate his speech from the "babbling, bubbling, chattering" (195.1) that abounds in *Finnegans Wake*.[11]

The voice of Anna Livia Plurabelle presents another difficulty, since it is heard at various times on two different levels—the voice of the wife of HCE and that of the spirit of the river Liffey. It would be well also to separate from these two voices the approximations or imitations of her speech that are put on or assumed by other characters. The ALP chapter (196–216), for instance, is primarily about Anna Livia, yet at no time does she speak within it. Rather, a kind of flowering "river-speech" is adopted by the two washerwomen who discuss her while doing their laundry on the bank of the river:

> She was just a young thin pale soft shy slim slip of a thing then, sauntering, by silvamoonlake and he was a heavy trudging lurching lieabroad of a Curraghman, making his hay for whose sun to shine on, as tough as the oaktrees (peats be with them!) used to rustle that time down by the dykes of killing Kildare, for forstfellfoss with a plash across her. (202.26)

Though the women are on one level alter egos of ALP, they are certainly individualized characters in this context, presented by the narrator, and their discussion serves to give the reader an initial description of Anna Livia and the flavor of her language.

10. Stuart Gilbert has noted that "each of the polymorphous personages of the work has his appropriate rhythm," *James Joyce's Ulysses* (New York: Vintage Books, 1958), p. 242, though style and tone might be more precise than rhythm.

11. HCE's major speeches may be found at the following locations: 36.20–36.24; 54.20–55.2; 82.21–83.3; 363.20–366.30; 532.6–554.9.

Just previous to this, Shem too has imitated his mother's speech in describing her: "little oldfashioned mummy, little wonderful mummy, ducking under bridges, bellhopping the weirs, dodging by a bit of bog, rapidshooting round the bends, by Tallaght's green hills and the pools of the phooka and a place they call it Blessington and slipping sly by Sallynoggin, as happy as the day is wet" (194.32). It seems that Anna Livia, as well as Earwicker, does have some effect on the other characters in the dream, since whenever they speak of her their own language takes on the rhythmic cadence, the alliteration and onomatopoeia that are characteristically hers. Obviously, however, the reader must be on the alert that he does not mistake these interludes for statements of ALP herself, for one soon learns that the adoption of her style by a character does not also mean the adoption of her sentiments. The washerwomen divulge the embarrassing rumor that she is "throwing all the neiss little whores in the world at him [HCE]" (200.29), and Shem will often use her style to denigrate his father, as two cases in point. These are things that the husband-sheltering Anna Livia would never do. She does not have the great influence over others that HCE has, and she is unable to change or counter ways of thinking that are contrary to her own. Campbell and Robinson call her "the eternally fructive and lovebearing principle in the world,"[12] and she should be seen as passive, as opposed to the active HCE.

The two voices or aspects of Anna Livia might best be defined from an examination of the speech that begins at 617.30 and closes at 628.16, the end of the book, since the section begins with ALP as the living, human citizen of Chapelizod but is continued at 619.20 by the spirit of the river: "Soft morning, city! Lsp! I am leafy speafing." The

12. *A Skeleton Key to Finnegans Wake*, p. 10.

first half of the speech is couched in the form of a gossipy letter, and the language might remind one very much of Molly Bloom:

> That we were treated not very grand when the police and everybody is all bowing to us when we go out in all directions on Wanterlond Road with my cubarola glide? And, personably speaking, they can make their beaux to my alce, as Hillary Allen sang to the opennine Knighters. Item, we never were chained to a chair, and, bitem, no widower whother soever followed us about with a fork on Yankskilling Day. Meet a great civilian (proud lives to him!) who is gentle as a mushroom and a very affectable when he always sits forenenst us for his wet while to all whom it may concern Sully is a thug from all he drunk though he is a rattling fine bootmaker in his profession. (618.20)

There is a realistic, slangy lilt to the passage, which Joyce had already captured with Molly and Martha Clifford (not to mention Nora Barnacle). Anna Livia's scatterbrained pride in the respect she and her husband draw from the town extends to the fine character of a citizen who frequents their pub, as compared to the slovenly ways of Sully, who had a hand in slandering HCE. Charmingly and realistically, however, she must admit that the latter is a fine bootmaker, whatever his damning flaws. She is quite forthright and unselfconscious, in contrast to her husband and her sons, and never does she lose her composure as they so often do. Since her mind is cluttered with the many associations and commitments of the mundane world, she manages to hold upon proportion and reality that is perhaps the strongest in her family.

Anna Livia, less voluble than her relatives, speaks quite rarely in *Finnegans Wake*,[13] though she is often in the thoughts of the other characters in the drama. When she does speak, her subject is always her husband and family, and she is

13. ALP's major speeches may be found at the following locations: 491.26–495.33; 565.18–566.6; 617.30–619.19; 619.20–628.16.

mainly concerned to protect her husband and rehabilitate
him in the eyes of the populace. As has been noted above, she
does not have the strength, or perhaps the inclination, to
break in upon the narrative of others, but whenever she is
called upon she will sing the praises of HCE. He was brave
enough to enlist for the Crimean War: "he stepped into the
breach and put on his recriution trousers and riding apron
in Baltic Bygrad" (491.34), and all the malicious rumors are
a plot of the nefarious Magrath and his henchman Sully, who
"smells cheaply of Power's spirits, like a deepsea dibbler, and
he is not fit enough to throw guts down to a bear" (495.4).

Anna Livia is the only one of the characters to speak well
and convincingly of Earwicker, for Shaun's approbation of
his father is always damaged and undercut by the sexual *double
entendres* that he cannot eliminate from his speech. What lends
a good deal of credence to what ALP has to say is the important fact that she tries to view her husband clearly, with all
his faults, and is still able to support him: "What about his
age? says you. What about it? says I. I will confess to his sins
and blush me further" (494.30). She does not bother to white-
wash him, never lapses into the maudlin, self-pitying confession that he himself may employ, and still feels justified in
remaining at his side. Also, she can comfort her children as
well as her husband, as in this moment with Shem: "You were
dreamend dear. . . . Sonly all in your imagination, dim. . . .
While elvery stream winds seling on for to keep this barrel
of bounty rolling and the nightmail afarfrom morning nears"
(565.18). Anna Livia's speech is herself—feminine and
motherly, protective, a bit coarse, with enough insight to
laugh occasionally at herself and those she champions. To
differentiate her further from her husband: "Every third man
has a chink in his conscience and every other woman has a
jape in her mind" (486.11).

The speech of Anna Livia as river spirit serves as a coda

within a coda, for, just as the final chapter of *Finnegans Wake*
takes us outside the narrative line and comments in general
upon it: "It was a long, very long, a dark, very dark, an all-
burt unend, scarce endurable, and we could add mostly quite
various and somewhat stumbletumbling night" (598.6), so
too the final speech takes us outside and above the specific
female Anna Livia Plurabelle to the voice of all-enduring
woman. The Dublin accents of ALP have been modulated by
the alliterative and cadenced tones of the feminine spirit of
the Liffey:

> Ho hang! Hang ho! And the clash of our cries till we spring to
> be free. Auravoles, they says, never heed of your name! But I'm
> loothing them that's here and all I lothe. Loonely in me loneness.
> For all their faults. I am passing out. O bitter ending! I'll slip
> away before they're up. They'll never see. Nor know. Nor miss
> me. And it's old and old it's sad and old it's sad and weary. I go
> back to you, my cold mad feary father, till the near sight of the
> mere size of him, the moyles and moyles of it, moananoaning,
> makes me seasilt saltsick and I rush, my only, into your arms. I
> see them rising! Save me from those therrble prongs! Two more.
> Onetwo moremens more. So. Avelaval. My leaves have drifted
> from me. All. But one clings still. I'll bear it on me. To remind
> me of. Lff! So soft this morning, ours. Yes. Carry me along,
> taddy, like you done through the toy fair! (627.31)

As the voice speaks of her rejection by those she loves, it
retains its relevance to the final position of Anna Livia, yet
it certainly cannot be accepted as the voice of an actual character. It expresses the frustrations of all wives and mothers,
yet it actually describes the rush of the river from the mountains to the sea. The river departs to renew and replenish
itself in the sea, while Anna Livia must regenerate herself in
her love for her husband and family. The actual tones of the
speech are close to those of Anna Livia, but there is a much
heavier emphasis here on "s" and "f" sounds to capture

onomatopoetically the sounds of the flow of the river and the stirring of the leaves of the tree, both symbols of ALP. Clive Hart describes the essence of Anna Livia as "the female principle of flux and continuity,"[14] and this final section, differing in both tone and content from what she has expressed previously, captures the spirit of ALP as both real woman and regenerative force. While the voices of the characters are within, and a part of, the actual dream drama, the speech of the river encompasses the events of the night-piece from without and transports the narrative from an individual to a universal perspective.

Thus we may see that the voices of the elder Earwickers are separate and distinct, each dealing with its own preoccupation and each reliant upon the action of the many dreams that take place on this single night. Though the consciousness of HCE has the greatest strength and vitality, the voice of his wife can be heard in its own right, as can the voices of his children, and no one character's mind is controlling them all. That they are individual can be seen both from the unique differences in modes and methods of speech, and from the definite topical preserves that each has staked out as his or her own. Once one realizes that HCE is not alone in his dreaming, one can account for many of the happenings in *Finnegans Wake* that were previously unexplicable. Many people dream, and, consequently, individual events have many interpretations and many effects. As Joyce explained to Miss Weaver in a letter of 1926: "One great part of every human existence is passed in a state which cannot be rendered sensible by the use of wideawake language, cutanddry grammar and goahead plot."[15]

14. *Structure and Motif in Finnegans Wake* (Evanston: Northwestern University Press, 1962), p. 202.
15. *Letters of James Joyce*, ed. Richard Ellmann, vol. 3 (New York: Viking Press, 1966), p. 364.

2
Some Other Sleepers at the Wake

Without a doubt it is the voice of Shaun, eldest son and favorite of HCE, that is heard most insistently and most often throughout the pages of *Finnegans Wake*. Besides answering most of the questions in Book I, chapter 6, and describing Shem in chapter 7 of the same Book, Shaun's dreaming mind is displayed at great length in the whole of Book III. He is certainly the most forward of the Earwicker family, and, the successor to his father in the Viconian scheme of things, he stands out as one of the most important characters in the novel. Adaline Glasheen notes that "with Shaun, Joyce scourges the intellectual and esthetic abuse of Irish Catholicism with a ferocity positively medieval,"[1] but, as well, Shaun's mind is made to stand for that of the typical bourgeois, in all its pettiness, repression, and self-importance.[2] Modeled in part on the character of Stanislaus Joyce, Shaun is a creature of his time and certainly a product of the paralysis of contemporary society. Here he is, lecturing his sister Issy on her recent, rather scandalous behavior:

1. *A Second Census of Finnegans Wake* (Evanston: Northwestern University Press, 1963), p. 237.

2. Ruth von Phul goes so far as to say: "Shaun the Post combines the antagonists and foils of all Joyce's books. . . . He is the bosom enemy, the inner adversary," "Circling the Square: A Study of Structure," *James Joyce Miscellany: Third Series* (Carbondale: S. Illinois University Press, 1962), p. 251.

I overstand you, you understand. Asking Annybettyelsas to carry
your parcels and you dreaming of net glory. You'll ging naemaer
wi'Wolf the Ganger. Cutting chapel, were you? and had dates
with slickers in particular hotels, had we? Lonely went to play
your mother, isod? You was wiffriends? Hay, dot's a doll yarn!
Mark mean then! I'll homeseek you, Luperca as sure as there's
a palatine in Limerick and in striped conference here's how.
Nerbu de Bios! If you twos goes to walk upon the railway, Gard,
and I'll goad to beat behind the bush! See to it! Snip! It's up to
you. (444.30)

Without fail, Shaun's speeches always evolve into lectures or
sermons,[3] and he feels most at home before an admiring
audience. His tone is inevitably self-righteous, and rarely
is he unsure of himself or does he attempt to ingratiate himself with his listeners as does his father HCE. Always cen-
sorious of others, his sentences are often strung together
as a series of precepts or commands, for he is convinced
that his own ethical code is the only one that can be allowed
in society. His voice is the voice of totalitarian authority:
"Allaboy Minor, take your head out of your satchel!"
(152.13); "Away with covered words" (188.25); "we'll go a
long way towards breaking his outsider's face for him"
(442.22). As might be expected, he admits to being a book-
burner, and he is scornful of those who have chosen an
artistic way of life—people like: "the divine comic Denti
Alligator" (440.6) and "Rinseky Poppakork" (497.28).

Though he adopts a moral tone and the stance of a prelate
to do so (shades of Buck Mulligan), he usually manages
inadvertently to ridicule his religious position with puns
and sly hintings. His sermon begins with "words taken
in triumph, my sweet assistance, from the sufferant pen

3. Shaun's major speeches may be found at the following locations: 126.ff.
answers Questions 1–3, 5, 7–9, 11; 169.ff; 260.ff. right marginalia; 293.ff. left marginalia;
299.21–300.8; 407.27–426.4; 431.21–457.24; 461.33–469.28; 477.32, answers inter-
mittently.

of our jocosus inkerman militant of the reed behind the ear"
(433.7), and his call for faith resembles that of a bookmaker:
"Keep cool faith in the firm" (434.2). Shaun is the only character in *Finnegans Wake* who is much concerned at all with religion, and he uses it solely as an instrument to insure respect
and obedience from those with whom he deals.[4] As Mamalujo
later point out: "his moraltack [is] still his best of weapons"
(602.10). However, like Earwicker, he deals in maxims
and clichés, and cannot avoid the same kinds of errors:
"put your swell foot foremost [with a hint of Oedipus]" (434.19);
" 'tis an ill weed blows no poppy good" (448.20). Rather
than ridiculing religion itself, as some have charged,
Joyce uses Shaun to expose the hypocritical ways in which
faith is manipulated.

Shaun, behind his puritanical mask, is quite concerned
with sex, and his main interest is his sister, Issy. It is in his
lectures to her, especially, that his meanness emerges,
for a leer always seems to accompany his slips: "First
thou shalt not smile. Twice thou shalt not love. Lust, thou
shalt not commix idolatry" (433.22). He dismisses his mother,
Anna Livia, as a flirt, with "her coy cajoleries, and her dabblin
drolleries" (139.24), but he goes so far in his dream as even
to propose to Issy. Typically, his romantic plea does not
seem of a very sincere nature: "I'd never say let fly till we
shot that blissup and swumped each other, manawife . . .
I'd plant you, my Gizzygay, on the electric ottoman in the
lap of lechery, simpringly stitchless with admiracion" (451.28).

What makes Shaun's advances reprehensible, while we
view those of HCE with a kind of sympathy, is that he seems
continually rational and aware of what he is saying at all
times. While Earwicker embarrasses himself with a burst
of emotion that he cannot overcome, Shaun retains control

4. Hugh Kenner calls him "the go-ahead organizer of the New Order," *Dublin's
Joyce* (Bloomington: Indiana University Press, 1956), p. 285.

of himself in almost every situation and knowingly constructs his arguments. He is a calculator and a manipulator. He does come close to losing his calm in a few instances, but each time he is able to convert the lapse into further attempts to convince. His frustrated cry of "Iy waount yiou!" (446.2) is immediately followed by: "yore ways to melittleme were wonderful," and a similar stumble, brought on by his intense love of food, is smoothed over as a joke: "It [health]'s more important than air—I mean than eats—air (Oop, I never open momouth but I pack mefood in it) and promotes that natural emotion" (437.19).

There is little love in Shaun—carnality is primary—and this is underlined most clearly in a strange interlude featuring Shaun (still appearing as Jaun), Issy, and Dave the Dancerkerl, a surrogate of Shem that Shaun creates.[5] After having apprised Issy at great length of his undying love for her, Jaun finds that he must depart for a time, but he will leave behind, to keep her company, his best friend, Dave, "my darling proxy" (462.16). The introductions accomplished: "This is me aunt Julia Bride, your honour, dying to have you languish to scandal in her bosky old delltangle" (465.1), Shaun proceeds to throw them together sexually, and even cheers them on: "Shuck her! Let him! What he's good for. Shuck her more! Let him again! All she wants!" (466.15)[6] (Compare Bloom watching Boylan and Molly in the Circe chapter: "Show! Hide! Show! Plough her! More! Shoot!" [*Ulysses*, p. 567].) The contrast between Shaun and Earwicker could not be more apparent, since, while the farthest the lat-

---

5. This voyeuristic impulse in Shaun links him with the Four Old Men, who are also apparent upholders of morality and social order.

6. Edmund Epstein equates Dave with Shem and the biblical David: "It is King David, both as the talmudic Messiah and as the romantic artist, the phallic attacker of the old-fogy Philistines, who is here shown in a sexual role that changes the balance of power in the family," *The Ordeal of Stephen Dedalus* (Carbondale: S. Illinois University Press, 1971), p. 136.

ter is able to go in his imagination is as "Daddy" Browning bringing presents to his Peaches, Shaun is wholly uninhibited in his imaginings about his sister. HCE's longings are brought about by an overflow of parental affection that embroils him with social taboos, but Shaun's desire is simply sexual satisfaction. HCE stutters and stammers; Shaun demands and asserts.

Shaun is perhaps at his most malicious when he is concerned with his favorite topic—his brother Shem. Some of the epithets he uses are: "Sham" (170.24); "O'Shame" (182.30); "Pain the Shamman" (192.23); and "Shem Skrivenitch" (423.15). The whole of Book I, chapter 7, is a scurrilous indictment of Shem, ending with Shaun, as JUSTIUS, asking for Shem's confession:

> Shem Macadamson, you know me and I know you and all your shemeries. Where have you been in the uterim, enoying yourself all the morning since your last wetbed confession? I advise you to conceal yourself, my little friend, as I have said a moment ago and put your hands in my hands and have a nightslong homely little confiteor about things. Let me see. It is looking pretty black against you, we suggest, Sheem avick. You will need all the elements in the river to clean you over it all and a fortifine popespriestpower bull of attender to booth. Let us pry. (187.34)

Certainly, Shaun's primary topic of conversation throughout the book is his brother, and he will go to great lengths to lower Shem in the estimation of his listeners. Whether with the tone of stern priest, pitying acquaintance, or understanding but grieved brother, Shaun always places Shem in the blackest light imaginable. Shaun, for instance, will be Burrus, "the real choice, full of natural greace" (166.15), while Shem will be Caseous, "the highstinks aforefelt and anygo prigging wurms" (163.9). He describes a switch from his statements to Shem's as: "From Miss Somer's nice dream back to Mad Winthrop's delugium stramens" (502.29). Many commentators have explored Joyce's use of Giordano Bruno's notion that an entity can attain to a knowledge of itself only through an understanding of, and fusion with, its opposite, in his delineation of the twins, and this can be used to explain much of Shaun's behavior. (In an interesting essay, Roland McHugh expands on the idea: "When the level of one force is high an external opposing personality appears by necessity, with an equally high level of the other force. . . . This gives the brother battle."[7] The main problem with the theory is that it becomes quite involved: "It is surely reasonable that Shemshaun being shembiased in the first half and shaunbiased in the second, Shem in the first half should be shemshaunbiased."[8] While Shem, as we shall see, seems aware of his need for his brother, and all he represents, to function creatively (to overthrow an old order or cycle and to begin a new), Shaun never seems quite able to grasp the concept. Consequently, of course, he curries the favor of those in power but is never able to feel truly secure within himself. He loses in spirit, though he may be victorious in physical fact.

Shaun usually concerns himself only with the antagonisms he feels toward his brother and acts on the basis of these, thus missing his chance for fulfillment. His one-sided oratorical triumphs are mainly hollow ones (as witness the abovementioned Dave the Dancekerl episode, which follows a long diatribe against Shem), but there are moments when a flash of understanding seems to play about his vitriolic brow. After introducing Dave, he makes the following statement in an offhand manner, without quite under-

7. "A Structural Theory of *Finnegans Wake*," *A Wake Newslitter* 5 (December 1968): 83.
8. *Ibid.*, p. 87.

standing it: "Got by the one goat, suckled by the same nanna, one twitch, one nature makes us oldworld kin. We're as thick and thin as two tubular jawballs. I hate him about his patent henesy, plasfh it, yet am I amorist. I love him" (463.15). This is just what Bruno and Joyce are postulating, but Shaun moves on immediately to another topic and union is again put by. Though it is true that the television pair Butt and Taff do accomplish the shooting of the Russian General as *"one and the same person"* (354.8), and that Burrus and Caseous win Cleopatra by fusing into "elusive Antonius, a wop" (167.1), these theoretical unities do not seem to affect the actual relationship of the brothers.

At the same time, it is not really possible to downgrade Shaun completely, since he is human in his desire to be liked by those around him. And certainly he cannot deny his bond with Shem: "I am no scholar but I loved that man who has africot lupps with the moonshane in his profile, my shemblable! My freer!" (489.26). The problem seems to be that the more devious side of his nature (here he plays Iago to Shem's Othello) must always gain the upper hand. He may recognize his ties to his family and fellow man, but the satisfaction of his ambition and his physical desires will always win out. He would like to play his brother's keeper with a vengeance.

The attribute of Shem that is most irksome to Shaun is the former's ability as a writer (though we never hear of anything he has published). Once again, Shaun cannot see that without the presence of the Penman his own symbolic role as the Post is meaningless. The writer must have the mailman or deliverer, and vice versa, if Joyce's thematic message is to reach its destination. Shaun, however, harps upon and denigrates Shem's talent in passage after passage, and even hopes to usurp the role for his own. He insinuates that all the ideas are his (as did Stanislaus Joyce): "robbing leaves out of my taletold book" (453.18), earlier says that Shem plagiarizes from many sources: "every dimmed letter in it is a copy" (424.32), and even condemns Shem's work as indecent: "it is not a nice production. It is a pinch of scribble, not wortha bottle of cabbis" (419.32). He himself could do much better, but, unfortunately, he rationalizes, he does not at the moment have a pen: "I'd write it all by mownself if I only had here of my jolly young watermen" (447.10). The stories he does tell to humiliate Shem—the Mookse and the Gripes, Burrus and Caseous, and the Ondt and the Gracehoper—all backfire and make him look ridiculous.

Time after time, critics caution that we must not view Shem as an admirable figure and Shaun as a despicable one—a valid point—but certainly we should also keep in mind the fact that Shem's bad points are painted in with the bold colors that Shaun, not Joyce, is choosing. It is Shaun who scorns "Shakhisbeard" (177.32) and "Sharadan" (184.24), not Joyce. Shaun's voice is never so sneering and sarcastic as it is when he relates Shem's pretensions to literature, for here is the one thing that Shaun cannot match. Even though Shem may be "all ears, an artificial tongue with a natural curl, not a foot to stand on, a handful of thumbs, a blind stomach, a deaf heart, a loose liver" (169.15), his vocation is something that Shaun's gibes cannot destroy. Bernard Benstock feels that "shaun must eventually relent; Shem *is* his own breastbrother, and Shaun must eventually realize himself his brother's keeper,"[9] but there seems little in the text to warrant such a conclusion. In fact, when asked if he would raise a finger to aid his dying brother, Shaun flatly answers: "No, blank ye! So you think I have impulsivism?" (149.11).

9. *Joyce-again's Wake* (Seattle: University of Washington Press, 1965), p. 240.

Now it is clear that some of the preceding statements, and some to follow, might be called moral or value judgments, and in essence this is just what they are. For too long now, critics have chosen to take Stephen's description in *A Portrait* of the uninvolved, aloof artist-god as Joyce's own. Certainly Joyce is not sitting back, paring his nails, and in all his works differentiation of value is implicit. To say that a novel discusses moral matters is not necessarily to say as well that it is moralistic or didactic. *Finnegans Wake* is not therapeutic—it will not solve our personal problems—but it does state its preferences pretty clearly.

It is interesting to note that Shaun in Book III rises, like his mother in the final chapter, from a fairly realistic to an archetypal level. He begins as the recognizable Shaun in III, 1, but passes on to the role of Jaun in III, 2. As a somewhat twisted Byronesque figure he remains familiar, but in chapter 3 he has metamorphosed into Yawn, a personification of infant sleep: "Yawn in a semiswoon lay awailing and (hooh!) what helpings of honeyful swoothead (phew!), which earpiercing dulcitude!" (474.11). Though his style and tone are not really altered as Anna Livia's are, he is stripped of the bulk of his social masks and becomes a much more sincere and real person, more in line with Benstock's description of him. In many instances he becomes a questioner, a new role for him, and even seeks to hide his brother from the Four Old Men: "he lives sameplace in the antipathies of austrasia" (489.10). This is certainly not meant to imply that Shaun undergoes any sort of spiritual conversion, but this point does seem to be the closest he will come to a recognition of his brother: "We were in one class of age like to two clots of egg" (489.19).

The voice of Shem is just as distinctive as that of any of the other members of the family, but in a different way, for, like that of Stephen Dedalus, it is usually extremely self-conscious of its own learning.[10] Shem's answer, as MERCIUS, to Shaun's JUSTIUS, might almost have used the "Proteus" chapter of Ulysses as a starting point:

> My fault, his fault, a kingship through a fault! Pariah, cannibal Cain, I who oathily forswore the womb that bore you and the paps I sometimes sucked, you who ever since have been one black mass of jigs and jimjams, haunted by a convulsionary sense of not having been or being all that I might have been or you meant to becoming, bewailing like a man that innocence which I could not defend like a woman, lo, you there, Cathmon-Carbery, and thank Movies from the innermost depths of my still attrite heart, Wherein the days of youyouth are evermixed mimine, now ere the compline hour of being alone athands itself and a puff or so before we yield our spiritus to the wind, for (though that royal one has not yet druck a gouttelette from his consummation and the floerpot on the pole, the spaniel pack and their quarry, retainers and the public house proprietor have not budged a millimetre. (193.31)

The echoes of Shakesperian blank verse and of the soliloquies of Melville's Ahab are immediately apparent, yet, as with Dedalus, the mind seems to become entangled with itself. One sentence in this speech proceeds for a labyrinthine forty-five lines (193.32–195.4). One is left with a sense that the speaker perhaps takes himself a little too seriously, that diction and phrasing almost devolve into a kind of Elizabethan pomposity. Yet such a speech is not entirely characteristic, for Shem is nothing if not versatile.

In each situation he adopts the stylistic mask or pose that he feels will suit the moment best. Though in the above instance he chooses to match seriousness with high seriousness, he answers Shaun's self-righteous parable of the Ondt

10. Shem's major speeches may be found at the following locations: 126.ff. asks Questions 1–12; 193.31–195.4; 260.ff. left marginalia; 293.ff. right marginalia; 286.26–287.17; 293.1–299.20; 304.5–306.7; 418.10 poem.

and the Gracehoper with a series of rowdy couplets, pointing
out Shaun's lack of a sense of humor:

> *Your feats end enormous, your volumes immense,*
> *(May the Graces I hoped for sing your Ondtship song sense!),*
> *Your genus its worldwide, your spacest sublime!*
> *But, Holy Saltmartin, why can't you beat time?* (419.5)

Shem is a master parodist, imitating his mother and father
or skipping from one literary genre or tone to another, to
answer, tweak, or avoid his antagonists, and he can easily
make the leap from a meditation on space and time to the
bawdy limerick: *"There was a sweet hopeful culled Cis"*
(267.left marginalia). Modeled on the character of Joyce
himself, Shem is at all times possessed of a sense of humor,
and, even more important, an ability to laugh at himself.
He does, it is true, have a tendency to indulge in occasional
self-pity,[11] yet his awareness of himself and of situations
enables him to retain a hold on a realistic point of view. In
the Mime of Mick, Nick, and the Maggies, for example, his
chagrin at not being able to guess the riddle and the derison
of the girls drive him to consider running away from home,
where he would "fire off, gheol ghiornal, foull subustioned
mullmud [Oscar Wilde], his farced epistol to the hibruws"
(228.32), give up politics and religion, and take to drink.
Reveling in his own misery, however, he soon sees the ludicrous nature of his pose and restores himself with a brusque:
"Can that sobstuff, whingeywilly!" (232.23). Such self-
awareness is not a characteristic of Shaun.

Perhaps the main reason for Shem's use of these many
and varied literary voices is the fact that, while he tries not

---

11. To say that he is "awash in self-pity," as does Adaline Glasheen, *A Second
Census of Finnegans Wake*, p. 191, perhaps oversimplifies Shem's relationship with
Shaun.

to show it, he is quite sensitive to the criticism of others and is quite aware that he does not and cannot conform to the middle-class mold. He uses his various voices as Wildean or Yeatsian masks that afford him a certain amount of emotional protection from the condemnation of those around him. Though Anna Livia may mother and protect him and Issy may occasionally flirt, Shaun is always on the lookout to embarrass him, and Shem also realizes that HCE is much more fond of his eldest son. Describing his father, Shem notes that he, "while satisfied that soft youthful bright matchless girls [Issy] should bosom into fine silkclad joyous blooming young women is not so pleased that heavy swearsome strongsmelling irregularshaped men should blottout active handsome wellformed frankeyed boys" (134.23)."[12] Thus Shem adopts these poses to place himself one step farther away from injury and to achieve a distance from which he may retaliate with scorn.

In such a way, it is quite possible that the Ass who narrates the first three chapters of Book III, as the beast of burden of the Four Old Men and as Bottom of "A Midsummer-Night's Dream," is actually Shem, who takes this opportunity to make light of his more serious brother. His opening: "Methought as I was dropping asleep somepart in nonland of where's please" (403.18) is a good deal reminiscent of Shem's Shakespearian imitations, and the awed tone of eulogy has just enough irony in it to be Shem's:

And I pledge you my agricultural word by the hundred and sixty odds rods and cones of this even's vision that young fellow looked the stuff, the Bel of Beaus' Walk, a prime card if ever was! Pep? Now without deceit it is hardly too much to say he

12. Along with the suggestion of HCE's liking for young boys, his preference for Shaun is established by the latter's description later as "the fine frank fairhaired fellow of the fairytales" (220.12). Shaun is the apple of his father's eye.

was looking grand, so fired smart, in much more than his usual
health. No mistaking that beamish brow! (405.11)

The final allusion to the dragon-slaying young fire-eater
of Lewis Carroll's "Jabberwocky," with all its penetrating
glee, might help to substantiate the identification. Shem
listens to the fable of the Ondt and the Gracehoper with
due respect, but is forced to conclude that "it falls easily upon
the earopen and goes down the friskly shortest like treacling
tumtim with its tingtingtaggle. The blarneyest blather in all
Corneywall!" (418.14). His most telling thrust, from behind
the mask that Shaun does not seem to recognize, is to ask
that he explain Shem's letter: "the strangewrote anaglyptics
of those shemletters patent for His Christian's Em" (419.18).
That Shaun is quick to exclaim that he can, and that he
makes a fool of himself in trying to do so, is a tribute to the
way in which Shem encourages his brother to expose himself in these sections. This Jaun chapter is almost certainly
Shem's reply to Shaun's attack in "Shem is as short for
Shemus" (169.ff.). Shem's subterfuges may not be wholly
aboveboard, but they certainly merit more approbation,
and display more wit and skill, than Shaun's below-the-
belt harangues. Along with Stephen Dedalus, Shem might
well say: "he fears the lancet of my art as I fear that of
his. The cold steelpen" (*Ulysses*, p. 7), since it is with the lance
of his own learning that he attempts to parry the bludgeons
of concerted, accepted opinion.

As is demonstrated by his choice of the role of MERCIUS,
Shem does feel deeply for his brother and is continually forgiving the latter's slights and injuries. When struck by
Shaun at the end of the "Lessons" chapter he replies: "Thanks
eversore much, Pointcarried!" (304.5), and later displays
humility to the Ondt: "*I forgive you, grondt Ondt, said the Gracehoper,
weeping*" (418.12). Shem's main concern is that his brother recog-

nize their mutual need, and time after time he explains their relationship. Though he may not like much about Shaun, their existences are bound up together: *"We are Wastenot with Want, precondamned, two and true,/Till Nolans go volants and Bruneyes come blue"* (418.30). There is more than a trace of masochism about Shem, but his forgiveness is the primary and necessary step in yet another attempt at getting Shaun to see reason.[13] The questions that he puts to Shaun in Book I, chapter 6, asking of the natures of the members of their household and the world in which they live, are designed to educate Shaun. His description of his mother's sexual organs, cloaked by a discussion of geometry, is not the simple, snickering prank of a child: "I'll make you to see figuratleavely the whome of your eternal geomater" (296.30). The essay topics that Shem postulates at the end of the chapter function in the same way. Needless to say, Shem does not succeed, and the warring of the brothers continues throughout *Finnegans Wake.* Yet Shem never seems daunted by his failures and continues in a manner almost obsessive, just as each of the characters is completely involved in one main topic of conversation or dreaming from which he cannot be swayed. The fact that one never really seems to pay much attention to the words of another has little bearing on the striving of each to be heard and understood.

The speech of the daughter, Isobel, or Issy, is one of the most recognizable in the novel,[14] yet it is probably also the voice of least importance among the major characters. Drawn from the "little language" of Jonathan Swift to Stella in the *Journal to Stella,* Issy's voice can be quite charm-

13. Campbell and Robinson's suggestion "that an indisposition to stand up even for his own rights is Shem's norm of action," *A Skeleton Key to Finnegans Wake* (New York: Harcourt, Brace, 1944), p. 191, underestimates his character.

14. Issy's major speeches may be found at the following locations: 143.31–148.32; 248.11–249.4; 260.ff. footnotes; 457.25–466.32; 527.3–528.13.

ing and often amusing, but it is devoid of any recognition of the issues and problems that are beguiling the members of her family. To Frank Budgen, "Sister Iseult is all the fascinating *ingenues* that ever lived, from the girls that were met in the Land of Nod to the latest platinum blonde out of Hollywood."[15]

> I swear to you by Fibsburrow churchdome and Sainte Andree's Undershift, by all I hold secret from my world and in my underworld of nighties and naughties and all the other wonderwearlds! Close your, notmust look! Now open, pet, your lips, pepette, like I used my sweet parted lipsabuss with Can Holohan of facetious memory taught me after the flannel dance, with the proof of love, up Smock Alley the first night he smelled pouder and I coloured beneath my fan, *pipetta mia*, when you learned me the linguo to melt. Whowham would have ears like ours, the blackhaired! Do you like that, *silenzioso?* Are you enjoying, this same little me, my life, my love? (147.25)

Basically, she is content to discuss her appearance and romantic intrigues in lisping babytalk before the mirror of her dressing table. She realizes that she is an object of desire and flirts with any man who comes across her path, and she should be seen as the type of mindless woman that Joyce had already created in Molly Bloom. As the sexual successor to Anna Livia, Issy is strictly a creature of emotion, who spends much of her time "at the movies swallowing sobs and blowing bixed mixcuits over 'childe' chaplain's 'latest' or on the verge of the gutter with some bobbed hair brieffrocked babyma's toddler" (166.13). It does not seem quite clear what Adeline Glasheen means when she says: "Issy is not . . . a charming or coherent talker. Conversation is a civilized art and she is at once below and above civilization," but Mrs. Glasheen is certainly right

---

15. *James Joyce and the Making of Ulysses* (New York: Smith and Haas, 1934), p. 293.

in calling Issy "a triumph of female imbecility."[16] She seems included as the attractive ornamentation that Joyce sometimes thought women should be, and as an object for the twins and their father to contend over. Here is the narrator's description:

> with her greengageflavoured candywhistle duetted to the crazyquilt, Isobel, she is so pretty, truth to tell, wildwood's eyes and primarose hair, quietly, all the woods so wild, in mauves of moss and daphnedews, how all so still she lay, neath of the whitethorn, child of tree, like some losthappy leaf, like blowing flower stilled, as fain would she anon, for soon again 'twill be, win me, woo me, wed me, ah weary me! deeply, now evencalm lay sleeping. (556.15)

Her mindless monologue in Book III, chapter 3, as Stella speaking to Vanessa and Alice in Wonderland to her looking-glass reflection: "Alicious, twinstreams twinestraines, through alluring glass or alas in jumboland" (528.17), becomes so boring to the inquiring Four Old Men that they impolitely fade her out: "(I'm fading!) . . . (I'm fay)" (528.11). In the same way, her inane footnotes to the "Lessons" chapter are ignored by both the boys, who are involved with more serious matters, just as the Mookse and the Gripes ignore Nuvoletta in their fable. This is certainly not to say that Issy is uninteresting or unimportant as a character, but she stands somewhat outside the action of the novel and never seems quite aware that it is going on. Strangely enough, she feels that she is all-important, that the desires of all are concentrated upon her, when, in actuality, the men wish only to use her, never to know her as a person. It is significant that Anna Livia does not even mention her once. As Issy herself says: "I enjoy as good as anyone" (298.n.1), and

16. *A Second Census of Finnegans Wake*, p. 124.

perhaps this is her saving grace, since she seems to be enjoying herself and is not at all troubled or disturbed, as are those around her. "It's only because the rison is I'm only any girl, you lovely fellow of my dreams" (146.5).

Finally, we might mention the Four Old Men, or Mamalujo, who do a great deal of talking and dreaming in *Finnegans Wake*.[17] As Mrs. Glasheen notes,[18] they usually speak in a definite order: Matthew, Mark, Luke, and John, though this is not always the case. Though each speaks with the accent of the section of Ireland he represents, it is usually quite difficult to tell them apart. In a letter to Ezra Pound,[19] for example, Joyce explains that the fourth question of Book I, chapter 6, is answered by the Four in order (140.8), and David Hayman's examination of Joyce's manuscripts reveals that the speeches of the Four beginning at (477.3) were set by the author in the same definite progression.[20] Yet, quarrelsome by nature, the Four will often interrupt each other and squabble among themselves, as here where Matthew first reproves Mark, and then Luke and John, for speaking out of turn: "Your crackling out of your turn, my Moonster firefly [Mark as the province Munster], like always. And 2 R. N. [Luke] and Longhorns Connacht [John], stay off my air! You've grabbed the capital and you've had the lion's shire since 1542 but there's all the difference in Ireland between your borderation, my chatty cove, and me [Matthew as Ulster]" (528.26). In relation to the realistic level of the narrative line, Mamalujo are four old seamen who drink nightly at Earwicker's pub and have

17. Mamalujo's major speeches may be found at the following locations: 94.32–95.26; 140.15–141.7; 373.13–382.26; 386.ff.; 477.ff.; 559.ff.
18. *A Second Census of Finnegans Wake*, p. 87.
19. *Letters of James Joyce*, ed. Richard Ellmann, vol. 3 (New York: Viking Press, 1966), p. 239.
20. *A First-Draft Version of Finnegans Wake* (Austin: University of Texas Press, 1963), pp. 231–32.

spent the evening discussing the rumors about HCE: "So you were saying, boys? Anyhow he what?" (380.6). Prying and gossippy in their behavior, they have dreams that take the form of inquisitions or examinations in which they question as many witnesses as possible in order. to get at the truth. Their tone is always a harsh one, and at times they almost come to blows with the person to whom they are speaking: "Will you repeat that to me outside, leinconnmuns?" (521.28).

Also, despite their alleged desire for the facts, it often seems that they are more interested in a good story or an undiscovered aspect of the Earwickers' personal lives. Their voyeuristic nature is constantly on display, and later they are even described as sinister: "it was in the back of their mind's ear, temptive lissomer, how they would be spreading in quadriliberal their azurespotted fine attractable nets, their nansen nets, from Matt Senior to the thurrible mystagogue after him and from thence to the neighbor and that way to the puisny donkeyman" (477.18). The Four never indulge in frivolity, though occasionally their speeches are humorous in themselves, because they are always intent upon their quest. As Clive Hart sums them up, they "are involved in trying to find a common denominator for their four points of view; but the only absolute they ever discover is the absolute uncertainty from which they began, the wholly relative nature of all the cycles."[21]

From the preceding view of most of the supporting speakers[22] who people the night of dreaming that encompasses

21. *Structure and Motif in Finnegans Wake* (Evanston: Northwestern University Press, 1962), p. 63.

22. Though the Manservant is not heard to speak directly, the maid, Kate the Slops, will at times complain of all the work she has to do: "who eight the last of the goosebellies that was mowlding from the measlest of years and who leff that there and who put that here and who let the‚kilkenny stale the chump" (142.2).

Finnegans Wake, we might conclude that such a multiplicity of perspectives and styles makes the novel much more complex than does any theory of a single dreamer. Whether or not this is desirable in such an already convoluted work is, of course, a moot point, but, in actuality, such a concept makes the book much easier to read and comprehend. Once one is able to separate one voice from another and to identify it, what at first seemed incomprehensible changes in the style and tone of Earwicker's monologue may now be revealed as quite logical shifts in point of view from one character to another. Such a reevaluation of the narrative structure frees one from the Herculean task of justifying Earwicker's mind as some kind of Jungian unconscious, for the more productive exploration of the themes of the novel as a whole. In practice, a narrative technique that employs shifts in speaker or point of view is accepted as conventional in the twentieth-century novel, and, once acknowledging these kinds of shifts, the reader should be able to approach more closely to the narrative line and to a deeper understanding of the individual characters. J. S. Atherton has commented that *Finnegans Wake* is "everyone's dream, the dream of all the living and the dead,"[23] and perhaps it is, but before we can arrive at such an overview we must approach through the channels of the individual dreaming minds that Joyce is exhibiting. Thousands upon thousands of people are quoted or touched upon, but there is a small and definite number of fictional characters who are conducting the proceedings.

23. "The Identity of the Sleeper," *A Wake Newslitter* 4 (October 1967): 83.

3

Their Master's Voice

There is another character or entity in *Finnegans Wake* as important as any of the main fictional personages: the omniscient narrator who is present at all times throughout the novel. It is he who completes the gaps around the characters' speeches and who sees into their dreaming minds with sympathy and understanding. The technique of employing such a narrator is, of course, quite common and acceptable in the tradition of the novel, but Joyce's permutations of this role make of the device something new and unique. As well as standing above and away from the action, this narrator is extremely aware of his position as an important link between the fiction and the reader. In the many ways he plays out his part, he almost assumes the status of a character in his own right. Our man is much like Tristram in Sterne's *Tristram Shandy*, though never playing an actual part in the fictional narrative, at one moment cool and aloof, at the next mocking, insulting, or sympathetic to the stress placed upon the reader's comprehension. The difference, however, is that Tristram views his entire production as farcical and artificial, and is content to titillate his audience, regardless of the final consequence, while maintaining an ironic, yet paternal, benevolence for his father and for his eccentric Uncle Toby.

Finnegans Wake is essentially a dramatic production,

employing all the techniques of movies and the legitimate stage, and its narrator is cognizant of the fact that he is the star of the drama. Discussing Dickens, Douglas Bush speaks of "the frequently theatrical quality of his comic characters' self-dramatization,"[1] and goes on to establish such characterization as a literary tradition stemming from Chaucer and Shakespeare. Our narrator fits snugly into this line, since his most salient trait is awareness, both of himself and of his role. Whether jovial or morose, anecdotal or professorial, his tone always reflects the fact that he is conscious of the footlights and works on many different portrayals of his role to suit each given situation. John B. Vickery would not agree, stating that "Joyce here asserts the artist's commonality with mankind implicitly but relentlessly by refusing to permit the order of his words to create a distinct narrator who is distanced from the ritual drama of death and revival."[2] His is a "command performance by special request with the courteous permission for pious purposes the homedromed and enliveneth performance of the problem passion play of the millentury, running strong since creation" (32.30).

Joyce's speaker has a sense of humor even more bizarre than Sterne's, but one is always conscious of the fact that the former is attempting to get certain thematic points across even in the most riotous situations. He seems deeply concerned on a personal level both with the narrative line and with our own reactions to it, never emotionally abandoning either the characters or us. He regards the events of the narrative as integral to himself. Walter Allen says that:

---

1. *Engaged and Disengaged* (Cambridge: Harvard University Press, 1966), p. 29.
2. "*Finnegans Wake* and Sexual Metamorphosis," *Contemporary Literature* 13 (Spring 1972): 226.

the great theme of the European novel, and perhaps especially of the English novel, has been man's life in society; more precisely, the education of men and women, in the sense of their learning to distinguish through their inescapable involvement in society, the true from the false both in themselves and in the world about them,[3]

and this enlightening, the narrator seems to feel, is his vocation in *Finnegans Wake*. He is at once in the action and outside of it, affected by events and untouched by them. Though he understands, and sometimes seems to feel affection for, the other characters, his focus is always outward, directed toward the reader. Tristram will allow us to write our own conclusion to a chapter, but this is something that could never occur in *Finnegans Wake*. Here we are presented with a huge mass of opinions and many points of view: we are asked to draw our own conclusions, but we are directed firmly toward the right ones every step of the way. The boundary or line of demarcation between the fictional world and our own is rarely recognized by our guide. He must constantly try to point us in the right direction. The narrator of *Finnegans Wake* has his feet firmly rooted in the ground of Earwicker's Chapelizod, but his head rises above all this into the clouds of the world of reality that the reader inhabits.

One can always sense a deep desire on the part of the narrator that he be heard and understood, that his depiction of the Earwickers will interest his audience and that his thematic intentions will be comprehended. He cautions us that "every word will be bound over to carry three score and ten toptypsical readings throughout the book" (20.14), and even will implore us to continue our efforts: "(Stoop) if you are abcedminded, to this claybook, what curios of signs (please stoop), in this allaphbed: (18.17). Often his tone is soothing

---

3. *Tradition and Dream* (London: Faber and Faber, 1964), p. xiii.

and conciliatory: "Now, patience; and remember patience is the great thing, and above all things else we must avoid anything like being or becoming out of patience" (108.8). Continually, he drops hints as to how the book is to be read and how it may be handled. We are apprised of its debt to movie techniques: "if you are looking for the bilder deep your ear on the movietone:" (62.8), given clues to the fact that many characters speak unidentified, each in his own original manner: "why, pray, sign anything as long as every word, letter, penstroke, paperspace is a perfect signature of its own?" (115.6), and advised that a cosmic view of these events is not always advantageous: "the farther back we manage to wiggle the more we need the loan of a lens to see as much as the hen saw" (112.1). Yet to say that the narrator does his best to assist the reader is not to imply that he will ever compromise or go out of his way to make things any easier. He writes no key to his own work. By the very nature of the dream situation, we are locked in with a different kind of language, which can and does play tricks with our waking world comprehension, and there is nothing the narrator can do to change this. He expects us to work with it and it to work upon us. Our reactions are anticipated: "You is feeling like you was lost in the bush, boy? . . . You most shouts out: Bethicket me for a stump of a beech if I have the poultriest notions what the farest he all means" (112.3), but we are expected to wrestle with the problem.

Yet another difficulty through which the narrator attempts to lead us is the very nature of a baffling rumor and half-truth. The stories of HCE's misdemeanors have multiplied a thousandfold, so that it seems impossible ever to sort them out. Objectively, the narrator documents them all for us, yet solemnly he warns that "the unfacts, did we possess them, are too imprecisely few to warrant our certitude" (57.16). Chapters 2 and 3 of Book I, which discuss the sin in the Park and the rumors that fly about the town afterwards, are thus extremely complicated and hard to folow, yet they are so, not because of the dream language or any subterfuge, but because of their own mazelike qualities. The Cad, after encountering Earwicker, tells his suspicions to his wife, who consults her confessor, who passes the story to a teacher named Philly Thurston, who lets it out to Treacle Tom and Frisky Shorty. Tom talks in his sleep and is overheard by Peter Cloran, O'Mara, and Hosty, the last spreading the story all over town and composing the infamous "Ballad of Persse O'Reilly." As the narrator counsels:

> Can it was, one is fain in this leaden age of letters now to wit, that so diversified outrages (they have still to come!) were planned and partly carried out against so staunch a covenanter if it be true than any of those recorded ever took place for many, we trow, beyessed to and denayed of, are given to us by some who use the truth but sparingly and we, on this side ought to sorrow for their pricking pens on that account. (61.28)

Unfortunately, we never hear what the rumor is as it grows from carrier to carrier, so there is no way to sort out the distortions. We know that the Cad is put off by the way Earwicker spits: "would a respectable prominently connected fellow of Iro-European ascendances with welldressed ideas who knew the correct thing . . . expectorate after such a callous fashion" (37.25), but throughout the chapter it is the circulation of the rumor, rather than its content, that is described.

The third chapter is concerned with various specific charges by specific individuals, but they are so farfetched and disconnected that the reader is left totally at sea. Once again the narrator will not deign to comment. The three soldiers, for example, state: "It was the first woman . . .

souped him, that fatal wellesday, Lili Coninghams,[4] by suggesting him they go in a field" (58.22), while a cabdriver calls him: "just a plain pink joint reformee in private life" (59.27). A long list of the names he has been called is just as unhelpful.[5] Through all this the narrator maintains the objective stance of a scientist, neither confirming nor denying the truth of any of this material. He does, however, at one point identify the position he expects us to take in the face of all this: "in this scherzarade of one's thousand one nightinesses that sword of certainty which would indentifide the body never falls" (51.4).

In essence, he is explaining to us that individual truths can never be isolated in this situation, and, indeed, that they are eventually irrelevant. Just as one fall or rise at any given time are all falls and all rises, it is sufficient that we realize that Earwicker has sinned. The exact nature of his fault is immaterial, since the consequences and effects on him will be the same no matter what he has done. HCE is being devoured by guilt, and this is what is important, what we should concentrate upon. If we become too involved with the intricacies of the rumors, with who said exactly what, or with any of the other labyrinthine motifs of *Finnegans Wake,* we shall never be able to achieve the distance from individual events that the narrator constantly assures us is necessary for any deeper comprehension of the novel. Once again he has provided a key to what is going on, but once again he will not take full responsibility for carrying us by the pitfalls of the narrative. If we wish to spend years of our time ferreting out Swahili words in the text, that is our business, not his. He helps as best he can, preparing us

---

4. Adaline Glasheen identifies her as the wife of the Cad, *A Second Census of Finnegans Wake* (Evanston: Northwestern University Press, 1963), p. 148.

5. This list is explicated by Hugh B. Staples in "Some Notes on the One Hundred and Eleven Epithets of HCE," *A Wake Newslitter* 1 (December 1964): 3–6.

for the statements of the characters themselves, assuming that we may be directed but not led by the ear. (Frank Budgen recalls Joyce as commenting: "I want the reader to understand always through suggestion, rather than direct statement."[6])

An obvious question that arises is just who is this narrator, but it is definitely not any easy one to answer. Certainly the voice has the ultimate knowledge and awareness of God, but no passage in the book allows us to make this identification with any real justification. The same might be said for identifications of Finn MacCool or Tim Finnegan. The fact that the narrator consistently adopts the pronouns "we" and "us" in a comradely, rather than editorial fashion, seems to point to an entity of more mundane origin. Possibilities range from Adam to Everyman, but it does seem that many of the narrator's characteristics are also those of Joyce himself. His intense desire to be understood, to write a book that the masses would appreciate as well as the literari, and his crushing disappointment at the critical disparagement of *Finnegans Wake*, are reflected by the narrator, and also by Anna Livia's cry: "Is there one who understands me?" (627.15). Richard Ellmann states that this "was Joyce's own question to Nora thirty-four years before in Dublin,"[7] and such similarities pop up on almost every page. This is not to say that the narrator *is* Joyce, though autobiographical material saturates the *Wake,* but he is certainly emotionally involved in the continual exhortings and pleadings to which the reader is exposed. J. S. Atherton's naming of "the universal mind"[8] as the dreamer in *Finnegans Wake* might better suit the narrator, for it is

6. *James Joyce and the Making of Ulysses* (New York: Smith and Haas, 1934), p. 21.
7. James Joyce (New York: Oxford University Press, 1965), p. 725.
8. "The Identity of the Sleeper," *A Wake Newslitter* 4 (October 1967): 84.

finally impossible, and probably unnecessary, to name him. He is our guide and perhaps even our friend, and it is his function, rather than his face, that is important.

The technique employed by the narrator to acquaint us with the Earwickers might be likened to the use of a movie camera with a telephoto lens. As the book opens, the perspective is quite distant and general, both in spatial and temporal terms. Our first view of Dublin is seemingly from high in the air, since we watch the river Liffey as it flows past Adam and Eve's Church and catch a glimpse of Howth Castle. Rather than introducing any of the characters, the first chapter traces the history of the many inhabitants of the area, from early Scandinavian invaders to the piratess Grace O'Malley to the Duke of Wellington to Tim Finnegan of the musical ballad. The second chapter unfolds the genealogy of Humphrey Chimpden Earwicker and finally arrives at his sin and the rumors that have sprung up around it. Still we have not met a character directly, though we have been moved closer to the action, and it is not until chapter 6, with Shem asking questions and Shaun and others answering, that a major character appears for any length of time.

Books II and III are those devoted to closeups, and here we are immersed entirely in the Earwickers' early evening actions and their dreaming thoughts and fantasies throughout the night. The narrator allows us full-scale looks at all the characters, displaying individual examples of Viconian and Brunonian generalizations for our examination. Book IV, the ricorso section and coming of day, however, reverses the movement from far to near, as once again we are transported back away from specific, contemporary action. St. Kevin makes his appearance, Patrick debates and defeats the druid Berkeley, and Anna Livia is transformed into the spirit of the river. The circle is completed, we are left where we began, as

Anna's monologue is broken off on the last page and picked up again by the narrator on the first.[9] Obviously, the narrator did not intend that we should become too closely involved with the characters, since basically he wishes them to be taken as examples or illustrations of a timeless cyclical process. When we view photographs in an exhibition, we are moved by the human qualities the faces represent, not by the specific individuals represented themselves. Certainly we cannot help but get used to them and feel some affection for them, but the cosmic point of view in which we are often placed makes total sympathy almost impossible. Here, for example, is his objective, movie-scenario presentation of the Earwicker's bedroom:

Scene and property plot. Stagemanager's prompt. Interior of dwelling on outskirts of city. Groove two. Chamber scene. Boxed. Ordinary bedroom set. Salmonpapered walls. Back, empty Irish grate, Adam's mantel, with wilting elopement fan, soot and tinsel, condemned. North, wall with window practicable. Argentine in casement. Vamp. Pelmit above. No curtains. Blind drawn. South, party wall. Bed for two with strawberry bedspread, wickerworker clubsessel and caneseated millikinstool. Bookshrine without, facetowel upon. Chair for one. Woman's garments on chair. Man's trousers with crossbelt braces, collar on bedknob. Man's corduroy surcoat with tabrets and taces, seapan nacre buttons on nail. Woman's gown on ditto. Over mantelpiece picture of Michael, lance, slaying Satan, dragon with smoke. Small table near bed, front. Bed with bedding. Spare. Flagpatch quilt. Yverdown design. Limes. Lighted lamp without globe, scarf, gazette, tumbler, quantity of water, julepot, ticker, side props, eventuals, man's gummy article, pink. (558.35)

It would be silly to postulate that HCE, ALP, Shem, or Shaun are flat characters, but certainly we never really worry very

---

9. J. Mitchell Morse was first to notice the shift in speakers in "On Teaching *Finnegans Waket*," *Twelve and a Tilly* (London: Faber and Faber, 1966), pp. 69–70.

much about HCE's sin or the rivalry of Shem and Shaun. The narrator sees to it that we maintain our distance, that we place them in a universal perspective as well as understanding and appreciating them.

In some senses he is much like the unseen, controlling narrator of *Ulysses*. As we progress into this latter novel, it becomes clear that it is misleading to call *Ulysses* a stream-of-consciousness novel like *The Sound and the Fury*, for example. The controlling narrator who stands behind Stephen, Bloom, and Molly allows us only selective entrance into their minds, and frames their musings as the Wakian narrator frames the statements of his sleepers. Style becomes the distancing mechanism in *Ulysses*, and actually, from the Cyclops chapter to Ithaca (over four hundred pages), we view the characters almost completly from outside, as we had in Wandering Rocks. Bloom does meditate at the conclusion of Nausicaa, but this is the only point at which stylistic parody does not force the reader back and away from the action. As the Wakian voice taunts his listeners, so does the narrator of *Ulysses* challenge us to identify the Man in the Macintosh and Martha Clifford. The key word would seem to be control, since both narrators are quite careful that what we see is what they want us to see.

It might also be mentioned that he is outside the particular Chapelizod dream situation, that he is not involved or probably even acquainted with the Earwickers. That he himself is dreaming or involved in deep meditation seems assured by the language he employs, but he dreams on a more selective and unemotional level than do the characters. The awareness of an audience that he always carries with him indicates that the id is not really in control, that he is able to manipulate, to act rather than be acted upon. He answers his own rhetorical question thus: "You mean to see we have been hadding a sound night's sleep? You may so"

(597.1). Our narrator consciously means us "to see," and, though we may *say* it was a sound night's sleep, "sound" refers only to the volume of the characters' voices that have kept us and him awake.

HCE and his family are first seen at the close of a day, and then as they sleep and wake fitfully, but our narrator never sleeps. He may doze, as he does at the end of several chapters: "When we sleep. Drops. But wait until our sleeping. Drain. Sdops" (74.19); "Loud, heap miseries upon us yet entwine our arts with laughters low! /Ha he hi ho hu./ Mummum" (259.7), yet each ensuing chapter finds him willing and able to lead us on. Each chapter is structured around this rhythmic movement toward sleep, a movement that is reversed in the final chapter. "Arts" is perhaps the key word here—"hearts," certainly, but primarily "art," or the ability to construct a meaningful fiction.

There is nothing random about what we read, for the narrator sets up the situations artfully, and behind him stands the artful Joyce emulating both Daedalus and Ulysses. HCE may lose control but the narrator never does. He is always calm and collected, bringing up another historical example or allusion, contrasting it to the stance of an individual Earwicker, and moving on to something else. He might best be likened to a stage manager, setting a scene, adjusting a costume, hurrying a character onstage, and watching attentively from the wings. Without him there could be no production.

Though they are not coached or controlled in what they are to say, the characters operate within the frame that the narrative voice defines and sets up. Rarely is there any transition from chapter to chapter in *Finnegans Wake*, as there is in more conventional novels. (Chapters in Books II and III do follow chronologically, but there are no other ties between them.) The shifts are not haphazard, each chapter being used to illuminate some important perspective on the family, but on first reading one never knows where he will be as one chapter succeeds another. (Basically, this too is the technique of *Ulysses*.) There is, for example, no fictive, narrative line at all in Book I, as we move from a description of Shem's letter in chapter 5 to the series of questions and answers, to a Shaunian description of Shem, to the washerwomen's description of Anna Livia. Adaline Glasheen says that Joyce called chapter 6 "a picture history from the family album,"[10] and the phrase could be applied to the whole of Book I. The narrator does not really allow a plot to develop; rather, he presents a series of tableaux, which he embellishes by allowing the figures speech and movement.

There is no plot to the descriptions of Shaun or the washerwomen, but there is a great deal of psychological or introspective movement within each. In every case the narrator turns his camera upon a specific individual and allows him free rein. Shaun, of course, is in his element: "Can you beat it? Whawe! I say, can you bait it? Was there ever heard of such lowdown blackguardism? Positively it woolies one to think over it" (180.30). The reason that there is little commotion or interruption in the speeches of Shaun or the washerwomen is that both Shem and ALP are essentially passive characters who do not feel goaded enough to defend themselves. The opportunity is always available but they decline it, just as, conversely, the stronger characters, Shaun and HCE, will leap to their own defense incessantly in the chapters that follow. The narrator certainly realizes this, but he expects that ensuing action and comment will mitigate the opinionated condemnations of these successive chapters. Once again, he is putting many views and opinions of characters and situations on exhibition, all of them valid to

10. *A Second Census of Finnegans Wake*, p. xxxiv.

a given speaker at a given moment, expecting us to construct a proper mosaic out of the fragments.

Omnipresent in Book I, our narrator assumes a different role for himself in Books II and III. As the performances of the characters attain to greater duration and larger importance, the narrator's status as a significant voice fades proportionately. He is rarely heard to venture an independent opinion in the middle sections. His position as narrator becomes typically conventional, and he does little more than set scenes and locate the characters spatially for their performances. He begins preparations for the "Mime of Mick, Nick, and the Maggies," for instance, in the style of a theater program: "Every evening at lighting up o'clock sharp and until further notice in Feenichts Playhouse. (Bar and conveniences always open, Diddlem Club douncestears.) Entrancings: gads, a scrab; the quality, one large shilling" (219.1), and thereafter remains in the background. He does not appear at all in the "Lessons" chapter, and is once more a stage manager in Book III, here fiddling with the lights, as he turns the narrative over to the Ass: "Come not nere! Black! Switch out!" (403.17).

Though again he does not interfere, he structures Book II, chapter 4 as a microcosm of the spatial movement of *Finnegans Wake* as a whole. Thus, as we begin, we view the ship from the vantage of the seabirds high in the air as Tristan and Isolde are carried across the sea: "Overhoved, shrillglee-screaming. That song sang seaswans. The winging ones. Seahawk, seagull, curlew and plover, kestrel and capercallzie. All the birds of the sea they trolled out rightbold when they smacked the big kuss of Trustan with Usolde" (383.15). From here we center in on Mamalujo, eavesdropping and assuming the narration: "they were the big four, the four maaster waves of Erin, all listening, four" (384.6), and it is they who provide the closeups of Tristan and the alluring Isolde: "a

strapping modern old ancient Irish prisscess ... nothing
under her hat but red hair and solid ivory ... and a firstclass
pair of bedroom eyes, of most unhomy blue" (396.7). The
courting completed, we once again move back, Mamalujo
relinquish the podium, and the narrator concludes from an
Olympian position: "And still a light moves long the river.
And stiller the mermen ply their keg. /Its pith is full. The way
is free. Their lot is cast" (399.31). The obvious parallels
remain to be drawn between Tristan and Isolde, HCE and
ALP, and lovers of past centuries, but the narrator no longer
draws them. He has retreated behind the narrative line and
will remain there until Book IV, when he attempts, in his own
way, to draw things together. The narrator chooses the scene
and the time in these sections, but from that starting point he
allows the characters to work things out as they will. Concurrently, he allows the reader to view the action unobstructed,
trusting that the aid he has given in Book I may move his
audience to a proper evaluation of the Earwickers' unrestrained caperings.

With Book IV the narrator returns, but he seems changed
from the voice we heard previously. Gone is his flagrant sense
of humor, and gone also seems his intense desire to keep us
involved in the narrative. It has been a long night. It is almost
as if he realizes that, having come this far, the reader needs
no urging to pay attention and is seriously working at putting
the pieces together. His purpose in this Book is a summing
up, but this final summation is a curiously inconclusive one:

between all the goings up and the whole of the comings down
and the fog of the cloud in which we toil and the cloud of the fog
under which we labor, bomb the thing's to be domb about it so
that, beyond indicating the locality, it is felt that one cannot with
advantage add a very great deal to the aforegoing by what, such
as it is to be, follows, just mentioning however that the old man

of the sea and the old woman in the sky if they don't say nothings about it they don't tell us lie, the gist of the pantomime. (599.29)

Unlike the narrator of a more conventional novel, who utilizes his last few moments with his reader to tie up loose ends of the plot line and perhaps even to point a moral, the narrator of *Finnegans Wake* only tells us that the truths of his book should have been self-evident before we began: "Our wholemole millwheeling vicociclometer . . . is known to every schoolboy scandaller" (614.27).

Positions reversed, the reader implores the narrator for information, rather than vice versa, but his only answer is calming reassurance: "What has gone? How it ends? Begin to forget it. It will remember itself from every sides, with all gestures, in each our word. Today's truth, tomorrow's trend. Forget, remember!" (614.19). In other words, we should allow what we have been shown to blend with our own experiences, and then its universal significance will be revealed. Since it is the relative, fluid nature of all historical events that Vico and Joyce are describing, there is finally no didactic statement that the narrator could make, even if he were inclined to do so. The closest he comes to this is only a statement of the mutual interdependence of the various spatial and temporal cycles: "Themes have thimes and habit reburns. To flame in you. Ardor vigor forders order. Since ancient was our living is in possible to be" (614.8). From his ultimately objective position the narrator leaves us with the river, the life-giving fluid upon which the earth survives. Individuals have disappeared, and only the essential forces of existence remain. It is almost as if the narrator too has learned from the progression of *Finnegans Wake*, so that he may attain to the calmness and depth of understanding that Joyce expects the reader to achieve. He, the narrator, is not refined out of existence; but rather, he hopes that what has gone before should speak for itself. He accepts it, and so should we.

Another reason our narrator leaves the last word to Anna Livia, rather than stepping to the front of the stage himself, might be explained by a comment he makes early in the final chapter: "The untireties of livesliving being the one substrance of a streamsbecoming. Totalled in toldteld and teldtold in tittletell tattle" (597.7). Anna Livia as the river is a physical, realistic example of the concept of existence that the narrator is presenting. In her trancelike state she is the "Streamsbecoming," beginning and ending, summing up her story and the story of humanity in gossip and rumor, a tattletale who reveals the secrets of us all. "Every talk has his stay" (597.19), says the narrator, and he ends his conversation by allowing ALP the final statement. We are left with another illustration rather than a close, a "the" rather than a period. As Samuel Beckett reminds us: "the danger is in the neatness of identifications,"[11] but it does seem that this apparent loose end is but a final reminder of the principle upon which the book is based. Take any individual in any given time and one can see that there are parallels in all the centuries of historical time and place,[12] all of which can be reduced to the primal features and forces of the landscape.

The narrator serves as a kind of master of the revels, a Prospero without the latter's supreme self-assurance, who stands above the action, directing it subtly toward a meaningful end. His hand is behind all that transpires, but it is a hand that the characters do not feel and the reader seldom sees. Unlike Prospero, however, who peoples an island with sprites and monsters to demonstrate his world view, the narrator of *Finnegans Wake* is content to work with the raw materials that the real world presents to him. Though the

11. "Dante . . . Bruno. Vico . . Joyce," *Our Exagmination Round His Factification for Incamination of Work in Progress* (Paris: Shakespeare and Co., 1929), p. 3.

12. Hugh Kenner condenses this to: "Finnegan's recumbency is the sleep of every superannuated hero, his resurrection every resurgence, his wake every hurlyburly of the practical world," *Dublin's Joyce* (Bloomington: Indiana University Press, 1956), p. 323.

characters undergo very little change throughout the narrative (they are basically the same at the end as they were at the beginning), it is the narrator himself who is different. In actuality he has learned nothing new, but, along with the reader, he has managed an acceptance of the concepts he believed were true when he began his production.

He comes to the novel, in other words, with a set of precepts that he proves both to the reader and to himself. His passage from a position of intellectual aloofness to a mingling with the inhabitants of mundane reality strengthens and justifies his cosmic overview at the end. His ideas have been tested among the individual raw materials from which they were created, and once again they have been shown to be consistent. Like the reader and like *Finnegans Wake* itself, he is returned to his starting point, but his and our lack of rest has proved more beneficial to us than the sleep of the Earwickers to them. Bloom and Molly have not changed a great deal at the end of *Ulysses*, and neither have Humphrey and Anna, but, once again, they demonstrate Joyce's conception of an unchanging universe. What he asks for is comprehension, not change.

4

The Dreams of the Dreamers

Existing on yet another level are the many characters who populate the interpolated stories in the novel. Though such madcap personages as the Prankquean, the Norwegian Captain, and Burrus and Caseous do no dreaming of their own, they are creations of several of the Earwickers and give an added life to these tales within the tale. Popping up seemingly at random, the stories introduce us to the Mookse and the Gripes, the Ondt and the Gracehoper, Willingdone and Lipoleum, and Buckley and the Russian General. Pleasing enough in themselves, the tales are manipulated by the characters to present their own points of view in fable and parable, and they can also tell us more about the Earwickers themselves.

The interpolations can best be understood if one equates them with one of the building blocks that Joyce used to anchor his book: the portmanteau word. As is well known, Joyce expanded upon Lewis Carroll's idea of composing one word that is a combination of many, thus compressing a great deal of meaning into a little space. So, too, while retaining its own individuality, each of the tales is a microcosm containing elements of the major themes and concepts that constitute the macrocosm of *Finnegans Wake*. In Joyce's own words, each is a "dodecanesian baedeker of the every-tale-a-treat-in-itself variety" (123.27). Utilizing some of the notions of Vico and

Bruno, he allows his characters and settings to vary from story to story, but essentially the tales discuss the same things: the fall of the father into ultimate disgrace and/or the brother rivalry of the twins. All, in one way or another, are sexual in nature[1] and concern the desire of the father for the mother or daughter, the brother for the brother or sister, the brother or sister for the father or mother, or simply the man for the man or woman. Often the interpolations contain several of these combinations, and they may at once have several applications to various levels of the plot. The task of explication is the reader's: "Now? How good you are in explosition! How far-flung is your folkloire and how velktingeling your volupkabulary!" (419.12).

Giambattista Vico's theory of the cyclic progression of history is as important to an understanding of the interpolations as it is to the construction of Joyce's book itself. By now, most of us are familiar with Vico's contention that the progress of man can be recorded in three ages, Divine, Heroic, and Civil (the beginning announced by a thunderclap), the whole sequence concluding with a brief waiting period, or recorso, before everything begins again. Such, in essence, is the structure of *Finnegans Wake*. The interpolations, too, are based upon this plan, for each the action "recurs in three times the same differently" (481.10)[2]. The tripartite structure is clearly defined in such a tale as the Prankquean's (21.5–23.15), since her three journeys to van Hoother's castle correspond with the three ages of Vico, and the period of the peace treaty serves as recorso. The Prankquean's three visits are paralleled by those of the

---

1. Margaret Solomon has extended this idea at length in *Eternal Geomater: The Sexual Universe of Finnegans Wake* (Carbondale: S. Illinois University Press, 1969).

2. Interestingly enough, John Peale Bishop links such circular structure to Irish folklore: "The circulatory form is one which seems to be especially sympathetic to the Irish mind, for many of the Irish fairy tales proceed in a circle, like the story of Oisin, where we are brought at the end back to the beginning," *Collected Essays* (New York: Random House, 1948), p. 158.

Gracehoper (414.18–419.10): "he took a round stroll and he took a stroll round and he took a round strollagain" (416.27), and the latter's adventures with the Ondt are presented in three scenes and a concluding poem. The stories of the Mookse and the Gripes (152.15–159.18) and Burrus and Caseous (161.15–167.25) both contain three dramatic sections and a conclusion, while the Norwegian Captain's three forays to the pub of the Ship's Husband and his three riddles or questions (311.21–332.35) fit his tale into the Viconian structure. In almost every case the recorso section of an interpolation is used to herald the coming of another tale or cycle or to remind us of those that have come before: "how kirssy the tiler made a sweet unclose to the Narwhealian captol" (Prankquean, 23.10),"Moo thought on the deeps of the undths ... if by grice he had luck enoupes" (Mookse and Gripes, 158.15), "by way of letting the aandt out of her grosskropper and leading the mokes home by their gribes" (Norwegian Captain, 331.15), "*you quit your mocks for my gropes*" (Ondt and Gracehoper, 418.32). Each interpolation is an example of the Viconian cycle that has no beginning or end, for Joyce realizes: "all that has been done has yet to be done and done again" (194.10). Like Vico's cycles, each interpolation is but a redescribing of the civilization of man, though here, as we shall see, the man is particularized as Earwicker.

"It follows," Vico announces near the beginning of Book I of the *New Science*, "that the first science to be learned should be mythology or the interpretation of fables, which were the first histories of the gentile nations."[3] Taking his cue from Vico, Joyce studs his novel with fables that contain within themselves the keys to his book, though on first reading they may seem unrelated to Chapelizod and the family of a local pub keeper. This is not to say that the fables assume more importance or require more scrutiny than the main narrative;

3. Quoted in Hugh Kenner, *Dublin's Joyce* (Bloomington: University of Indiana Press, 1956), pp. 329–30.

but what we can learn from them can be applied with great benefit to the central events of the saga of the Earwickers. One explanation of the stories' obscurity, however, may be given by Vico himself:

> The first age invented the fables to serve as true narratives, the primary and proper meaning of the word *mythos*, as defined by the Greeks themselves, being "true narration." The second altered and corrupted them. The third and last, that of Homer, received them thus corrupted.[4]

The fables of *Finnegans Wake* are not corrupted, but we do exist in the age of Homer, and Joyce forces his reader to interpret or piece them together for himself. Getting at the meaning of the fables entails an examination and understanding of history, and this is exactly what Joyce desires of his reader.

Also, just as the cycles of Vico can be universalized to include all peoples in all ages, so too can the interpolations. Each character is of a different nationality, and each story takes place in a different historical setting. Besides the obvious heritages of such as the Norwegian Captain, Chinese creeps into the discourses of the Romans, Burrus and Caseous: "she's very fond of Burrus but, alick and alack! she velly fond of chee" (166.30). German is spoken in the Ondt and Gracehoper: "Nichtsnichtsundnichts!" (416.17) as well as in several other tales; the Prankquean speaks French: "her petty perusienne" (21.17); and the Norwegian Captain converses in a strange composite language called "translatentic norjankeltian" (311.21). Times vary from pre-Christian Rome (Burrus and Caseous) to twelfth-century Ireland (Mookse and Gripes) to nineteenth-century France (Willingdone and Lipoleum). Literary forms, too, move from folklore

---

4. *The New Science of Giambattista Vico*, trans. T. G. Bergin and M. H. Fisch (New York: Vintage Books, 1961), p. 256.

(Prankquean) to fable (Ondt and Gracehoper) to television play (Norwegian Captain). Though the story of Earwicker should not be interpreted as merely the epic of Everyman, the themes with which he is involved are eternal. The interpolations, as contrasting views of the life of HCE and his family, are applicable to all times and places, and they serve to transfer the drama to a cosmic stage.

As a corollary to the thought of Vico, Joyce employed Giordano Bruno's ideas that, again, history is cyclical and that something can attain to a knowledge of itself only through an understanding of, and fusion with, its opposite. This thesis is most relevant in *Finnegans Wake* to the struggles of the twins, Shem and Shaun, for it is apparent that neither may really triumph over the other—they must combine their efforts if any of their projects are to come to fruition. The interpolations that deal with the brother conflict bear this out, since each entity that appears is quickly complemented by its opposite. The Mookse and the Gripes fable is a prime example, opening with an invocation of "Bruno Nowlan" (152.11) and closing with the turnabout "Nolan Browne" (159.22). Also, the sight of the Mookse parallels the hearing of the Gripes: "The Mookse had a sound eyes right but he could not all hear. The Gripes had light ears left yet he could but ill see" (158.13). The contrasts are more clearly defined as the levels of identity deepen: the Mookse is Shaun, Pope Adrian IV, St. Michael, St. Peter, Tory, Dog, Stone; the Gripes is Shem, Lawrence O'Toole, Satan, St. Paul, Whig, Cat, and Tree. These strings of multiple identity and opposition serve to describe the situations at hand through the simultaneous presentation of a myriad of similar instances. Each situation must, in a sense, be read vertically as well as horizontally.

Paradoxically, these oppositions or antagonisms, rather than alienating the brother figures, tend to draw them closer together. In the Mutt and Jute dialogue (16.9–18.16), the two characters exchange identities in order to continue their discussion: "Let us swop hats and excheck a few strong verbs weak oach eather" (16.8). In the tale of Buckley and the Russian General[5] (338.3–355.7), Butt and Taff, in order to accomplish the shooting of the General, become "*One and the same person*" (354.8), united as Buckley.[6] Shem and Shaun are "samuraised twimbs" (354.24), who can work together only when they have a common goal: the overthrow of their father. The deposition of the father by the sons, exemplified in the struggle of Cronus and Zeus, is another of Bruno's theses, one that can be found in each of the interpolated stories. It is only here, in the tales, that the brothers achieve this unity, so that the fables act as a signpost for them as well as for the reader.

The exact nature of the sin of HCE is still clouded in supposition, and perhaps this is the way Joyce wanted it. No matter what precisely did happen in Phoenix Park between HCE, the two girls, and three soldiers, the effects of the guilt engendered there are of primary importance. His transgression of fall from grace haunts Earwicker throughout the book, coloring his actions and his interpretation of those of others. Conversations are centered around rumor and misrepresentation, and the facts of the adventure in the Park only become more and more obscured. Though the interpolations that do deal with HCE's disgrace view his fall from several perspectives, they serve to provide insight into the causes and effects of this fall upon the protagonist, and may even help in clearing up some of its mystery.

The Museyroom episode (8.9–10.23) is a good example of

5. For an intensive exploration of this tale see Nathan Halper's "James Joyce and the Russian General," *Partisan Review* 18 (July 1951): 424–31.

6. Discussed by Bernard Benstock in "The Quiddity of Shem and the Whatness of Shaun," *James Joyce Quarterly* 1 (Fall 1963): 26–33.

this, for Earwicker's demise is displayed to the public in the guise of the Willingdone's disgrace at the hands of the Jinnies and the "three lipoleum boyne" (8.21). The focus here is primarily upon HCE as the Willingdone—Lipoleum does not appear—and thus a situation is set up parallel with that in the Park. The Jinnies, as temptresses, taunt the willingdone about his wife's conduct on the homefront: "Fieldgaze [*Wie geht's*] thy tiny frow. Hugacting" (9.5), perhaps offering themselves as compensation, but they are curtly rejected in his return message: "fairly ann [*fait rien*]" (9.14). From this it does seem possible that perhaps poor Humphrey is innocent of promiscuity, at least in deed, after all. The Willingdone's fall comes about through the efforts of Shimar Shin (Shem and Shaun), rather than as a result of sexual temptation. Willingdone's crude joke: "hanking the half of the hat of lipoleums up the tail on the buckside of his big white harse" (10.10), so infuriates the opposition that they blow his horse out from under him, and he is thrown into the mire. (It is possible that the joke consists of the Willingdone himself defecating into the hat, the Irish "hat trick," shades of the Prankquean's "pea trick" and the Russian General.) The salient thematic element in this episode is the struggle of the sons to overthrow the father with a combined effort, and his fall comes about when he refuses to let well enough alone. The Willingdone's excessive attempts to reject the Jinnies and to insult his adversaries serve only, like HCE's extensive denials and justifications, to enmesh him more deeply.

Several pages later, in the tale of the Prankquean, Earwicker is transformed into Jarl van Hoother, and his fall is presented in a different light. John Peale Pishop asserts that the tale "contains the most important elements of the situation which lies beneath the sleeper's anguish."[7] Once

7. *Collected Essays*, p. 152.

again HCE is sexually tempted, this time by the three visits of the Prankquean, and once again he is able to resist. His will power, however, seems to draw strength from the fact that he is more enamored of masturbation: "laying cold hands on himself . . . shaking warm hands with himself" (21.11), than he is of heterosexual love, and this debility foreshadows the waning of ALP's attraction for her husband. The story differs from the Museyroom in that the prime antagonist now is the Prankquean as Anna Livia Plurabelle, who uses her sexuality as a ruse to capture his children and influence them against him. The Jinnies of Lipoleum change sex and become Jimminies, or the twins.[8] The three children, Tristopher, Hilary, and the dummy (Issy), serve as the passive, watching soldiers, while ALP incorporates into herself the attributes of the girls in the Park.[9]

When van Hoother finally does take action at this treachery, he manages only to disgrace himself by inadvertent defecation in his angry excitement: "he clopped his rude hand to his eacy hitch and he ordurd" (23.3), and is forced to make peace. The father is overthrown once more, here through the influence of the mother, and again a joke is at the center of things, for Jarl van Hoother is unable to answer the riddle of the Prankquean, which would have brought him dominance: "why do I am alook alike a poss of porterpease?" (21.17).

HCE is assailed from all sides, and it soon becomes evident that, despite his sexual peccadilloes, his flaw lies essentially in the relationships within his family and his own insecurity.

---

8. This change is discussed in greater detail in my article "The Prankquean in *Finnegans Wake,*" *James Joyce Quarterly* 1 (Spring 1964): 14–18.

9. Analyses of the Prankquean and her riddle have proliferated. Some of the more relevant are: E. L. Epstein, "Chance, Doubt, Coincidence, and the Prankquean's Riddle," *A Wake Newslitter* 6 (February 1969):3–7; Ronald J. Koch, "Giordano Bruno and *Finnegans Wake,*" *James Joyce Quarterly* 9 (Winter 1971):237–49; Grace Eckley, "Petween Peas Like Ourselves: The Folklore of the Prankquean," *James Joyce Quarterly* 9 (Winter 1971):177–88.

Conflicts rage around him, but he seems unable to understand them until it is too late. Both the Museyroom and the Prankquean point to the fact that Earwicker's demise is the ault of no overt action of his own. Both Willingdone and arl van Hoother attempt to ignore their adversaries, and it s their inactivity that results in their respective failures. It is Earwicker's own inability to act that contributes to his deline. He is certainly guilty of sin, but in most cases the sin is f omission rather than commission. No doubt he would ave liked to make advances to the girls in the Park, but in ll probability he was guilty only of poor judgment in chooing a bush behind which to relieve himself. Tormented by uilt and fear, he allows the clouds of suspicion to rise around im, helping them on with his incriminating denials. He seems nuch like the child who overturns the cookie jar and greets is mother at the door with the statement that nothing has appened during her absence. The interpolations show us hat, in actuality, the encounter in the Park is of less imporance than the relationships between HCE, his wife, and his hildren. Here are to be found the true causes of his spiritual all, and it is here that he is most unable to cope with situaions. Like the Willingdone, he talks himself into a corner; ke van Hoother, he hesitates and is lost.

The theme of brother rivalry apparently fascinated Joyce, nd he traces its working throughout history. Two stories, he Mookse and the Gripes and Burrus and Caseous, center round his problem, and they seem to take place at a time vhen the father has been overthrown and the brothers are truggling over the spoils. It is important to remember that oth incidents occur in the same chapter, are narrated by haun, and are daydream or wish fulfillment, since the father s already out of the way and things are slanted so that Shem eems easily defeated. The episodes convey a great deal of nsight into the character of Shaun, tell us more about the true

nature of the rivalry, and show that Shem is not to be s‹
quickly eliminated as Shaun might wish. The essence of thei‹
relationship is again shown to be Bruno's contrariness of oppo‹
sites, hate in love and love in hate: "I Shaun hate him abou‹
his patent henesy, plasfh it, yet am I amorist. I love him" (46:‹
17).

The Mookse (Shaun) adopts the role of the invader o‹
usurper, cloaked in the persona of Pope Adrian IV, as ha‹
often been recognized, and attempts to extend his dominanc‹
over the Gripes (Shem), who represents the Irish branch o‹
the Catholic Church. The struggle between them is a‹
intellectual one, with the Mookse relying upon many theolo‹
gical sources to argue rings around the Gripes, who can onl‹
taunt his opponent "about aulne and lithial [Anna Livia]'
(154.4), the mother who often displays her preference for him‹
The Gripes continually admits the rightness of the positio‹
of the Mookse, as will the Gracehoper later on, but it i‹
here, in his moment of triumph, that Shaun allows victory t‹
slip from his grasp. He cannot refrain in his pedantry fron‹
extending the discussion *ad infinitum:* "bullfolly answere‹
volleyball" (157.7). Even the blandishments of the endearin‹
Nuvoletta cannot sway the Mookse, and he babbles on a‹
twilight falls. The aforementioned homosexuality is presen‹
in tone and intimation, rather than in actual occurrence, a‹
the Gripes is ordered to "abase you, baldyqueens" (154.12)‹
and the Mookse gestures with his "jewelled pererect" (155.23)‹
The battle must be declared a stalemate, for the twins meta‹
morphose into drying laundry and are gathered up from th‹
riverbank by an old washerwoman (ALP). In essence, thei‹
mother ends the meaningless struggle and carries them off t‹
bed where they belong. Joyce is declaring, through the fable‹
that the rivalry of the brothers cannot result in victory fo‹
either, that neither brother can win since each needs the othe‹
in order to define himself.

The Mookse and the Gripes episode takes on even more significance when one realizes that the appearance of Nuvoletta adds a further thematic level to the story. Besides appearing as Issy, watching the contest of the boys, she is also Anna Livia Plurabelle: "her muddied name was Missisliffi" (159.12), foreshadowing the final chapter of the novel. From this perspective, the twins symbolically represent HCE, and their spurning of the female is the rejection of ALP by her husband, Earwicker. Like Anna Livia, Nuvoletta is forced to return to the sea, to renew herself from whence she came. Nuvoletta's cry as she leaps into the stream: "Nuée! Nuée!" (159.9) transforms her suicide into a rebirth, underlining the cyclical continuity of the Earwickers' relationship and that of *Finnegans Wake* itself. Through subtle shading, ALP can be both mother and daughter, Shem and Shaun both father and son. The utilization of Bruno is self-evident. Here again one perceives the prime function of the interpolations—the fusion of the main strands of the narrative into a single unit that can illustrate all of them at the same time.

In the Burrus and Caseous piece, the names have been changed, but the situation appears the same. Caesar is dead, "having been sort-of-nine-knived" (162.5), and the scene is set by the images of war that pervade the first few passages. As might be expected in a companion picture, however, the mirroring techniques in this story reverse the significance of the events that the reader has just seen acted out by the Mookse and the Gripes. As Joyce admits, he is "pudding the carp before doevre hors" (164.17). Shem, as Caseous, is again deplored, while Shaun, as Burrus, is lauded, but any violent rivalry is practically nonexistent. Instead, the two are involved in the kind of forced alliance that enmeshed their historical counterparts, Brutus and Cassius. Again a girl is involved in the Drama, but Margareena is a poor substitute for Nuvoletta. She is a cheap shopgirl with no illusions about love, who spends much of her time "avidously reading about 'it' but evidently on the look out for 'him' " (166.11). Rather than ignoring the girl as did the Mookse and the Gripes, Burrus and Caseous contend for her affections, but they find that it is the female who is in control of the situation. Margareena, as Cleopatra, spurns them both for Antonius, as Joyce proposes his own reworking of Shakespeare's Roman plays. Burrus and Caseous are left alone to learn how to "be tolerant of antipathies" (163.15). In actuality, however, Antonius is not a new character at all; he is the entity formed by the fusion of Burrus and Caseous as Bruno's plilosophy again comes into play. Antonius has a "personal interest in refined chees of all chades at the same time as he wags an antomine art of being rude like the boor" (167.2). As with Butt and Taff, two opposing principles meld to achieve a common goal: "the *qualis* equivalent" formed by "*talis* on *talis*" (167.5)[10].

The dominant note of this section is artificiality and disguise, for it is made apparent that Margareena is not all that she appears to be. Notwithstanding the shallowness of her character, she is in reality a lesbian, concealing "her own more mascular personality by flaunting frivolish finery over men's inside clother" (166.24). She uses the affair with Antonius-Burrus-Caseous only as a cloak to hide her more devious activities. At the same time, suspicion is cast upon Burros and Caseous, who are described as "too males pooles (164.4), or two male prostitutes. The perverted sexuality speaks for itself, and this, along with the theme of concealment, is a parallel to HCE's behavior in the Park and his meeting with the Cad following the incident. We see that the promiscuity and sexual guilt symbolically represented here are common to the sons and daughter, as well as to the father, and that any sort of sexual fulfillment in the world of the Earwickers is negligible.

---

10. Bernard Benstock views this fusion basically the same way in *Joyce-again's Wake* (Seattle: University of Washington Press, 1965) p. 239.

Neither the Mookse and Gripes nor Burrus and Caseous presents any resolution of the conflict, since in neither does one of the brothers come out ahead of the other. It is the fable of the Ondt and the Gracehoper that draws the various thematic strands of the rivalry together conclusively. On the surface the story appears to be but another of the clashes of the brothers, with Shaun as the thrifty Ondt rightfully refusing solace to Shem as the frivolous Gracehoper who has played away the summer. Shaun, again the narrator and perhaps plagued with delusions of grandeur, intends to rule all by himself and to make his reign and realm much greater than "Beppy's" (415.36) or Pappy's. Finally, the Ondt, "that true and perfect host" (417.24), to accomplish his end leaves his brother to die of starvation as the winter approaches.

It is at this point that Joyce reveals the true purpose of the story, since here the narrative point of view shifts and Shem is allowed room for his own thoughts on the proceedings. In an episode abounding with allusions to philosophers of the past, Shem emerges as the spokesman for the present of *Finnegans Wake*. The poem concluding that fable is an artistic production, naturally a creation of the Penman. The Gracehoper nobly forgives the Ondt for the latter's ill treatment of him, admits his own foolish behavior, and strives in the body of his piece to acquaint the Ondt with the reality of their relationship. He insists that each of them desperately needs the other: "Can castwhores [Castor] *pulladeftkiss if oldpollocks* [Pollux] *forforsake 'em*" (418.23). Though the unification results in something less than an aristocrat: "*Homo Vulgaris*" (418.26), oneness is requisite if either is to function productively. Here is Joyce's most personal and direct statement on the Brunonian conflict of the twins. He has, for the moment, identified himself with the Gracehoper: "hoppy on akkant of his joyicity" (414.22) and "blind as a batflea" (417.3), to underline this theme: "*We are Wastenot with Want, precondamned, two and true,/ Till Nolans go volants and Bruneyes come blue*" (418. 30).

From the abovementioned allusions to the fall of the father, it must seem that more is involved here than the brother rivalry alone. The Gracehoper is also employed as HCE, whose fall is described once more. The amorous intentions of the Gracehoper, or Earwicker, flourished during the summer months when, along with Floh, Luse, Bienie, and Vespatilla, he had "Auld Letty Plussiboots [ALP.] to scratch his cacumen" (415.3). With the coming of autumn or later life, however, he is left alone by them all, just as HCE is to be deserted by ALP in the fourth and final section of the book. True to the structural pattern of the interpolated stories, Joyce touches upon all of the Earwickers, moving his reader closer to the core of this family's existence.

The tale of the Norwegian Captain, a television play on a set "as modern as tomorrow afternoon" (309.14) in HCE's pub, has been saved for last in this discussion, since it is the most difficult of the stories to comprehend, even on the literal level. Adaline Glasheen, too modestly, says she "really do(es) not know what happens in the . . . episode,"[11] and Clive Hart feels that "the Norwegian Captain is . . . an incarnation of Earwicker's anti-self, the Man-Servant (indentified with the Cad) who, like Shem, is always associated with the Norwegian language."[12] While there is something to say for Hart's theory, William York Tindall thoroughly confuses the issue by thinking that the Norwegian Captain and Ship's Husband are one and the same character and asserting that "he (the Captain) marries the tailor's daughter."[13] With the hope of clearing up some of this uncertainty, I present my own chronology of events.

11. *A Second Census of Finnegans Wake* (Evanston: Northwestern University Press, 1963), p. 187.

12. *Structure and Motif in Finnegans Wake* (Evanston: Northwestern University Press, 1962), p. 125.

13. *A Reader's Guide to James Joyce* (New York: Noonday Press, 1962), p. 285.

Part I: the Norwegian Captain, a Scandinavian sea rover, appears in the pub owned by the Ship's Husband and, after several drinks, asks where he can purchase a suit of clothes; he is directed to Kersse the Tailor, who takes his measurements and assures him that the garments will be properly fitted (311.5–36).[14] The often-quoted story of Joyce's father about the tailor and the hump-backed sea captain functions here; the Captain, a joker like the Prankquean, runs out without paying for the suit: "holey bucket, dinned he raign" (312.12), ignoring Kersse's imprecations; the Tailor is made the butt of the humor of the onlooking patrons of the pub (312.13–14), and finally decides that the Captain is dead: "following pnomoneya he is consistently blown to Adams" (313.12); in the interim the Ship's Husband prospers and the drinkers discuss Finnegans accident and Kersse's relationship with the young daughter of the Ship's Husband, who "wends to scoulas in her slalpers" (314.35).

Part II: the Norwegian Captain returns from his voyage: "Howe cools Eavybrolly! . . . Skibbereen has common inn" (315.20–34) and is acclaimed by the tipplers, who appreciated his earlier prank: "Heirs at you, Brewinbaroon! Weth a whistle for methanks" (316.9); he is welcomed back by the Ship's Husband and, happy at his reception, orders food and drink for the house: "He made the sign of the feaster. Cloth be laid!" (317.11); the bill for all this merrymaking mounts steadily, but the Captain is unaware of it, for he is musing on the Ship's Husband's daughter and the pleasures of matrimony: "Take thee live all save the wive? I'll think uplon, lilady" (318.3); the Captain is soon drunk and leaves for the outhouse as the spree continues in all its intensity; the enjoyment of the freeloaders increases at this bounty, but the Ship's Husband realizes that he has extended too much credit

14. Somehow or other, Mrs. Solomon decides that "the attempts to 'fit' the captain with the 'suit' are homosexual encounters," *Eternal Geomater*, p. 35.

and "swished to the lord he hand't" (319.32); the Captain returns to the barroom and publicly curses the Tailor for a fop:
"adepted to nosestorsioms in his budinholder" (320.4), before once again taking to his heels and running out on the
bill: "soaking scupper, didn't he drain" (320.30). At this
point the production pauses for station identification, and
the drinkers in Earwicker's pub take this opportunity to order refills (320.36–321.2).

Part III: Kersse enters the pub dressed in dandified fashion,
having been to the steeplechase, and is jeered by the crowd:
"Tick off that whilehot, you scum if a botch" (322.5); it turns
out that Kersse is in actuality a Welshman, "welsher," who
attempts to dress like a native Irishman: "had been mocking
his hollaballoon a sample of the costume of the country"
(322.6); the Tailor answers with threats of what would happen
to the Captain if he ever returned, and he swears that no one
alive could have fitted the Captain's humped back: "that
hell of a hull of a hill of a camelump bakk" (323.23); now
the Captain does return: "Heave, coves, emptybloddy!"
(324.11), and the drama is interrrupted momentarily for a
weather report, a newscast that foreshadows the Captain's
marriage: "Birdflights confirm abbroaching nubtials"
(324.36), and a commercial; the play resumes with the Ship's
Husband, who apparently has heard of the Captain's longing
for a wife, offering him the hand of his daughter. There seems
a suspicion that Kersse has already gotten the girl pregnant,
for "either you does or he musts and this moment same"
(325.19), decrees the father; the Ship's Husband declares that
marriage will civilize the Captain and, on the spot, baptizes
him as a Catholic and an Irishman: "I popetithes thee, Ocean
[Oisin]" (326.6); though the Captain doesn't like this: "he was
haltid considerable agenst all religions" (326.21), the ceremony is a *fait accompli*, and the Ship's Husband now turns to
Kersse and attempts to reconcile him with the Captain; he then

goes on to describe his daughter's charms to the Captain and assures him she will "work her mireiccles and give Norgeyborgey good airish timers" (327.30); she will want children and the Captain will have to "beat his barge into a battering pram with her wattling way for cubblin" (328.2), but all will be well.

Part IV (Recorso): the populace rejoices at the prospect of the wedding: "Dub did glow that night" (329.14), and the play ends with the bride's comments upon the marriage and honeymoon. Strangely, Mrs. Glasheen feels that "the Captain is castrated and that Kersse is a female or turns into a female."[15] The first statement may be spiritually true, but the last does not seem justified by the text.

The story of the Norwegian Captain is told in Book II, the very center of *Finnegans Wake*, and it functions as the thematic keystone that unites the dealings of Earwicker, Anna Livia, Shem, Shaun, and Issy. From one perspective the adventures of the Captain are those of HCE in his youth. (He is humpbacked, stutters, is called "Hombreyhambrey" (317.10), and has probably inherited the pub from the father of ALP.) The Captain's courting of the daughter parallels HCE's wooing of Anna Livia (who appears as "Anna Lynchya Pourable" (325.4)). It may seem somewhat hard to believe that the buccaneering Captain of this tale could have degenerated into the spiritless Earwicker, yet the seeds of his decline are sown within the story. His settling down, itself, into conventional Dublin may be seen as a fall, and the honeymoon scene demonstrates that he has already begun to lose control of his marital affairs. At the same time, however, rather than being completely pessimistic, this story too is Viconian: "the first course, recoursing" (322.36), and Earwicker in his prime is quite admirable. He *is* godlike and heroic as we first meet

15. *A Second Census of Finnegans Wake*, p. 138.

him, and he does manage to vanquish his adversary in a kind
of war and a kind of love. That he must arrive at the mundane
civil age is inevitable. He is what he is—simply a man—and
Joyce's tale helps to illuminate the character's erstwhile
heroism and to explain his eventual and gradual demise.

On another level, the vying of the Captain and Kersse for
the daughter of the Ship's Husband reiterates the struggle of
the brothers for the favor of Issy. Shem, as the Captain, is
the bold and rebellious nonconformist who opposes Shaun,
as Kersse, the respectable, bourgeois tailor who stands as
one of the conventional pillars of society.[16] This is the only
instance where Shem seems victorious, but the Ship's Husband goes to great lengths to reconcile the antagonists and to
impress upon them their interdependence: "Brothers
Boathes, brothers Coathes, ye have swallen blooders' oathes"
(325.25). To triumph, Shem is forced to accept the civilizing
aspects of society in his baptism and retirement from the sea,
and, on closer examination, we find that Shem alone does not
conquer at all. Once again, as in tale after tale, the brothers
blend into a single entity to achieve consummation.[17] The
bridegroom who demands entrance at Issy's door on the first
night of the honeymoon is a composite formed of Shem and
Shaun: "Knock knock. War's where! Which war? The
Twwinns" (330.30). Here the brothers reap the benefits to be
gained from alliance, and the fertility of their actions reflects
ironically upon the increasing sterility of their father. Such
is the cyclic nature of all existence, here again described as

16. For Roland McHugh: "in the earlier part of the episode the three are distinguished by spellings of the word 'said.' Pukkelsen, the Norwegian Captain (sagd), is
Shem; Kersse the Tailor (sazd), is Shaun. . . . The Ship's Husband (sayd), is Shem-
shaun," "A Structural Theory of *Finnegans Wake*," *A Wake Newslitter* 5 (December
1968): 85.

17. Benstock sees the problem as an aesthetic one: "reconciliation seems dependent upon the artist's willingness to share his creative inspiration and the willingness
of the bourgeois to accept the significance of that inspiration." *Joyce-again's Wake*, p. 244.

Shem and Shaun embark upon the circle that is coming to an end for Humphrey Chimpden Earwicker.

At this point it should become clear that the term *interpolated*, which has been used to describe these episodes, is a misnomer, for they certainly do not distract the reader from the main narrative of *Finnegans Wake*. On the contrary, they are pauses in the temporal and spatial flow of the action where Joyce redefines and reillustrates the essential elements of his work. The technique draws upon the tradition of the conventional novel—the "old Man of the Hill" pause in *Tom Jones*, to cite just one example, functions in exactly the same manner. Simple on their surfaces, they are convoluted at their cores; they are simple fables that could *almost* be read to children, and they are unravelings of the book's mystery. Our dreamers certainly have pleasant and unusual dreams.

5
Riddling, Writing, and Reason

The mystery and confusion that pervade the very fabric of *Finnegans Wake* insure that asking and questioning play a major role in the unfolding of the narrative. The Four Old Men, for example, lead the actual inquisitors, and they never cease in their squabbling interrogation of a myriad number of witnesses. In other instances, to name only a few, the Prankquean asks her riddle, the Cad asks for the time, and Shem asks Shaun for forgiveness. Needless to say, none of these questions is answered satisfactorily, if indeed they are answered at all, and perhaps Joyce is implying that the solutions that the characters cannot supply are left to the perception of the reader. We might recall Fritz Senn's: "the game of *Finnegans Wake,* at any rate, is an ignitious one, and once we become ignitiated there is no simple way to stop the process."[1] It might almost be said that one of the first of these questions: "What then agentlike brought about that tragoady thundersday this municipal sin business?" (5.13) sets the problem that is dealt with by the whole of *Finnegans Wake,* since in its implications it includes Adam, Finnegan, Humphrey Chimpden Earwicker, and all of us.

On page after page we are bombarded with questions, riddles, anagrams, guessing games, as Joyce's rendition of

1. "A Reading Exercise in *Finnegans Wake,*" *Levende Talen* 269 (June-July 1970): 479.

"life's robulous rebus" (12.34) goes its own way, hurrying along to a second and a third query before we have had time to consider the first. The vital difference between the characters is still clouded in doubt at the conclusion of the novel and the reader completing the final page is certain that he has been expected to pause often enough to ponder and to accomplish some solutions. The last question of the book is allotted to Anna Livia: "Is there one who understands me? One in a thousand of years of the nights?" (627.15), and it should not be taken as a rhetorical one. Like Scheherazade in the *Arabian Nights*, Joyce might continue his puzzles and paradigms indefinitely, but his intention is to stimulate us to investigate their meaning, not only to amuse. We must first recognize that such questioning situations exist before we can begin to deal with them. The novelist's technique is thus to permeate the narrative with questions that apply to the characters themselves and even with some that are put to the reader, hoping that he will understand why the fictional personages cannot answer theirs while dealing with those which pertain to him alone.

Discussing the use of riddles in Irish literature, Vivian Mercier finds in them

> a reminder of the oral nature of druidic lore and traditional Irish poetry and storytelling. The *fili* [Irish poet] had to know hundreds of tales by heart, and no doubt he was catechized orally to test his knowledge of them before he obtained his "degree" in poetry; almost inevitably the question became an integral part of the tale itself, or of any other traditional lore.[2]

It is likely that Joyce would be familiar with such a tradition, and the riddles and questions thus serve a double purpose in displaying the skill of the poet as well as drawing the reader on to insight. There definitely seems a relation to druidism

2. *The Irish Comic Tradition* (Oxford: Oxford University Press, 1962), p. 81.

here, as we shall see in the dialogue of Saint Patrick and the Druid Berkeley (611.4–613.4). Continuing, Mercier discusses an idea "imbedded in the popular beliefs of the Irish . . . that wisdom can be demonstrated by the propounding or answering of seemingly insoluble riddles,"[3] and once again there is a bearing on *Finnegans Wake*. It would seem that Joyce is quite consciously working in a tradition, utilizing those elements of his Irish literary heritage which he can reshape in the creation of a contemporary novel. Just as he borrows from Vico or Bruno or psychoanalysis, he turns back to the culture of his homeland to aid in structuring his work. Finnegan asks: "Did ye drink me doornail?" (24.15), a washer-woman asks: "O/ tell me all about/ Anna Livia! I want to hear all/ about Anna Livia" (196.1), and a rhythm of question and answer is developed that can be demonstrated himself throughout the book.

Not content with limiting himself to Ireland, Joyce makes use of traditions of questioning from many lands and times, as with the "Willingdone Museyroom" (8.10) which he transforms into the Chapel Perilous of the Grail Knight. Typically for Joyce, the symbols presented that Jessie L. Weston[4] records as Cup, Dish, Lance, and Sword appear at the entrance of the museum as "the Cap and Soracer . . . pike and fork" (8.12). All appear in different form in Earwicker's Chapelizod, but all contribute to a major theme, which Joyce is continually strengthening and augmenting with bits and pieces from everywhere. To illustrate this technique further, we might examine two of the major questioning motifs that have to do with Shem, our later-day *fili*. (Shem has "bardic memory," even though Shaun does term it "low" [172.28].) In one instance he asks a riddle that no one is able to answer: "When is a man not a man?" (170.5), and in another he asked

3. *Ibid.*, p. 86.
4. *From Ritual to Romance* (New York: Vintage Books, 1957), pp. 65–80.

to guess the correct color in a children's riddling game and fails. Time after time throughout the book references are made to the two situations. Their importance has not yet been adequately explored, since on examination we find that each centers, from a different perspective, on the core of what Joyce is demonstrating thematically in *Finnegans Wake*. In a letter to Miss Weaver, Joyce described in a general way Shem's predicament in the children's game:

> The scheme of the piece I sent you is the game we used to call Angels and Devils or colours. The Angels, girls, are grouped behind the Angel, Shawn, and the Devil has to come over three times and ask for a colour. If the colour he asks for has been chosen by any girl she has to run and he tries to catch her. As far as I have written he has come twice and been twice baffled.[5]

The color that Shem is not able to guess in his three tries is "heliotrope," and it is really no small wonder that he fails from the kind of clue he is given: "Up tightly in the front, down again on the loose, drim and drumming on her back and a pop from her whistle. What is that, O holytroopers? Isot givin yoe?" (223.9). After hinting at "red": "Hast thou feel liked carbunckley ones?" (224.35), he answers incorrectly: "monbreamstone?... Hellfeursteyn?... Van Diemen's coral pearl?" (225.22), and loses the game. (The riddle had been rephrased earlier during the trial of Festy King, but Shem does not seem to have recognized it: "Lindendelly, coke or skillies, spell me gart without a gate? Harlyadrope" [89.18].) The children laugh and make fun of him—Issy later sneers: "He, angel that I thought him, and he not aebel to speel eelyotripes, Mr. Tellibly Dibilcult!" (303. n. 1)—and Shem is bathed in ridicule. What is important here is that throughout the episode Shem has seemed more concerned

---

5. *Letters of James Joyce*, ed. Stuart Gilbert (New York: Viking Press, 1957), p. 295.

with the nature of questions and questioning than he has with the specific riddle itself.

Before making his answer he wonders why he is once again placed in this position: "What's my muffinstuffinaches for those times?" (225.11), and he answers himself with a description of existence: "Breath and bother and whatarcurss. Then breath more bother and more whatarcurss. Then no breath no bother but worrawarrawurms. And Shim shallave shome" (225.12). He seems to realize that man's existence is characterized by doubt and questioning, by an inability to fix upon a black-and-white definition of essentials, and that this individual situation is but one in an endless series that makes up the life of a sensitive and perceptive human being. The Rainbow Girls have little interest in "punns and Reedles" (239.35), but, from this point in the novel on, Shem attempts an answering, which Shaun and his more carefree cohorts never do. Whether or not he can accomplish this answering may be another matter, but at least he continues to try.

This seemingly trivial incident in the children's games is of such great significance because it bears directly on, and contains the key to, the Patrick-Druid Berkeley debate, which Joyce himself felt expressed the essence of his novel:

> Much more is intended in the colloquy between Berkeley the arch druid and his pidgin speech and Patrick the [?] and his Nippon English. It is also the defense and indictment of the book itself, B's theory of colours and Patrick's practical solution of the problem.[6]

Basically, the episode describes the defeat of Shem as the Arch Druid by Shaun as Saint Patrick[7] and the ensuing

6. *Ibid.*, p. 406.
7. Strangely enough, Adaline Glasheen reverses these identifications to make Shem a champion of the Church, a role he never plays, *A Second Census of Finnegans*

Catholicizing of Ireland, but the point over which they argue is color and its apprehension. The Druid is the first to state his case, and he says that individual colors are all that may be perceived by man in his fallen state, which seems to please man well enough. The Druid himself aspires to the greater vision of the perception of them all together, the appreciation of white light in its entirety. Such unity of vision and perception, he feels, is the only way man can begin to grasp the totality of reality. This is the argument with which he hopes to overcome the invader, Patrick. Colors, says the Druid, do

> not appear to full up together fallen man than under but one photoreflection of the several iridials gradationes of solar light, that one which that part of it (furnit of heupanepi world) had shown itself (part of fur of huepanwor) unable to absorbere, whereas for numpa one puraduxed seer in seventh degree of wisdom of Entis-Onton he savvy inside true inwardness of reality. (611.15)

Patrick does not seem to grasp this line of reasoning too well, dismissing it as "a handcaughtscheaf of synthetic shammyrag" (612.24), and instead of replying he plays upon the superstitions of the people in attendance. Kneeling down, he makes obeisance to the sun, "the sound sense sympol in a weedwayedwold of the firethere" (612.29), and he wins the day as a pragmatic Machiavelli since the ignorant populace shifts its allegiance without the blink of an eye.

Shem's downfall, however, is not in Joyce's estimation any defeat at all, since his vision is whole, not fragmented as is Shaun's. Paradoxically, Shaun chooses the sun, or darkness since one cannot look at it, and thus he exemplifies a dogmatic

Wake (Evanston: Northwestern University Press, 1963), p. lxiii. Bernard Benstock states rightly that: "Shem and Shaun share aspects of the Irish saint" throughout the novel, *Joyce-again's Wake* (Seattle: University of Washington Press, 1965), p. 13, but he later agrees that Shem is Berkeley here.

refusal to question a mystery and the concomitant stamping out of the poetic and scientific imaginations. He desires only the here and now, what is before him, and he cannot be bothered with questions of the aesthetic or spiritual. The tie with the children's guessing game is sounded at the beginning of this section as: "Heliotrope leads from Harem" (610.36), and becomes even more definite when one remembers that heliotrope, as well as being a shade of purple, is also a definition of any plant that turns toward the sun.[8] The reaction of the onlookers to Patrick's play is: "Good safe firelamp! hailed the heliots" (613.1), and thus they become identified with Shem's adversaries in the children's game. As "heliots," they are sun worshipers, adherents of the politician Tim Healy, who sided against Parnell, and "helots," or slaves, rather than leaders of men.

Just as before, Shem here symbolically cannot or will not recognize heliotrope or the sun, for his view of what is important refuses to accept such a split in unity, a cessation to questioning. To him, "Good safe firelamp" can never equate with "God save Ireland." The "safe" is not that with which he is concerned. Shem may be defeated in fact, but he is the victor in spirit, as was Leopold Bloom before him. Joyce is here discussing the value of questioning—answered, rewarded, or not—as opposed to dogmatic acceptance of sterile precepts that can only leave man in darkness. Shem never answers the problem put to him, but this is ultimately unimportant, since it is the attempt that gives meaning to his existence. Rather than gazing at the ground in submission, Shem is the character who turns his eyes to the heavens: *"looking through the roof towards a relevution of the karmalife order*

---

8. Mrs. Solomon, true to her basic thesis, says that heliotrope "certainly applies to the sons' 'troops'—their privates—and to sexual games sons and 'trollops' play before marriage," *Eternal Geomater* (Carbondale: South Illinois University Press, 1969), p. 32.

privious to his hoisting of an emergency umberolum in byway of para-
guastical solation to the rhyttel in his hedd" (338.5). The ideas and
ethics of the brothers seem to have changed little as they
passed from childhood to manhood.

By the same token, just as Shem cannot answer the "heliotrope" riddle, the riddle he asks is never answered either; "the
first riddle of the universe: asking, when is a man not a man?"
(170.4). The question is stated in altered form in six other
places in the book: "where was a hovel not a havel" (231.1);
"When is a Pun not a Pun?" (307.2); "whereem is man . . .
nother man" (356.13); "when is a maid nought a maid"
(495.6); "Here is a homelet not a hothel" (586.18); "when is
a man nought a nam" (607.11), but the answer is always
supplied by Shem: "when he is a—yours till the rending of
the rocks,—Sham" (170.23). As a first step in solving the
riddle for ourselves, in getting at what exactly it does mean,
we might follow Clive Hart's direction:

> The solution to Shem's first riddle of the Universe becomes
> clear only when all of its parts—that is, all of *Finnegans Wake*—
> have been assembled and examined together. The whole book
> is a mass of cross-corresponding material which the reader
> must synthesize in order to understand; like the "messages,"
> no one part of it is comprehensible without the rest.[9]

After such a sound statement, however, Hart himself does
not provide a solution. But Bernard Benstock does,[10] and
his conclusions should be examined at the beginning of this
discussion. Benstock feels that Shem considers himself a
"sham," and it is for this reason that Shem makes a denigrating
evaluation of his own character. Benstock, however, justifies
his statement with the insults that Shaun, in fact, casts out.

9. *Structure and Motif in Finnegans Wake* (Evanston: Northwestern University Press, 1962), p. 157.

10. *Joyce-again's Wake*, pp. 207–9.

Also, Benstock feels that the riddle is sexual in nature, equating "rending of the rocks" with procreation, and asserting that puberty will make Shem genuine: "as a child he is certainly a *sham*, but only until puberty, only *till the rending of the rocks.*"[11] How being a child makes Shem a sham is hard to understand, and it does seem that "rending of the rocks" might refer simply to death or the Last Day (Joyce continually puns on "Ragnarok," the Norse final destruction of the world, throughout the novel). If we accept Hart's idea that all occurrences of the riddle must be recognized and assessed together, and such a technique of leitmotif is certainly basic to Joyce's writing in *Finnegans Wake,* one must ask where the sexual significance lies in "When is a Pun not a Pun." The *Wake* is quite sexual in nature, and the riddle in application may be too, but to limit it in this way is perhaps to overlook some of its more universal thematic significance. In the same way, to mistake Shaun's monologue as Shem's admission of his own failings may lead to a misunderstanding and underestimation of Shem's stature as a character in his own right.

Leo Knuth feels that with the riddle Shem "is referring to himself. . . . He is a sham, because his creations are but imitations assuming the appearance of reality."[12] The riddle that Shem asks, rather than being pointed back at himself, is directed outward, to *any* man, and thus it attempts to make a point about the nature of humanity instead of being a further definition of Shem's own character. It is really quite simple and means exactly what it says—a man is not a man in the true sense of the word when he chooses to turn his back on things that are innately valuable, and instead lives a life of hypocrisy and injustice. "Sham" is the primary reading, for this is the case where a pun is not a pun. Shaun cannot answer it because he does not wish to admit, either consciously or

11. *ibid.,* p. 208.
12. "Shem's Riddle of the Universe," *A Wake Newslitter* 9 (October 1972): 82.

unconsciously, its obvious application to himself, to the repressive and artificial kinds of precepts and ways of life which he stands so squarely behind.

The riddle is not simply an indictment of Shaun, however, for it applies to all men of the same stamp, men who may differ in face and name but who are interchangeable in their baseness: "whereom is man . . . nother man, wheile he is asame" (356.13). It can apply specifically to the Earwicker household: "Here is a homelet not a hother" (586.18), governed by the repressed and convoluted HCE, or it can be turned on any residence. It can apply to male or female and expose the shallowness of Issy and demonstrate the genuineness of ALP, but the difficulty in solving it rests in the minds of those who refuse or are afraid to examine it, rather than in the riddle itself. Its final variation as "the first and last rittlerattle of the anniverse" (607.10) reflects the continuous and circular structure of *Finnegans Wake,* for, as the book comes to a close and we are returned back to the first page, "nam" is a reverse spelling of "man," and the solution given is "Watch!" (607.12). (Utilizing Leo Knuth's suggestion that *an am* in Gaelic is "the time," we should realize that on another level Shem's riddle recalls the Cad's accosting of Earwicker in Phoenix Park.) The exposition of *Finnegans Wake* is the solution, as the book begins once again and we are privy to the innermost thoughts of the characters to watch many of them reveal themselves as shams. As J. Mitchell Morse explains it:

this theme is repeated throughout *Finnegans Wake:* the power arrogance and corporate assurance of those who presume to speak for God, opposed by the intelligence, skepticism and lonely self-respect of the creative individual. There are weaknesses on both sides: on the individual's, the importunity of the flesh and the hesitancy that comes of understanding the complexity of his relationship with others; on the side of those who presumably speak for God, the blindness of action uninhibited by doubt, thought, understanding or compassion.[13]

This is one of the most basic oppositions of *Finnegans Wake,* and this is what both the riddles are used to illuminate. Since the riddle is Shem's, it thus seems that he possesses a higher degree of perception into the nature of things than that with which he is usually credited, and perhaps his importance in the novel should be upgraded. Though it is the elder Earwicker who receives the bulk of the attention in most of the writing about the *Wake,* he is, in fact, always being acted upon, and never once in the narrative seems able to grasp what is going on around him. Bumbling and goodnatured, he stumbles backward through the novel, but it is Shem who can evaluate more correctly those he encounters, and it is certainly he who speaks most directly for James Joyce. Though it is true that Shaun rather than Shem instigates much of the action in the work, Shem's aloofness should not be seen as indifference, for he pares his wits rather than his nails. Unheeded and seemingly defeated, he withdraws, but Joyce would never grant any sort of significant victory to the Shauns of this world. In *A Portrait* Stephen Dedalus is driven out of Ireland and in *Ulysses* Leopold Bloom is displaced in Molly's embrace by Blazes Boylan, yet never do we view them as vanquished. So too should Shem-Glugg-Berkeley transcend his outward loss of stature.

As a corollary to the riddles, we might examine Shem's role in the construction of ALP's Letter, in itself a riddle since no one seems quite sure what it contains. Like "when is a man not a man?", bits and pieces of the missive pop up on almost every page, and Clive Hart's description of it is perhaps most apt: "However numerous and diverse its sources, the Letter

13. *The Sympathetic Alien* (New York: New York University Press, 1959), p. 80.

remains primarily an expression of the nature of Anna Livia, the female principle of flux and continuity."[14] The scribe, though, is Shem, under ALP's direction; as one theory has it: "the secretary bird, better known as Pandoria Paullabucca [ALP], whom they thought was more like a solicitor general, indiscriminatingly made belief mid authorsagastions from Schelm the Pelman to write somewords to Senders about her chilikin puck" (369.25). At different times, just about every character writes a letter of some sort, reaching out for communication with each other:

> All the world's in want and is writing a letters. A Letters from a person to a place about a thing. And all the world's on wish to be carrying a letters. A letters to a king about a treasure from a cat. When men want to write a letters. (278.13)

The main problem seems to be that the letters are never delivered, whether by interference, accident, or indifference.

In this, the most important letter, ALP is attemping to explain to her husband the natures of their children, to explain in essence the basic characteristics of all people. That he never reads it is the result of several factors (that it is disguised as a letter to Santa Claus and that Shem, the ill-favored son, has written it are no help), but most important is the fact that Shaun the Post is entrusted with its delivery. By his very title, this is Shaun's special role in life, but in this enterprise he is not successful. At one point the letter is described thus: "Letter, carried of Shaun, son of Hek, written of Shem, brother of Shaun, uttered for ALP, mother of Shem, for Hek, father of Shaun" (420.17), before the misadventures of its delivery are recorded. Shaun, narrating this sequence, recalls that he:

14. *Structure and Motif,* p. 202.

Tried Apposite House. 13 Fitzgibbots. Loco. Dangerous Tax
9d. B.L. Guineys, esqueer. L.B. Not known at 1132 a. 12 Norse
Richmound. Nave unlodgeable. Loved noa's dress. Sinned, Jetty
Piersse. Noon sick parson. 92 Windsewer. Ave. No such no. Vale
Finn's Hot. Exbelled from 1014 d. Pulldown, Fearview. Opened
by Miss Take. (420.21)

And so it continues until he gives up in disgust. Bernard Benstock feels that the Letter has been "stolen by the bourgeois
politician Shaun for the purpose of passing it off as his own in
order to reap the reward of making the universal secrets acces-
sible to and palatable for his constituents and followers,"[15]
and that this may be one of Shaun's covering stories, but it
seems more likely that he honestly fails. Shaun possesses
neither the acumen nor the perseverance for such a mission.
Not a bit concerned with the importance of the Letter's contents, he is mainly concerned that Shem may derive some sort
of fame or benefit from its writing and treats the whole thing
as a joke: "outragedy of poetscalds! Acomedy of letters!" (425.
24). Ironically enough, he holds the truth in his hands, but he
does not even bother to look at it.

As was the case with his riddle, Shem's performance in the
Letter goes for naught in *Finnegans Wake*, since no one ever
gets the opportunity of reading it. Once again, however, his
extremely crucial role is that of the demonstrator of the truth,
the artist who exhibits his work in the hope that someone will
understand. This is his position from beginning to end in the
novel, though in instance after instance he is scorned or
misunderstood. That this is true might perhaps be attributed
to the enormity of Shem's undertaking and to the shortsight-
edness of his listeners, rather than to any shallowness or
inability of his own. As William T. Noon puts it: "the poet's
ability to imitate in parable this act of God's fatherly act of

15. *Joyce-again's Wake*, p. 9.

creation cannot be more than symbolic, for like all analogies with the infinite, finite human making is always enigmatic and at best but a shadow of the divine analogate."[16] Shem consistently labors on, rephrasing and restructuring the truths he hopes to make known, setting them before the characters and the reader in as many different forms as he can possibly devise. His refusal to despair at his inability to break through must be seen as a tribute to his own deep understanding of human nature, since never does he give up his efforts as a bad job. He may laugh in scorn, but never does he decide that it is useless to begin again, and in this he is certainly the ideal offspring and lieutenant of Anna Livia, the symbolic epitome of the life-force. Campbell and Robinson state that "Shem's business is not to create a higher life, but merely to find out and utter the Word,"[17] their "merely" somewhat out of place in describing the highly significant role of a prophet. As the narrator explains, we must "leave the letter that never begins to go find the latter that ever comes to end, written in smoke and blurred by mist and signed of solitude, sealed at night" (337.11). It is the Letter that will lead us to the ladder, but we must go to find it.

Thus the patterns of riddles and questions that cross and recross each other in *Finnegans Wake* are certainly more than a sop for the puzzle fan or some kind of attempt at dadaistic humour, as several have charged. They are central thematic functionings, which manifest their significance in their forms. By asking a question or posing a riddle, Joyce, as well as expecting us to answer each particular problem, hopes to set up in his reader a habit of questioning that will be in continual operation as he moves through the novel. Though they are not necessarily related in their content, the many questions and riddles are all part of a definite thematic technique. To

16. *Joyce and Aquinas* (New Haven: Yale University Press, 1957), p. 129.
17. *A Skeleton Key to Finnegans Wake* (New York: Harcourt, Brace, 1944), p. 13.

Joyce's way of thinking, a children's riddling game is, in a sense, just as important as a questioning of existence, since it is the intellectual process, and not the individual answer, that brings one closer to an enduring truth. The inner light, which both Shem and the Druid possess, is accomplished through continual reassessment, not the bowing to a blinding light, and this seems to be one of the major statements that *Finnegans Wake* has to present.

Adaline Glasheen explains: "From the start of *Finnegans Wake* we have not chased after a presence or an affirmation, but after a missing meal, after rational, truthful explanation of what can be called Historical Truth or Man."[18] The knowledge we seek is not concealed in a difficult anagram or a wit-teasing riddle, but rather is contained in the whole of the book itself, in the recognition of the fact that no black-and-white answers will be forthcoming, as Shaun seems to expect. Absolutes are nebulous and amorphous here, but the more one questions, Joyce seems to say, the more one can begin to understand. "Now? How good you are in explosion! How farflung is your folkloire and how velktingeling your volupkabulary!" (419.11).

---

18. *A Second Census of Finnegans Wake,* p. lix.

Afterword

We find through the examination of only a few of the narrative techniques or devices that the more we uncover Joyce's structural designs the tighter appears the overall structure of *Finnegans Wake*. Clive Hart has noted that "neither before nor since *Finnegans Wake* has the literary *leitmotiv* been used so consistently or to such brilliant effect,"[1] and he documents over a thousand of these motifs, but it also should now be apparent that blocks of the narrative action link up in much the same way, as do the riddles and the interpolated stories.[2] A glance at David Hayman's study[3] serves to substantiate the vigorous linguistic planning that went into the novel, but only after tracing these above-mentioned blocks of action can one get a fuller idea of the vast amount of control that has been imposed over the book's form. On the surface, the creation of a dream situation, with its implications of Freudianism and the subconscious, might presuppose a situation of formal anarchy, but, from this discussion of narration and point of view, one finds that this is not at all the case. Though

1. *Structure and Motif in Finnegans Wake* (Evanston: Northwestern University Press, 1962), p. 161.
2. It should be noted that Hart later qualifies his position quite a bit: "In the simplest sense of the term, some, at least, of *Finnegans Wake* may lack control; Joyce may have abandoned it to chance," "*Finnegans Wake* in Perspective," *James Joyce Today,* ed. Thomas F. Staley (Bloomington: Indiana University Press, 1970), p. 162.
3. *A First-Draft Version of Finnegans Wake* (Austin: University of Texas Press, 1963).

each character is fictively free to say or to do anything he wishes, he is actually tightly bound by the limits that the narrator sets up, and the narrator in turn is subject to the uses that the master Joyce intends for him.

Accordingly, once one accepts a formal design of many dreamers dreaming continuously and consecutively, the book becomes more comprehensible and much easier to read. This, of course, is not to say that such a critical stance makes the reading of *Finnegans Wake* "easy," or that it will become standard fare for the casual reader, but only that one of the major difficulties—who says what at which time, and why—may not remain such an insurmountable problem. Working from a different perspective, William T. Noon has arrived at the same conclusion: "the alert reader soon perceives that the illusion which Joyce is striving to create is not the problem of incoherent dreaming but of most consciously controlled and patterned comic art."[4] Most important, perhaps, is the fact that all of the characters who populate the dream with HCE become more alive and understandable when we can enter into their minds too. No longer must we accept what once says or thinks about another without weighing such statements against the supposed culprit's self-defense or actual behavior. As a consequence, our views of several of them should be reassessed, since stereotyped descriptions, too long a commonplace in discussions of the *Wake,* may no longer be precisely on the mark.

In actuality, it appears that Earwicker himself may not be of such individual importance as we may have believed. A majority of the actions and thoughts of the other characters are centered around his resurrection and rejuvenation, but it is the efforts of these characters in this enterprise, the process of revival itself, that dominates the reader's attention. The

4. *Joyce and Aquinas* (New Haven: Yale University Press, 1957), p. 137.

struggle of the forces of life against those of death-in-life is being depicted here. Ironically, Shaun, the favorite son, would doom the father were it not for Shem and Anna Livia, and therefore it is the latter who is granted the final speech of death and resurrection. Earwicker's regeneration is a triumph for them, an accomplishment in which he has really played little part, and he does not tower above and control what is going on around him, as many have thought. Indeed, when we can examine the separate, individual voices in the dream situation, we find that the narrator, not HCE, is the person in charge and that he is the leading actor in this drama.

It should also be clear that Shem is not such a wastrel and ne'er-do-well as Shaun insists. In fact, Shem is definitely the more attractive of the two. His all-important role in the novel has been described in detail in the section dealing with the riddling motif, and certainly his cool wit alone should elevate him in the eyes of *Wake* readers. The perfect balance of the complementary duality of the twins will have to be newly weighted in his favor, since, whatever his lack of endearing qualities, he remains the link between Anna Livia, her family, and the reader. Concurrently, it must naturally follow that Shaun should be denied a goodly amount of his critical stature. He is the bulwark of the bourgeois, as has always been claimed for him, but, after examining his speeches, it is obvious that he represents all of its vices and none of its virtues. He is economical to the point of perversion, and respectful of law to the point of a blind obedience that borders on fascism. He has more Lynch and Mulligan in him than he does Leopold Bloom.

Along with this, Shaun has no respect for the institutions of marriage and family, no respect for the elderly, and he cares about nothing but his own advancement. The preceding vitriol is not meant as a blanket denunciation of Shaun as a character, but he certainly stands for little that Joyce consid-

ers positive in *Finnegans Wake*. Shaun continually employs
a kind of posing rhetoric to cloud his failings, but, when we
realize that other voices are pricking the bubble of his respect-
ability, we can see him in a much clearer light. He is not "the
fine frank fairhaired fellow of the fairytales" (220.12); perhaps
commentators have been too fair themselves.

Finally, we might say that exploring these narrative techniques only reinforces our conviction that little occurs in *Finnegans Wake* without a purpose. Altering Giodano Bruno's
motto ("*Hilaris in tristia, tristis in hilaritate*") a bit, substitut-
ing "seriousness" or "relevance" for "melancholy," the
humorous things in the novel are meant to amuse, but even
they are charged with a thematic significance of their own.
The Prankquean and the Norwegian Captain, the games of
Glugg and Chuff, move on many levels, all the way from
emotional humor to intellectual insight. Such is always James
Joyce's technique in *Finnegans Wake*—nothing, no matter how
small, is without its underlying function and significance. As
Samuel Beckett describes it: "Here form *is* content, content
is form. You complain that this stuff is not written in English.
It is not written at all. It is not to be read—or rather it is not
only to be read. It is to be looked at and listened to."[5]

---

5. "Dante . . . Bruno. Vico . . Joyce," *Our Exagmination Round His Factification for Incamination of Work in Progress* (Paris: Shakespeare and Co., 1929), p. 14.

Bibliography to Part One

Allen, Walter. *Tradition and Dream*. London: Faber and Faber, 1964.

Atherton, J.S. *The Books at the Wake*. New York: Viking Press, 1960.

————. "The Identity of the Sleeper." *A Wake Newslitter*, 4 (October 1967): 81–83.

Beckett, Samuel, et al. *Our Exagmination Round His Factification for Incamination of Work in Progress*. Paris: Shakespeare and Co., 1929.

Begnal, Michael H. "The Prankquean in *Finnegans Wake*." *James Joyce Quarterly* 1 (Spring 1964): 14–18.

————. "The Narrator of *Finnegans Wake*," *Eire-Ireland* 4 (Fall 1969): 38–49.

Benstock, Bernard. *Joyce-again's Wake*. Seattle: University of Washington Press, 1965

————. "The Quiddity of Shem and the Whatness of Shaun." *James Joyce Quarterly* 1 (Fall 1963):26–33.

Bishop, John Peale. *Collected Essays*. New York: Random House, 1948.

Budgen, Frank. *James Joyce and the Making of Ulysses*. New York: Smith and Haas, 1934.

Burgess, Anthony. *ReJoyce*. New York: W. W. Norton, 1965.

Bush, Douglas. *Engaged and Disengaged*. Cambridge: Harvard University Press, 1966.

Campbell, Joseph, and Robinson, Henry M. *A Skeleton Key to Finnegans Wake*. New York: Harcourt, Brace, 1944.

121

Daiches, David. *The Novel and the Modern World.* Chicago: University of Chicago Press, 1960.

Eastman, Max. *The Literary Mind.* New York: Viking Press, 1932.

Epstein, Edmund. *The Ordeal of Stephen Dedalus.* Carbondale: S. Illinois University Press, 1971.

Gilbert, Stuart. *James Joyce's Ulysses.* New York: Vintage Books, 1958.

Glasheen, Adaline. *A Second Census of Finnegans Wake.* Evanston: Northwestern University Press, 1963.

Gross, John. *James Joyce.* New York: Viking Press, 1970.

Halper, Nathan. "James Joyce and the Russian General." *Partisan Review* 18 (July, 1951): 424–31.

Hart, Clive "*Finnegans Wake* in Perspective." *James Joyce Today,* ed. Thomas F. Staley. Bloomington: Indiana University Press, 1970, pp. 156–65.

———. *Structure and Motif in Finnegans Wake.* Evanston: Northwestern University Press, 1962.

Hayman, David. *A First-Draft Version of Finnegans Wake.* Austin: University of Texas Press, 1963.

Kenner, Hugh. *Dublin's Joyce.* Bloomington: Indiana University Press, 1956.

McHugh, Roland. "A Structural Theory of *Finnegans Wake.*" *A Wake Newslitter* 5 (December, 1968): 79–85.

Mercier, Vivian. *The Irish Comic Tradition.* Oxford: Oxford University Press, 1962.

Morse, J. Mitchell. "HCE's Chaste Agony." *Yale Review* 56 (March 1967): 397–405.

———. "On Teaching *Finnegans Wake.*" *Twelve and a Tilly,* ed. Jack P. Dalton. London: Faber and Faber, 1966, pp. 65–72.

———. *The Sympathetic Alien.* New York: New York University Press, 1959.

Noon, William T. *Joyce and Aquinas.* New Haven: Yale University Press, 1957.

Senn, Fritz. "A Reading Exercise in *Finnegans Wake.*" *Levende Talen* 269 (June–July 1970): 471–83.

Solomon, Margaret. *Eternal Geomater: The Sexual Universe of Finnegans Wake.* Carbondale: S. Illinois University Press, 1969.

Staples, Hugh B. "Some Notes on the One Hundred and Eleven Epithets of HCE." *A Wake Newslitter* 1 (December 1964): 3–6.

Thompson, Francis. "Portrait of the Artist Asleep." *Western Review* 14 (Summer 1950): 245–53.

Vickery, John B. "*Finnegans Wake* and Sexual Metamorphosis." *Contemporary Literature* 13 (Spring 1972): 213–42.

Von Phul, Ruth. "Circling the Square: A Study of Structure." *James Joyce Miscellany: Third Series.* Carbondale: S. Illinois University Press, 1962, pp. 234–61.

———. "Who Sleeps at *Finnegans Wake?*" *James Joyce Review* 1 (June 1957): 27–38.

Wilson, Edmund. *The Wound and the Bow.* New York: Galaxy Books, 1965.

PART TWO

Queer Mrs Quickenough and
Odd Miss Doddpebble:
The Tree and the Stone in
Finnegans Wake

Grace Eckley

Acknowledgments

Permissions to quote have been granted by Cooper Squar(
Publishers, Inc. for extracts from *The Mythology of All Races
Eddic*, by John Arnott MacCulloch; by Ernest Benn Limitec
for extracts from *The Lost Language of Symbolism* by Harolc
Bayley; by Oxford University Press for extracts from *Jame*
Joyce by Richard Ellmann; and by The Viking Press, Inc
and The Society of Authors, London, for extracts from *Fin*
negans Wake by James Joyce.

List of Abbreviations

CP *Collected Poems*. New York: The Viking Press, 1957.
D *Dubliners*. New York: The Viking Press, 1961.
E *Exiles*. Introduction by Padraic Colum. New York: The Viking Press, 1951.
AP *A Portrait of the Artist as a Young Man*. New York: The Viking Press, 1964.
U *Ulysses*. New York: Random House, 1961.
FW *Finnegans Wake*. New York: The Viking Press, 1939.

1

"a weird of wonder tenebrous" (281.2)

On the Anna Livia Plurabelle chapter (1.8) of *Finnegans Wake*, Joyce asserted that he was willing "to stake everything." To its most obvious characteristic of melodic sounds imitating the flow of water, he responded, "if it were meaningless it could be written quickly, without thought, without pains, without erudition; but I assure you that these twenty pages now before us cost me twelve hundred hours and an enormous expense of spirit."[1] Expense of time and spirit did not cease with that statement in 1927, however, while Joyce continued to revise the chapter until, as A. Walton Litz noted, it had gone "through seventeen distinct stages of revision between 1923 and 1938."[2]

Joyce explained the basic concepts of the chapter early in 1924 when he wrote to Miss Weaver,

> It is a chattering dialogue across the river by two washerwomen who as night falls become a tree and a stone. The river is named Anna Liffey. Some of the words at the beginning are hybrid Danish-English. Dublin is a city founded by Vikings. The Irish name is *Baile Atha Cliath*. Ballyclee = Town of Ford of Hurdles. Her Pandora's box contains the ills flesh is heir to. The stream is

1. Richard Ellmann, *James Joyce* (New York: Oxford University Press, 1965), p. 610.

2. *The Art of James Joyce: Method and Design in* Ulysses *and* Finnegans Wake (New York: Oxford University Press, 1961), p. 100.

quite brown, rich in salmon, very devious, shallow. The splitting up towards the end (seven dams) is the city abuilding. Izzy will be later Isolde (cf. Chapelizod).[3]

In his concept of the chapter, then, Joyce envisioned the entire book; for only three of those sentences apply strictly to the Anna Livia Plurabelle chapter. But chapter 8 is unique for its structure, composed entirely of dialogue, and for its characters—two washerwomen who appear nowhere else in the book except by reference. Hugh Kenner once remarked that the chapter is not "representative of the entire book,"[4] but its structure (dialogue) sets the novel's repeated pattern of progression: accusation-defense and (or) interrogation-reply. And the washerwomen, in their combined functions of telling the story of Anna Livia and transforming into the brothers Shem and Shaun (the tree and the stone), represent Joyce's view of artistic and material creation and establish characteristics for determining Shem and Shaun identities throughout the novel.

Joyce said he got the idea for the chapter while listening to two washerwomen shout across the Eure;[5] this overheard scrap of conversation from unknown persons, when translated into dramatic form, becomes the mysterious washerwomen who rise like weird sisters ("the dumb speak"—195.5) and metamorphose into a tree and a stone at the chapter's close. A would-be passer-by (i.e., the reader of *Finnegans Wake*) hears not only the history of Anna Livia but also the transformations ("I feel as old as yonder elm"—215.34–35; "I feel as heavy as yonder stone"—215.36-216.1) and the descent

3. Stuart Gilbert, ed., *The Letters of James Joyce* (New York: Viking Press, 1957), p. 213.

4. Quoted in Fred Higginson, *Anna Livia Plurabelle: The Making of a Chapter* (Minneapolis: The University of Minnesota Press, 1960), p. 4.

5. Ellmann, p. 575 n.

of night (as the women call "Night!" to each other) conveyed by dialogue.

At a common level the women who tell only what they have heard of ALP and HCE represent the desired objectivity of the oft-spoken but ne'er-so-well-as-here-expressed wish, "If these stones—or trees—could speak," a proposed topic for the children's composition ("If Standing Stones Could Speak"—306.22-23). Washing the linen and repeating the gossip, they develop two other truisms—the familiar clothing metaphor to confirm the common reliance on appearance (and Joyce's use of clothing to represent persons is a major *Wake* motif) and the rumors to confirm the convention that rumors historically yield more credibility than facts. The washerwomen have never seen Anna Livia, but know her well by reputation. By merely repeating the story, however, they sustain the objectivity required of the narrator of the traditional epic: and the chapter as a unit has all the elements of the conventional epic, including a beginning *in medias res*, objectivity in the telling by the washerwomen, the epic stature of hero and heroine, elevated diction, transcendence of time and place, the supernatural, a feast (199.10-3), three journeys, and a catalogue of Anna's gifts. On that level also the women, as characters in the story, project the required contrast between the larger-than-life hero and heroine and others as ordinary personalities. Structurally, longer passages of their verbal exchanges, as their different personalities clash, provide the transitions in time between units of the story of Anna and Earwicker. On the story level (the chapter as a unit also has all the elements of the conventional short story) the telling by one washerwoman offers the history of Anna's reputed activities, of her romance with Earwicker, and of her attempts to gain revenge on slanderers of his name.

Although the women do not appear elsewhere in the novel,

the dirty linen, metaphorically being washed in public as gossip circulates, does; and the variations of Earwicker's indiscretion are as necessary a part of the novel as the indiscretion itself. While men gather in the pub-courtroom to discuss and judge his behavior, the dispersal-washerwomen gossip about Anna Livia's romantic life. From Joyce's point of view, the washing, actually a whitewashing, is a routine phase of human existence for all persons: "Mopsus or Gracchus, all your horodities will incessantlament be coming back from the Annone Washwashwhose, Ormepierre Lodge, Doone of the Drumes, blanches bountifully and nightsend made up, every article lathering leaving several rinsings so as each rinse results with a dapperent rolle, cuffs for meek and chokers for sheek and a kink in the pacts for namby" (614.1–7).

After the washing, according to Earwicker and his customers in the pub, the world cycle starts afresh: "Of this Mr A (tillalaric) and these wasch woman . . . nothing more is told until now. . . . And then. Be old. The next thing is. We are once amore as babes awondering in a wold made fresh where with the hen in the storyaboot we start from scratch" (336.12–18). His listeners quickly agree and call for the truce, adding, just as the washerwomen concentrate on drying at the close of their chapter, "Drouth is stronger than faction" (336.20). As a phase in the Viconian cycle of existence, the third old man, Luke Tarpey, recounts the means by which gossip circulates among the women: "Maid Maud ninnies nay but blabs to Omama: . . . this ignorant mostly sweeps it out along with all the rather old corporators: . . . the maudlin river then gets its dues: . . . thence those laundresses" (586.6–13). The Earwicker children at their chapter 10 study and letter-writing appropriately close their letter with a reference to the washerwomen who will inaugurate a new era: "Till later Lammas is led in by baith our washwives, a weird of wonder tenebrous as that evil thorngarth, a field of faery blithe as this flowing wild" (280.36–281.1–3). The children's note for a passage with allusions to the Anna Livia Purabelle chapter (287.4–11) labels that section "Wolsherwomens at their weirdst."

The Old Norse *garth* was a guarded and protected place, and so also is Phoenix Park, the setting of this novel. But "tenebrous as that evil thorngarth" suggests the exact opposite, and Phoenix Park is also the scene of the famous Park murders and of Earwicker's crime. In the trial the interrogation includes "In the middle of the garth, then?" (90.14–15). With persons, as with scenery, appearances are unreliable, and appearances are determined by clothing. "A talor would adapt his caulking trudgers on to any shape at see" (375.34–35) summarizes the deception of appearances; while exposure through torn clothing may accomplish the same purpose as "everything comes out in the wash," for "Every ditcher's dastard in Dupling will let us know about it if you have paid the mulctman by whether your rent is open to be foreclosed or aback in your arrears" (586.15–18).[6] Washing means the review of past indiscretions, rather than the intentional commission of them and "each rinse results with a dapperent rolle," as if rinse by rinse or layer by layer the facades of civilization are being removed in the washing process. Before giving testimony on Earwicker's crime the Wet Pinter lets down "his rice and peacegreen coverdisk" (86.35–36) and Pegger Festy testifies only "as soon as the outer layer of stucckomuck had been removed at the request of a few live jurors" (91.01–02). The washing cycle after the fact also means "forget and forgive," an appropriate sentiment for

---

6. Since Margaret Solomon has discussed the sexual aspects of the tree and the stone, I do not repeat that level of meaning except where necessary. In the passage quoted, according to Mrs. Solomon, fore clothing and back clothing indicate genital and anal (hetero and homosexual) activities. See *Eternal Geomater* (Carbondale: Southern Illinois University Press, 1969), p. 101.

a new beginning. But the new cycle or season (a "later Lammas") requires both washerwomen, because each cycle contains the opposites that the women themselves, or the park, represent.

In contrast with Pope's exaltation of forgiveness in "To err is human, to forgive divine," Joyce's position on erring and forgiving is essentially that all equally err and all must equally forgive. The exact nature of Earwicker's sin—be it spying, praying,[7] urinating, anticipating,[8] masturbating, accosting, or revealing—matters little as the cycles of history turn. Near the close of their dialogue, one washerwoman calls "forgivemequick" and the other responds "forgetmenot." Similarly, as Luke declares that washing and drying of garments brings about a close of phase in the cycle of human existence, he cautions forbearance in regard to judgment; no one is free of sin and all garments (collars and cuffs and overalls) require cleaning (even ironing and storage) as a matter of survival into the next cycle:

> Forebeer, forbear! For nought that is has bane. In mournens-laund. Themes have thimes and habit reburns. To flame in you. Ardor vigor forders order. Since ancient was our living is in possible to be. Delivered as. Caffirs and culls and onceagain overalls, the fittest surviva lives that blued, iorn and storridge can make them. Whichus all claims. Clean. Whenastcleeps. Close. And the mannormillor clipperclappers. Noxt. Doze. (614.7–13)

So the outgoing Anna Livia observes the universality of error among men and urges washing and forgetting: "All men has done something. Be the time they've come to the weight of

---

7. J. Mitchell Morse suggests that the sin need not be sexual but a pantheistic "chaste ecstasy" misunderstood by the viewers. See "HCE's Chaste Ecstasy," *Yale Review* 56 (March 1967): 397–405.

8. HCE is once found guilty of "those imputations of fornicolopulation with two of his albowcrural correlations on whom he was said to have enjoyed by anticipation when schooling them in amown" (557.16–19).

old fletch. We'll lave it. So" (621.32–33). Nor does she overlook her own sex's propensity toward error: "Allgearls is
wea. At times" (626.3). Her anticipated union with the sea
confirms the association of washing and renewal (resurrection): "If I seen him bearing down on me now under white-
spread wings like he'd come from Arkangels, I sink I'd die
down over his feet, humbly dumbly, only to washup" (628.9–
11).

Not until the ricorso did Joyce give the washerwomen
names; they are "Queer Mrs Quickenough and Odd Miss
Doddpebble," who live at the Laundersdale Minssions
(620.19–21). As their dialogue progresses, without the aid of
divisive quotation marks, their personalities seem one of a
kind; they are salty old gossips who complain of back pains
and varicose veins, who cast perceptive glances upon the
evidence of the city's sex life revealed in the soiled laundry
while they "Tista suck" in wry disapproval and enjoy every
detail of salacity. Their poor grammar, their knowledge of
sin and sense of decency, add to the humor of the conversation: "Proxenete and phwhat is phthat?" (198.17); "It's just
the same as if I was to go par examplum now in conservancy's
cause out of telekinesis and proxenete you" (198.20–22); "For
coxyt sake and is that what she is? Botlettle I thought she'd
act that loa" (198.22–23). At the same time their good hearts
and kind intentions lend an element of pathos: "Wait till
the honeying of the lune, love! Die eve, little eve, die! We
see that wonder [the dawn approaching] in your eye" (215.3–5).
They know all the city's scandal and fill the conventional
role of the servants who maintain loyalty while they tell
of high life below stairs. When they disagree they call each
other names: "Were you lifting your elbow, tell us, glazy
cheeks, in Conway's Carrigacurra canteen?" (214.20–21);
"Was I what, hobbledyhips?" (214.21). But their own names
derive from their characters; the teller of the tale is indeed

quick with her tongue ("You're a bit on the sharp side"—
212.29; "I'm on the wide"—212.29–30), and Miss Doddpebble's odd limp derives from a scandalous indiscretion of her
own: "You won your limpopo limp fron the husky hussars
when Collars and Cuffs was heir to the town and your slur
gave the stink to Carlow" (214.28–30). But they part friends.

The story Mrs. Quickenough tells of Anna Livia stresses
her creative role through sexuality and productivity and her
wifely role in disregard for her own name and health to serve
her husband. It begins *in medias res* after HCE's disgrace
("Well, you know, when the old cheb went futt and did what
you know"—196.6–7), but objectivity requires qualification:
"Or whatever it was they threed to make out he thried to two
in the Fiendish park" (196.9–11). The story then moves backward in time to Anna's youth and forward to her retaliation
against all scandalmongers. The speaker remembers Earwicker's character in his youth in a way that resembles
Oedipus's addressing the suppliant Thebans in haughty sentence: "And the cut of him! And the strut of him! How he
used to hold his head as high as a howeth" (197.1-3). And
the washerwomen continue—how he walks, and how he
talks, of whom he was born, and whether he's married. The
romantic journey includes all possible danger, like that of
Beowulf crossing the swamps in search of Grendel's dam,
"by dredgerous lands and devious delts" (197.22), past several
landmarks, his "boat of life" launched "from the harbourless Ivernikan Okean" (197.29). Embarked on a sea voyage
with fornication aforethought, Humphrey Chimpden Earwicker, the conquering hero, keeps his epic proportions
while Anna Livia keeps her river identity: "That marchantman
he suivied their scutties right over the wash, his cameleer's
burnous breezing up on him, till with his runagate bowm-
priss he roade and borst her bar" (197.33–34). Nor does
Anna Livia fail to respond: "When they saw him shoot swift

up her sheba sheath, like any gay lord salomon, her bulls they were ruhring, surfed with spree" (198.3–5). Essentially a landlubber, he is remarkably at home in the water: "A bairn of the brine," of course. And quickly Anna Livia is seen in her "proxenete" role, enticing young girls to keep HCE happy, a program exciting enough to elicit an unrestrained "Tell me mohrer. Tell me moatst" (198.28) from the candid listener. HCE, plunged into despair from seven years of labor, "as glommen as grampus," wears the face of a land destitute in archetypal winter, a land physically and spiritually dead, "with the tares at his thor and the buboes for ages and neither bowman nor shot abroad and bales allbrant on the crests of rockies and nera lamp in kitchen or church and giant's holes in Grafton's causeway" (198.29–32),[9] and the signs of woe and desolation continue to accumulate so that "You'd think all was dodo belonging to him how he durmed adranse in durance vaal" (199.9). Faithful Anna continues to purl around "in a Lapsummer skirt and damazon cheeks, for to ishim bonzour to her dear dubber Dan" (199.13–14), plying him with special foods till she weakens herself with the effort ("to plaise that man hog stay his stomicker till her pyrraknees shrunk to nutmeg graters"—199.20–21), only to meet his derisive refusals: "he'd kast them frome him, with a stour of scorn" (199.24–25). Next she tries music and song in her very best voice, which would "bate the hen that crowed on the turrace of Babbel" (199.30–31) but "not a mag out of Hum no more than out of the mangle weight" (199.32–33). HCE's dour indifference then forces Anna to renewed efforts. As "dochter of Sense and Art" she decks herself to rival the prom beauties; wearing all the spring colors of

9. "The night of the big wind" was in 1576 or on January 6, 1839, according to the Dublin Annals. See James S. Atherton, *The Books at the Wake* (London: Faber and Faber, 1959), p. 93. See also John V. Kelleher, "Notes on *Finnegans Wake* and *Ulysses,*" *The Analyst* 10 (March 1956): 2.

"changeable jade," she chooses especially romantic and temptingly nostalgic songs and continues standing in her doorway to coax young love in to help cajole HCE out of his winter despondency. The questions of the listening washerwoman continue. How does she coax them in? By "legging a jig or so on the sihl" of her door and dramatizing "how to bring to mind the gladdest garments out of sight" (200.25–26) to arouse an indifferent male. And what does she say? At this point the technical structuring becomes especially obvious; a whole flourish of exclamation, such as "I'm dying down off my iodine feet until I lerryn Anna Livia's cushingloo" (200.35–36) precedes and announces like fanfare Anna's special message to the world—the same as that found by a hen in the park[10]—and here distinguished by italics.

In her message (201.5–20), Anna swears in nature imagery, "by earth and the cloudy," and, considering that the washerwomen's gossip on either of her banks would doubtless wear out anyone, she thrusts them an ironic return—"I badly want a brandnew bankside"—and refers to her shrunken, unappealing figure, "and a plumper at that!" Worn out she admits she is with waiting for her "old Dane hodder dodderer," her "life in death companion" and poor provider to "wake himself out of his winter's doze and bore me down like he used to." A busy little housekeeper, she considers a loan from a gentlemanly "lord of the manor or a knight of the shire" to tide the family over the lean months. Recognizing the comforts of home, especially the snug riverbed, she nevertheless casts a longing glance at the gay young life where, rather than confinement within banksides and the cares of house mis-

---

10. The letter is found in a midden heap located at Phoenix Park. Kate Strong leaves "her filthdump near the Serpentine in Phornix Park" (80.06), which is a "wolfsbelly castrament to will hide a leabhar from Thursmen's brandihands or a loveletter" (80.13–14). Cf. "trouved by a poule in the parco" (201.1–2).

tress, she could spread out on the beach or plain and "feale
the gay aire of my salt troublin bay and the race of the say-
wint up me ambushure." Her last words return to youth,
vigor, sexuality. In short, Anna's message recapitulates the
springtime vegetation rituals—lamenting the dead winter,
awakening spirits to new life, stimulating productivity.

Next come the spring freshets and discussion of children;
Anna has spawned so many aleveens that, thinking of death,
"We won't have room in the kirkeyaard," and of life, "She
can't remember half of the cradlenames she smacked on
them" (201.31–32), but more are expected. So much prolifera-
tion now arouses suspicion that "she must have been a gada-
bount in her day" and sends us tumbling backward in time
through a possible variety of paramours—"Tinker, tilar,
souldrer, salor, Pieman Peace or Polistaman" (202.14–15),
both single and plural ("in a tactic attack or in single com-
bat"); but the answer is that Anna herself cannot remember
who was first. The washerwomen recall her youth in Wicklow
valley in an attempt to place the first incident, and the geographic locations range from there to wild speculation of
meetings of land and water, and the names of mountains and
rivers range three provinces and the realm of Neptune
(203.9–13).[11] Nevertheless, as Joyce made clear in his notes
to *Exiles*,[12] innocence is a state of mind; and the psychological impact of experience comes for Anna with the
seduction of the hermit priest.[13] Like HCE's famous and

11. The Mourne (Ulster), Slieve Bloom (Leinster), Lake Conn and Lake Cullin
with the River Moy (Connacht), and Braye, fictitious. Bray Head is in Munster
and Bray near Dublin. "Where Neptune sculled and Tritonville rowed" extends
speculation into mythology.

12. "Richard having first understood the nature of innocence when it had been
lost by him fears to believe that Bertha, to understand the chastity of her nature,
must first lose it in adultery." See *Exiles*, p. 119.

13. Michael Arklow is Anna's only ascertainable first love whose name is specified.
Berhard Benstock writes, "that she has had a single lover prior to marriage is a
pattern already established in *Ulysses* where Mulvey equals Michael, and in 'The

mysterious fall, the hermit's fall results from his merely relaxing physical austerity for a moment and occasions the same sort of condemnation: "O, wasn't he the bold priest? And wasn't she the naughty Livvy?" (204.4–5). But the history of Anna's reputation goes farther back to natural provocation when as a person she was licked by a hound, or as a river she fell into a pool.

The washerwomen break the telling of this scandalous legend to exchange disapproving witticisms about the parallels of contemporary licit and illicit love, such as Mrs. Magrath's (Lily Kinsella's), as evidenced in the laundry. They think they recognize her drawers by the odor: "O, may the diabolo twisk your seifety pin! You child of Mammon, Kinsella's Lilith! Now who has been tearing the leg of her drawers on her?" (205.10–12). Next they take up the story with the announcement of HCE's disgrace in the *Wakeschrift* (the weekly newspaper and pun on *Finnegans Wake*), complete with the titter among the town's citizenry; Earwicker's "fall" becomes the hottest item at the local breakfast tables. Caught in what the washerwomen have found to be the natural affairs of prototypal humanity, Earwicker nevertheless suffers the scorn of the righteously indignant; all over town they turn his picture upside down ("his ikom etched tipside down"—205.27–28)[14] and generally abuse his name, and "the mauldrin rabble" gather "around him in areopage" (206.1) and merit Anna's retaliation. She swears "she's be level with all the snags of them yet" (206.5). Having given her all to creation and preservation, she next assumes the role of destruction.

Here occurs another break in the story, and every time the narrator pauses for breath the listener urges her on. This time,

Dead' where Michael Furey is Gretta's romantic past." See "A Covey of Clerics in Joyce and O'Casey," *James Joyce Quarterly* 2, no. 1 (1964): 24.

14. The picture ("ikom") hung upside down in folklore means punishment of a disliked person, probably by giving him a headache.

she yields to the suspense with "By the holy well of Mul-
huddart I swear I'd pledge my chanza getting to heaven
through Tirry and Killy's mount of impiety to hear it all,
aviary word!" (206.18–20). But the narrator feels she is being
ridiculed and exclaims, "If you don't like my story get out
of the punt" (206.21). The misunderstanding, though unjusti-
fiable resentment for one, brings from the other instruction
on proper breathing, necessary for working and talking.
The story resumes with the account of Anna's dressing to
distribute gifts.

The sections that describe Anna's preparations (206.29–
207.11) and her appearance (207.28–208.36) are remarkable
for the interweaving of human characteristics with the geography of the landscape, though the unpleasantness of river-
become-sewer does not escape recognition; Anna departs
with "a clothespeg tight astride on her joki's nose and she
kep on grinding a something quaint in her fiumy mouth"
for the length of the river, "ffifffty odd Irish miles" (208.23–
26). The listener exclaims, "Sweet gumptyum and nobody
fainted!" (208.27–28). The special effort at dressing and the
sending the maids on an errand make of the occasion a ruse
as well as a ritual: "as soon as the lump his back was turned,"
she departs. Carefully the populace scrutinize the queen and
record all the details; this is the news of the fashion pages,
told with reactions of eyewitnesses. "Everyone that saw her
said the dowce little delia looked a bit queer" (208.29–30)
sums up the female view, while the idle lounging male element is reported to ogle her as she passes "in contemplation
of the fluctuation and the undification of her filimentation"
(209.2–3). From their position on the North Wall, two of
Dublin's psychic cripples, "Wit-upon-Crutches." and "Master
Bates," decide with much ingenuity that her face has been
lifted.

As Anna begins her journey with her mealiebag slung over

her shoulder, river imagery continues both in her own person—"dribbling her boulder through narrowa mosses, the diliskydrear on our drier side and the vilde vetchvine agin us" (209.19–21)—and in the spectators—"the rivulets ran aflod to see" (209.30). Nor do either gifts or receivers of gifts merit much praise: from the "sacco of wabbash she raabed" she gives "all for sore aringarung, stinkers and heelers, laggards and primelads, her furzeborn sons and dribblederry daughters, a thousand and one of them" (210.1–5).

The list of gifts (209.36–212.19) and receivers ends with itemizing persons important to the structure of the entire novel (the twenty-nine leapyear girls and the three children— Shem, Shaun, and Issy, who complete the novel's central five characters) and returns to several fertility-virility images: "the grapes that ripe before reason to them that devide the vinedress"; Issy, "her shamemaid"; Shaun, "love shone"; and Shem, "her penmight," in continuing but doubtful existence, "life past befoul his prime" (212.16–19).

With due recognition of increase, "a bakereen's dusind with tithe tillies to boot" (212.20–21), the women discuss incidentals to their occupation, including scraps of literature that drift their way, "dodwell disgustered but chickled with chuckles at the tittles is drawn on the tattlepage" (202.33– 34). The tittles include a mixture of languages and titles for humorous effect.[15] An expressed wish for more story elicits the response that everything must end—or does it? "Well, you know or don't you kennet or haven't I told you every telling has a taling and that's the he and the she of it" (203.11–12) loses its finality in the joining of "he and she." The close of the day assimilates Tennyson's New Year with

15. Ellmann translates the garbled Italian of 212.34–36: "God said, Let there be man, and man was. God said: Let there be Adam, and Adam was." See Ellmann, p. 479 n.

the washing effort and the dawn: "Wring out the clothes! Wring in the dew!" (213.19–20).[16] The washing finished and the clothes spread on the bank to dry bring special care for the hotel sheets because "a man and his bride embraced between them" (213.24–25). The conversation, becoming more disjointed, turns to the changes which come with passing time interspersed with the practicalities of counting the laundry, and increasing problems of hearing. "Oronoko! What's your trouble?" (204.10)[17] from one precedes the other's statement of her sighting of the ghostly "Finnleader" and prompts more wry sacrilege of national and liturgical implication: "Ireland sober is Ireland stiff. Lord help you, Maria, full of grease, the load is with me!" (214.18–19). The washerwomen are in their best character here, with one accused of tipsiness and the other pleading the self-defense of the martyred wife: "Amn't I up since the damp dawn, marthared mary allacook,[18] with Corrigan's pulse and varicoarse veins, my pramaxle smashed, Alice Jane in decline and my oneeyed mongrel twice run over, soaking and bleaching boiler rags, and sweating cold, a widow like me, for to deck my tennis champion son, the laundryman with the lavandier flannels?" (214.22–28). There is a concluding flurry of identifications from the *Wake*, including the "four old codgers" (214.33), the setting (the Poolbeg lighthouse—215.01), and Irish history (the hedgeschools—215.2). Amid these allusions, space and time, with no pretensions to grandeur, move to astronomical dimensions as the women promise,

16. See Benstock, *Joyce-again's Wake* (Seattle: University of Washington Press, 1965), p. 199.

17. For extended analysis of "Oronoko," see Litz, p. 106.

18. Joyce parodies the Blessed Margaret Mary Alacoque also in *Ulysses*, p. 202, as "Blessed Margaret Mary Anycock." See Donald T. Torchiana, "Joyce's Eveline' and the Blessed Margaret Mary Alacoque," *James Joyce Quarterly* 6, no. 1 (1968): 22–28.

"We'll meet again, we'll part once more. The spot I'll seek if the hour you'll find. My chart shines high where the blue milk's upset" (215.5–7). And darkness descends.

The final comments on Anna Livia and Dirty Dan accord them the grace of queerness, pay tribute to their increasing numbers of whom a city is built, and give special attention to the varieties of human individuality among that progeny as well as recognition of the ever-turning cycles of history. Durational time slows to a standstill for the washerwomen, a slowing represented in failure of the senses—"My sights are swimming thicker on me by the shadows to this place" (215.9–10); "Can't hear with the waters of" (215.31); "My foos won't moos" (215.34); "I feel as old as yonder elm" (215.34–35); "I feel as heavy as yonder stone" (215.36–216.1)— while the waters continue to flow. As primordial stillness invades all being, the eternal questions remain: "Who were Shem and Shaun the living sons or daughters of?" (216.1–2). And the eternal asking beseeches of the stillness, "Tell me, tell me, tell me, elm!" (216.3). And stillness moves on the face of the waters. Creation came from water and night.

2
A-Anna-*ailm* and the Lost Word

Briefly, the story the women tell of Anna Livia—a beautiful and humorous story—links Joyce's view of woman as cosmological creatrix with woman as sexual creature. Throughout the chapter, the functions of questioner and answerer, that is, of listener and teller, are quite evident, while at the same time, although they occasionally disagree, the women serve the unified purpose of telling the tale of Anna Livia. And their dual accomplishment of washing and spreading the linen on the banks to dry is the fitting close of one era (Book I), which also ushers in the new era (Book II).

As chapter 8 closes, the creative force becomes identified with the teller-tree; the created force is the listener-stone. A series of attitudes expressed in chapter 8 determine by what subtle and overt means Joyce enlists sympathy with the creator-Shem-tree through Anna's character and how he develops tension with the created-Shaun-stone through the artist's need for an audience or a preserved record. The two persons as *separate* entities function so closely, dependent upon each other, that distinctions are difficult to maintain; but in the metaphors of tree and stone, unlike Yeats who wrote "How can we tell the dancer from the dance?", Joyce offers the father figure for unity *in sequential experiences* and the sons for duality, coexistent but not combined.

To understand Queer Mrs. Quickenough and Odd Miss

Doddpebble requires examination of the meaning of Anna as creatrix and Anna-Shem as tree with their (or its) created counterpart the Shaun-stone. These concepts can be traced from Joyce's earlier works, and they show why the sex change from women to men (to tree and stone, Shem and Shaun) occurs at the close of chapter 8. Rather than transsexualism, the process described is metamorphosis; and, in Joyce's application, it requires a gap in time. The artist awakens the "dumb" to speak at the close of chapter 7. Chapter 8 then represents a cycle in time and indicates that the qualities of either parent may be born in son and/or daughter of the succeeding generation; personalities may then combine or change to emerge in another form. In the Brunonian concept, opposites unite only in the One or God; and Joyce consistently marks physical changes or "mergences" only after such an "identity of undiscernibles" (49.37 which is death, as in "her wife Langley . . . disappeared from the sourface of this earth" (50.6–10) and "her widower in his gravest embazzlement" (375.26). Such is the concept that Joyce explains (614.31–615.1) in connection with Vico as an "ex-progressive process" and "subsequent recombination." The transformation of the washerwomen, then, demonstrates the totality of Joyce's argument at the same time the women represent, also, Joyce's characterization of the artist and his view of creation.

Anna's identity as water both gives her universality, based on water myths, and makes her a creatrix of the universe. The Greek creation myths explained that "all living creatures originated in the stream of Oceanus which girdles the world"[1]; and the circling of the ocean (Joyce's "commodius vicus of recirculation"—3.2) extends by nature to all liquid matter flowing through the entirety of living organisms

1. Robert Graves, *The Greek Myths* (Baltimore: Penguin Books, 1955), 1: 30.

in milk, blood, sap, urine—the last a favorite analogy for Joyce as in the "rain, rain, rain" escapade of the Prankquean. With variations the concept appears in many ancient cultures, including the Egyptian god Hu, the Chinese dragon, the Hebraic *Genesis*, the Indian *Vedas*, the Irish Domnu. In Scandinavian myth, the earth itself was said to have emerged from the sea.[2] Graves theorizes about the female Michal of Hebron as Adam's creatrix, and Anna Livia had a Michael in her past who dipped his hands in her cool waters. In Gnostic theory, Jesus was conceived in the mind of God's Holy Spirit, who was female in Hebrew and, according to Genesis 1:2 "moved on the face of the waters."[3] Names of male gods are frequently masculinizations of names of goddesses and represent a turning of the cultural tide from matrilineal to patrilineal succession. Among other uses of the name Anna, "the simple form Ana, or Anah, occurs as a Horite clan name in Genesis 36; though masculinized in two out of three mentions of her, she is principally celebrated as the mother of Aholibamah ('tabernacle of the high place')."[4] Anna (pronounced Ah-na) is in the spiritual Onn or Om or Aum,[5] and Joyce borrows from creation myths when, in his letter, he calls Anna's distribution of gifts a "Pandora's box." Elsewhere the *Wake* discloses Joyce's fondness for matriarchal and matrilineal terms, such as "annadominant" and "preadaminant"; and his inversion of "Adam and Eve's," the Dubliners' popular nickname (derived from a pub) for St. Francis' Church, to "Eve and Adam's" (3.1) at the beginning

2. John Arnott MacCulloch, *Eddic: The Mythology of All Races* (New York: Cooper Square, 1964), pp. 324–27.

3. Graves, *The White Goddess* (New York: Vintage, 1958), p. 158.

4. *Ibid.*, p. 411.

5. For this modulation, see Harold Bayley, *The Lost Language of Symbolism* (New York: Barnes and Noble, 1912), 1: 236–66. For the Brahman *Aum* in the *Wake*, see Clive Hart, *Structure and Motif in Finnegans Wake* (Evanston: Northwestern University Press, 1962), pp. 96–104.

of the *Wake* affirms his intention that the female represent the origin of cosmic life.

As Anna modulates to Onn or Om, comparison of ancient alphabets in many available charts shows the confusion of the letters A and O (Bayley calls it "A often approaching O"). Further, to say they represent only the first and the last is to do them great injustice. Bayley explains, "in the Revelation of Jesus Christ [Rev. 1:8] it is asserted, 'I am Alpha and Omega, the beginning and the ending, saith the Lord, which is, and which was, and which is to come, the Almighty.' In all languages the great A seems to have stood for a symbol of the Aged, Unaging, Constant, and Everlasting Hill, the Immutable El, the Unchangeable First Cause."[6] Anna, with the O that begins the Anna Livia Plurabelle chapter, has both the delta and the mountain shape and represents both origin and continuation of life. Bayley here explains why Anna as the river ALP is sometimes also called a mountain, properly designated by the Gaelic word *alp* (as in "Alp has doped"—209.09). Joyce explains this when Earwicker is a Mr. A or fallen Adam; he is represented "in sigla as the smaller Δ, fontly called following a certain change of state of grace of nature alp or delta" (119.19–21). Eddic myth describes the sea as a Mountain-giant (*bergbui*).[7] Bayley adds, "That a mountain-top was regarded as a symbol and a physical similitude of the sacred A is evidenced to some extent by generic terms for mountain, such as the Greek *akra*, the great Fire A; Savoyade *crau;* Slavonic *gara;* Anglo-Saxon *law*, i.e. *el aw*, 'Lord Aw'; Japanese *jama* or *yama san*, 'Holy unique Sun A'; Latin *montana;* Spanish *montanha* and *sierra*."[8] *Alpha* and *Omega*, or the A (*Aleph*) and T (*Tau*) of the Hebrew alphabet as symbol of First and Last, he writes, "was

6. Bayley, p. 348.
7. MacCulloch, p. 171.
8. Bayley, p. 348.

not restricted to Christianity, but has been found among Egyptian documents. The expression 'last' is generally mis-understood in this connection, the truer implication being the end of the last days and the dawn of a new era or be-ginning."[9] Anna at the close of *Finnegans Wake* inaugurates the dawn, as well as the beginning of the book. As river she flows past both tree and stone; and Earwicker, a unified Shem-Shaun, lives as a tree and dies as a stone. Since A equals mountain, alp, and Earwicker, and O signifies the circularity of river and book, the A-O motif of *Finnegans Wake* means continuity rather than polarity.[10]

For Irish origins of Anna's name and character, Graves explains the oldest Irish alphabet, the Beth-Luis-Nion (Birch-Rowan-Ash) as a tree and calendar alphabet; and he shows the arrangement of vowels among the consonants to des-ignate the progress of the year, with *O* intended to express the spring solstice. *A* meant the birth tree, the elm or silver fir, and meant fertility; its Mediterranean counterpart, the palm tree (which grows lustily in Ireland's subtropic climate), means phoenix and gives the geographic name Phoenicia (its roots requiring salt, it grew near water) or, in Joyce's terms, the Phoenix Park by the river Liffey. By its Hebrew name *tamar*, it was the Tree of Life in the Garden of Eden. Its Irish name, silver fir, gives the Gallic Fir goddess, whom Graves describes as "Queen of the Druids and mother of the whole tree calendar."[11] The other letters as names of trees all have significance for the characterizations of ALP and HCE (*L*, for example, designated the rowan tree or the Irish "tree of life" and its time coincided with Candlemas

---

9. *Ibid.*, p. 73.

10. For the A–O motif as polarity in *Finnegans Wake,* see Edmund L. Epstein, "Interpreting *Finnegans Wake:* A Half-Way House," *James Joyce Quarterly* 3, no. 4 (1966): 252–71.

11. Graves, p. 199.

"to mark the quickening of the year"; *P*, near the close of the year, was the dwarf elder, which provided reeds for thatched houses), but it is the Gaelic letter *A* or *ailm* as pine or silver fir that Joyce translates into the *Wake's* elm. Anna begins and continues both life and letters (the alphabet). When Anna's plurality evokes the listener's comment, "They did well to rechristien her Pluhurabelle" (201.35), the name not only suggests multiplicity in English but also has a Gaelic root *bile* meaning sacred tree[12] and a German root *Hure* meaning prostitute.[13]

As Anna is creatrix, water, and green tree, so her association with art becomes clear, both through the alphabet as beginning of letters and recorded expression of life in Joyce's work and through his personal attitudes, as explained in Ellmann's biography. These matters in turn will reveal the tree-Shem aspect of the telling washerwomen's transformations.

As far back as the beginning of *Chamber Music,* Joyce placed on the first page of text a poem that introduces the sound of water and love in association with water:

> There's music along the river
> For Love wanders there   (*CP* 9)

The first motif (the sound of water) will develop into Anna's manuscript of rippling sounds and the second (love in association with water) into the blending of sexual and artistic creativity. In the *Portrait* Stephen's water-fertile image of the temptress, who inspired his first poem, marks the union of the female (girl in the stream) with water and art. The image

---

12. Brendon O Hehir, *A Gaelic Lexicon for Finnegans Wake* (Berkeley: University of California Press, 1967), p. 106.
13. Helmut Bonheim, *A Lexicon of the German in Finnegans Wake* (Berkeley: University of California Press, 1967), p. 63.

"enfolded him like a shining cloud, enfolded him like water with a liquid life: and like a cloud of vapour or like water circumfluent in space the liquid letters of speech, symbols of the element of mystery, flowed over his brain" (*AP* 223). The mystical "word made flesh" plagues Stephen Dedalus in *Ulysses*, where he again links the creatrix with creative writing: "As we, or mother Dana, weave and unweave our bodies . . . from day to day, their molecules shuttled to and fro, so does the artist weave and unweave his image" (*U* 194). Anna Livia's inspirational and seminal powers range from the prime of life to old age. She can persuade "hot Hammurabi, or cowld Clesiastes" to "burst bounds agin, and renounce their ruings, and denounce their doings, for iver and iver, and a night" (139.25–28).

The mergence of grammar and biology in the diagram of Anna Livia's vagina gives Greek equivalents for A and L, marks π (the Latin *ph*) opposite the P, and represents in the diagram the A.L.P. and the Greek αλπᾶ or Latin *alpha* as beginning, appropriately, of both life (Anna as A.L.P.) and letters (the alphabet). Bayley writes,

That the letter A had some recondite significance is evident from the words of Jesus found in the Apocryphal Gospel of Thomas: "And he looked upon the teacher Zacchaeus, and said to him: Thou who art ignorant of the nature of the Alpha, how canst thou teach others the Beta? . . . Hear, O teacher, the order of the first letter, and notice how it has lines, and a middle stroke crossing those which thou seest common; (lines) brought together; the highest part supporting them; and again bringing them under one head; with three points (of intersection); of the same kind; principal and subordinate; of equal length. Thou hast the lines of the A. And when the teacher Zacchaeus heard the child speaking such and so great allegories of the first letter, he was at a great loss about such a narrative, about his teaching.[14]

14. Bayley, p. 348 n.

Bayley adds that Sir John Rhys called the three lines of the A "three beams of light" and remarked that from them all other words (i.e., letters) are derived.[15]

In the same way that the fusion of grammar and biology demonstrates that to learn the logic of language is to learn the lesson of life (the tree, the part played by Mrs. Quickenough), Joyce was turning the lesson of Irish life into art (the stone, the part played by Miss Doddpebble). To testify that the cultural milieu of his past forced attention to lost manuscripts, the *Portrait* begins with reference to the *Tain Bo Cuailgne:* "there was a moocow coming down along the road and this moocow that was coming down along the road met a nicens little boy named baby tuckoo" (*AP* 7). The meeting of Joyce and the story told by his father gathers significance as time passes; the old woman of Ireland who brings milk to Stephen, Haines, and Buck Mulligan in the tower focuses several aspects of nationality. With her ignorance of the national language, she is "maybe a messenger" (*U* 13) and in spite of Stephen's scorn stands for him as a symbol of Ireland: "Silk of the kine and poor old woman, names given her in old times. A wandering crone, lowly form of an immortal serving her conqueror and her gay betrayer, their common cuckquean, a messenger from the secret morning" (*U* 14). She steps climactically into their doorway at the moment when the conversation, led by Buck Mulligan, has ridiculed subjects continued into *Finnegans Wake:* the enthusiasm for the old lost culture and ancient history ("Five lines of text and ten pages of notes about the folk and the fishgods of Dundrum. Printed by the weird sisters in the year of the big wind"—*U* 12–13), and the emerging recognition of a possible universality in the similarities of thought and custom ("Can you recall, brother, is mother Grogan's tea and water pot spoken of in the Mabinogion or is it in the

15. *Ibid.*

Upanishads"—*U* 13), even though Mulligan aims for satire. When Joyce sets his world of *Finnegans Wake* in motion, his fallen Finn-Finnegan lies extended on the landscape and at his own wake, with the music of Anna "all the livvylong night" (7.1–2) to wake him in the double sense of mourning and arising. Ultimately Anna represents creating life (the tree), and Finn-Finnegan in sleep or death represents solidified art and petrified life (the stone); but Joyce introduces these concepts gently. With the situation already described, the stream of life could flow much as indicated with "idlers' wind turning pages on pages," and one could assume the extant records (13–14) sufficient for all time, except for the knotty problem of the letter, which becomes a metaphor for lost knowledge. Somewhere, always, there have been thought to exist mysterious writing of origins of the universe and un-revealed histories, sometimes both called "keys," explaining things unknown to man, but "Somewhere, parently, in the ginnandgo gap[16] between antediluvious and anna-dominant the copyist must have fled with his scroll" (14.16–18),[17] or its destruction came by way of natural or ac-cidental causes or intentional burying: "The billy flood rose or an elk charged him or the sultrup worldwright from the excelsissimost empyrean (bolt, in sum) earthspake or the Dannamen gallous banged pan the bliddy duran" (14.18–21). Similarly the *Book of Kells* was buried,[18] the *Book of*

16. Joseph Campbell and Henry Morton Robinson identify "ginnandgo gap" as the *Ginnunga-gap* of the Icelandic Eddas. See *A Skeleton Key to Finnegans Wake* (New York: Viking Press, 1961), p. 46 n.

17. Antediluvian books are mostly pictographic tablets found at Kish, Fara, and Ur. Also, Halley stresses the necessary recopying of perishable leather and papyrus "books" as a reason for the loss of many ancient manuscripts. See Harry H. Halley, *Bible Handbook* (Chicago: Henry H. Halley, 1957), pp. 44 and 55.

18. *The Book of Kells* was "stolen by night . . . and found after a lapse of some months, concealed under sods." See *The Book of Kells*, p. 4., quoted in Atherton, p. 63. Malachy, as new archbishop and successor of Patrick, went north to Armagh in 1132 and was immediately engaged in a conflict with a jealous rival to the suc-

Armagh stolen in 1132 (the year of the twins' birth). The Greeks had an unknown poet, and Hebrew myth formed the background of the Bible with its mysterious references to lost scrolls.[19] As the *Book of Kells* was discovered in the sod, or the Dead Sea Scrolls in a cave, or Hammurabi's Code in the ruins of a buried city (a realistic "midden heap" of fallen civilization), so a Belinda Doran (bliddy duran), her name obscured or varied as history repeats itself, may scratch up a manuscript with origin unknown and meaning unfathomed. At the same time, the letter is one person's letter to the world, as the outgoing Anna sighs, "Sometime then, somewhere there, I wrote me hopes and buried the page . . . and left it to lie till a kissmiss coming" (624.3–6). These are the serious backgrounds for Shaun as mail carrier (though as Shaun the Post he is both Postman and stone, that is, "deaf as a post") and for Miss Doddpebble as stone, in that the most durable record of the past is that represented in stone. That the creative force (either Anna or Shem as artist) has the talents to rouse the dead (the stone or the message from the past) stresses the importance of the Shem-Shaun tension. The stone and the manuscript are represented in "hot Hammurabi" and "cowld Clesiastes"; Hammurabi was the Babylonian king who received laws from the sun-god Shamash and wrote "Hammurabi's Code"—a cuneiform tablet now in the Louvre and which dates from approximately 2000 B.C.; Ecclesiastes records the aged Solomon's existential view that "All is vanity" (cf. 374.22–23). Creativity itself is transformed into stone, or into the stone attitude.

cession, a man named Niall, who carried away until 1137 "the Staff of Jesus, Patrick's bell, and *The Book of Armagh*." See D. D. C. Pochin Mould, *Ireland of the Saints* (London: B. T. Batsford, 1953), p. 115.

19. Robert Graves and Raphael Patai list as lost or suppressed pre-biblical sacred documents The Book of the Wars of Yahweh, Book of Yashar, The Book of the Story of Adam, and several others. For an example of such a reference in the Bible, see Joshua 10:13: "Is not this written in the book of Jasher?" See *Hebrew Myths: The Book of Genesis* (New York: McGraw Hill, 1963), p. 9.

Literally, Joyce's concern with lost manuscripts and legends ˋas an origin in *logos* itself. Biographically, the same conˋern marks an affiliation with the Irish Renaissance, which ˋe was just beginning to appreciate by 1909, the year of the ˋeturn to Dublin when he gathered materials for *Exiles* and *Jlysses*[20] and experienced the traumatic revelation by ˋosgrave of Nora's alleged companionship with him.[21] Of ˋhat return, Ellmann describes the biographical in terms of ˋhe literary: "Joyce, like Gabriel Conroy, was now making ˋis journey westward," and the experience dramatically ˋlarified several attitudes, especially toward Nora, and thereˋy inspired subsequent writing.

To testify that Joyce's literary (and mythical) woman ˋxisted in personal experience, Ellmann offers an analysis of ˋoyce's attitude: "in the figure of the Virgin he had found a ˋother image which he cherished. . . . When Joyce met Nora ˋarnacle in 1904, it was not enough for her to be his misˋess; she must be his queen and even his goddess; he must ˋe able to pray to her."[22] Citing the refusal of formal ˋarriage with Nora and the 1909 challenge to her fidelity as ˋeans of testing her love and assuring her acceptance of ˋeven the worst in him," Ellmann recounts Joyce's attempts ˋ learn her most secret thoughts, to learn "what it is to be a ˋoman" while writing letters about " 'adoration' and 'desecraˋion' of her image."[23] Ellmann further explains, "What ˋas unusual about his attitude was not that he saw his wife as ˋis mother or that he demanded fulfillment of either role. ˋhe novelty lay in his declining to confuse the two images ˋnd instead holding them remorsefully apart, opposing them ˋ each other so that they became the poles of his mind."[24]

20. Ellmann, p. 300.
21. See *ibid.*, pp. 288–99.
22. *Ibid.*, p. 285.
23. *Ibid.*, p. 304.
24. *Ibid.*, p. 305.

As Ellmann indicates, therefore, Molly Bloom represents the sexual aspects of woman (although she is maternal as well) and Anna Livia Plurabelle represents the maternal aspects (although she is sexual as well). As the washerwomen describe Anna Livia, her fidelity after her "marriage" is not questioned; on the contrary she incites rumors—as she purposefully makes herself a cuckquean—with her overzealous attempts to make her husband happy. In the last monologue, Anna as eternal mother expects replacement of herself in a daughter as she remarks, "Yes, you're changing, sonhusband, and you're turning, I can feel you, for a daughterwife from the hills again" (627.1–3).

While Ellmann acknowledges that Joyce's god of creation "is really a goddess,"[25] and Anna is a creatrix, Joyce's male characters are not great artists. In the world's cosmogonies (for example, the Egyptian, where the creator raised himself from Nu, the Ocean), water existed before god; or the creator used some primal matter of which the cosmos was previously fashioned and for which man was charged with the maintenance and continuation of that world. As the river returns to its source, so creative man, or the artist, returns to woman, his symbol of all creative power. On the cosmological level the mother figure is the creative universe itself, as in Gea-Tellus, the persona of Molly Bloom as Bloom lies beside her. In the *Wake* the characterization of Anna Livia as mother and river makes her a metaphor for the artist's need to unite himself with the universe; that is, she becomes a metaphor for his cosmic pride, in order that he may express that universe.

Since Joyce's cosmogony is one of continuing creation, the imminent union of the potential artist with fecund matter becomes his ultimate expression of that cosmogony. This is

25. *Ibid.*, p. 306.

why, I believe, a summation of Joyce's creative men reveals their potential, not their achievement: Gabriel Conroy of "The Dead" writes book reviews; Stephen of the *Portrait*, composing the villanelle, determines to become a writer; Richard Rowan of *Exiles* is an aspiring author; Stephen of *Ulysses* has written little more than a postscript to Mr. Deasy's letter, while Bloom's mania is the absorption, rather than the creation of knowledge.[26] In *Finnegans Wake* Shem as artist and person must be constantly ridiculed (as in "Shem was a sham"—170.25), subjected to answering Shaun's riddles, forced to write on his own body. As creator he defers always to women. After Shaun-Justius berates him (187–193) he introduces Anna Livia because in her they have origin, union, and hope (194–195). He "lifts the lifewand and the dumb speak" (195.5) for the washerwomen to tell the tale of Anna Livia; by reference to her he explains the secret of life in the chapter 10 grammar-biology lesson; and her monologue closes the book.

To demonstrate a world of imminent creation, *Dubliners*, *Ulysses*, and *Finnegans Wake* all conclude with a main character in a reclining position—in bed—like the awakening Adam of Michelangelo's masterpiece waiting to be touched into new life. Each seems suspended in a state of anticipation, just barely sensing the threshold of transformation; and the suspension combines the finality of an altered perspective with the uncertainty of expectation. Each lies in bed thinking his own thoughts while his spouse beside him sleeps. Gabriel Conroy, in this position, with his wife's startling revelation uppermost in his mind, recalls past events with their shifting scenes and personalities and makes an imaginative panoramic sweep of snowy Ireland until the living and the dead, the near and the far seem blended in a common-

26. I am indebted to Bernard Benstock for this observation.

alty of experience and sentiment. Molly Bloom ponders mak
ing a place for the unexpected new acquaintance, Stephen
Dedalus, in the family circle, while her recollections of the
past merge the mountains of Howth and Gibralter, and
earlier loves with the love of Leopold Bloom. Anna Livia
as wife of Earwicker, in her closing monologue lies beside
him in bed thinking into the future ("I could lead you there
and I still by you in bed"—622.19–20) and, as river flowing
out to sea, anticipates his "bearing down" on her "like he'd
come from Arkangels" (628.10). The state of anticipation
coincides with the dawn—Gabriel after a party, Molly after
Leopold's return home, Anna Livia after a late pub-closing
and love-making. In this view, Joyce's intensification of the
state of anticipation by concluding *Finnegans Wake* with a
suspended sentence was the final stroke of genius harmoniz-
ing form and content.

The quality of animated suspension, at its furthest extent,
means transformation; and at the close of the central chapter
of *Finnegans Wake* Joyce wrote his most obvious transformation, that of the washerwomen into the tree and the stone,
Shem and Shaun, an artist-audience duality who represent
the quick and the dead. Hence the washerwomen's names are
Mrs. Quickenough and Miss Doddpebble, and the latter's
name, analogous to the German Tod, means "dead stone."[27]
Again, this artist-audience duality may be seen emerging from
Joyce's earlier characterizations.

Each story in *Dubliners* is commonly conceived as containing a revelation (epiphany) for its main character; some of
the characters, such as the boys of the first three stories, are
capable of recognizing truths about themselves and others
and therefore have potential for change. The child of "The
Sisters" learns that a shattered chalice with its "grave" respon-

27. Again, I am indebted to Bernard Benstock.

sibilities means a shattered mind. The child of "An Encounter" learns about sadism and, by contrast, the merits of an ordinary friend, Mahony. The boy of "Araby" attempts a noble gesture for the sake of the girl next door and out of futility sees himself "a creature driven and derided by vanity." For Jimmy of "After the Races" self-awareness dawns finally with a game of cards, and in "Two Gallants" Lenehan's low aspirations are confirmed by the payoff of Corley. Such persons as the vote-gatherers in "Ivy Day in the Committee Room" and Mr. Farrington of "Counterparts" remain incapable of self-recognition and serve as examples of "paralysis"—the quality that Joyce will later exemplify in the dead stone.

Of the story "The Dead," Bernard Benstock has distinguished three kinds of dead: "the deceased, the moribund, and the living-dead," and the last he defines as "those who remain alive, but fail to live."[28] Gabriel's dawning awareness moves him out of this last category, but in a sense the living death may follow a completion of all experience that equates with lack of anticipation of new life. Such is Gabriel's analysis of the sleeping Gretta: "So she had had that romance in her life: a man had died for her sake." In contrast with what he imagines as Gretta's sense of completion from having unintentionally gleaned the maximum sacrifice from another person (Michael), much experience awaits him: "He had never felt like that himself towards any woman but he knew that such a feeling must be love." Attitudes may congeal into the stone atmosphere, or what Richard Rowan calls "the darkness of belief," leaving nothing to question and nothing to "tellabout." In youthful innocence Stephen of the *Portrait* writes into his diary the sense of urgency about the anticipatory state, in contrast with that which is over,

28. "The Dead," in *James Joyce's Dubliners*, ed. Clive Hart (New York: The Viking Press, 1969), p. 153.

completed: "The past is consumed in the present and the present is living only because it brings forth the future." To represent the past, the stone exists in the *Wake*.

A short time earlier Stephen had a "troubled night of dreams" which, before leaving Dublin, he wants to "tell-about":

> A long curving gallery. From the floor ascend pillars of dark vapours. It is peopled by the images of fabulous kings, set in stone. Their hands are folded upon their knees in token of weariness and their eyes are darkened for the errors of men go up before them for ever as dark vapours.
>
> Strange figures advance from a cave. They are not as tall as men. One does not seem to stand quite apart from another. Their faces are phosphorescent, with darker streaks. They peer at me and their eyes seem to ask me something. They do not speak. (*AP* 249–50)

The "images of fabulous kings, set in stone" will correspond with the record of the past. Their sense of weariness and the darkened eyes will be replaced, as the dawn of the new era approaches, with the "wonder in your eye" which the washer-woman sees. Those who emerge from the cave, with their eyes asking, will finally turn to the teller-artist for their answers.

At the close of *Dubliners, Ulysses,* and *Finnegans Wake,* the sleeping partner has just ceased telling his story: Gretta has revealed her youthful romance; Bloom is labeled "Narrator" and Molly "Listener" at the close of the Ithaca chapter; and HCE has told one last version of his romance with Anna before he closes the pub (546–554). The wakeful partner of the monologue continues the narration; and this reversal of roles provides a realistic basis for the teller-artist to function subtly as waker of the sleeping-completed-dead. The necessity for the waking-sleeping (or the Shem-Shaun) tension thereby forms the foundation for a novel developing the monomyth of recurrent life. Apparently it is no coincidence that Joyce's three books close with "Pillow Talk"—where the Irish epic, the *Tain Bo Cualigne,* begins; much "pillow talk" (57.34) marks the gap in time before Earwicker rearises.

In contrast with the paralyzed Dubliners, the wakeful Gabriel Conroy at the close of "The Dead" makes one decision strikingly different from attitudes expressed earlier when he determines that "the time had come for him to set out on his journey westward." The meaning of the ambiguous snow, that is, Gabriel's exact intention at the close of "The Dead" remains somewhat mysterious, I believe, because Joyce at this stage in his writing had not yet fully developed the technique of anticipation which, in this and later works, provides a part of those powerful, lyrical endings. Certainly Joyce provides more information of Molly's and Anna Livia's destinies; and even the listening washerwoman anticipates more story as she changes her request from a story of Anna to a story of the sons. But Gabriel's attitude has qualities basic to Joyce's characterization of the artist.

Gabriel's state of mind at the close of "The Dead" emerges from an altered prospect, composed of anticipation, and takes the form of a strong resolution (to go west). In a correspondingly decisive manner, Stephen in the *Portrait* resolves "to forge in the smithy of my soul the uncreated conscience of my race." Richard Rowan of *Exiles* seems to feel that the intensity of real living, that is, when life is lived at its fullest, depends not on finality of attitude or achievement; rather, brushing past his wife's eagerness to tell all, he concludes with a preference for suspension in a "restless living wounding doubt." Nevertheless, the creative qualities for Joyce logically belonged in the female figure; and he wrote, first, using this approach, Molly Bloom's acceptance of a new state, the married state, in her "yes I said yes I will Yes" to Leopold

Bloom, and second, Anna Livia's dying down "only to wash-up" at the close of *Finnegans Wake* as she loses her river identity while seeking union with the sea. Gabriel, like Molly and Anna Livia, concludes sensitive and wakeful. The sleeping partner of each, like the "paralyzed" persons of the earlier *Dubliners* stories, will find the furthest extent of his characterization in the stone. The "living and the dead," the sensitive and the paralyzed, the waking and the sleeping who inhabit Gabriel Conroy's world and upon whom the snow falls become, in the *Wake,* the tree and the stone.

3

"why the elm and how the stone" (563.21)

His dependence upon feminine inspiration was expressed by Joyce when he wrote to Nora, "I know and feel that if I am to write anything fine or noble in the future I shall do so only by listening at the doors of your heart."[1] The concept of union of artist with primal matter, accordingly, depends upon a metaphorical sexual relationship between Shem and Anna Livia.[2] The fourth-chapter radio program includes a suggestive second question, "Does your mutter know your mike?" (139.15), a question answered in sexual terms, concluding with a night climaxed with a triumphant exclamation, "Amin!" ["Am in!"] (139.28). Later Shem explains his mother's female anatomy to Shaun. Conversely, according to Mrs. Quickenough, Shem is Anna's "penmight." To exemplify his theme of continuing creation, Joyce can describe almost everything in sexual language; and Mark's description of "Finn his [Phoenix] park" becomes an account of sexual intercourse between the poet-tree and the river-Anna: "Of these tallworts are yielded out juices for

1. Richard Ellmann, *James Joyce* (New York: Oxford University Press, 1965), p. 315.

2. Not an uncommon concept; nor is it original with Joyce. Bayley quotes the *Wedding Song of Wisdom* on entering the House of God: "where, when they come, they must cast away their garments, and all become Bridegrooms, obtaining their true Manhood through the Virginal Spirit." See Harold Bayley, *The Lost Language of Symbolism* (New York: Barnes and Noble, 1912), 2:286.

jointoils and pappasses for paynims. Listeneth! 'Tis a tree story. How olave [Gaelic *ollave*, poet], that firile [Gaelic *men*], was aplanted in her liveside" (564.20–22). Shaun, for his part, aspires to sexual and literary conquest when he lectures Issy about "robbing leaves out of my taletold book." He adds, "may my tunc fester if ever I see such a miry lot of maggalenes!" (453.18–19).

With characteristic thoroughness, Joyce, to arrive at his comprehensive presentation of tree-creativity, begins with natural associations and tree myths and goes on to create additional meanings. Leaves, for example, suggest love in *Finnegans Wake*—Anna Livia cherishes one remaining leaf as she flows out to sea; Bayley explains, "Many leaves are formed like hearts, and the word *leaf* is identical with *love* and *life*. It is scientific fact that a tree *lives* by its *leaves,* and it is Swedenborg's leading dogma, 'That Love is the Life of Man.'"[3] In the Earwicker pub such an association describes persons enjoying life and laughter at a passing frivolity ("all the leaves alift aloft, full o'liefing, fell alaughing" —361.18), but only until the soberer matter of Earwicker's crime intrudes on the hilarity in the form of Constable Sackerson: "And they leaved the most leavely of leaftimes and the most folliagenous till there came the marrer of mirth and the jangtherapper of all jocolarinas" (361.26–28). Leaves and trees mean love to Issy who, even while arrayed in spiritual glory as a nun, is still a "child of tree, like some losthappy leaf" (556.19):

> Everyday, precious, while m'm'ry's leaves are falling deeply on my Jungfraud's Messongebook I will dream telepath posts dulcets on this isinglass stream (but don't tell him or I'll be the

3. Bayley, p. 274. He also quotes the passage from Swedenborg's *Divine Love and Wisdom* associating the heat of the sun, noticeable in leaves, with the warmth of love. Also, according to Bayley, Iggdrasil "resolves into *ig dur az il,* the "mighty, Enduring, Light God.""

mort of him!) under the libans and the sickamours, the cyprissis
and babilionias,[4] where the frondoak rushes to the ask and
the yewleaves too kisskiss themselves and 'twill carry on my
hearz' waves my still waters reflections in words over Margrate
von Hungaria, her Quaidy ways and her Flavin hair, to thee,
Jack, ahoy, beyond the boysforus" (460.19-27).

The nine hazels that grew beside Connla's Well and
dropped flowers of beauty and nuts of wisdom into a fountain
(and gave the salmon his spots) now are transferred to
Phoenix Park. The water represents Anna Livia, of course;
the tree's leaves, punning the pages of a book, represent the
work and the knowledge the creative artist (Gaelic *ollave*)
holds the key to; the "hedjes of maiden ferm" in the Earwicker family suggest Issy. Telling or singing, like the babble
of water or the sound of wind in the trees, all represent the
voices of creation or artistic expression; hence the Chaucerian
"mine auctor sung it me" introduction to this passage:

These brilling waveleaplights! Please say me how sing you
them. Seekhem seckhem! They arise from a clear springwell
in the near of our park which makes the daft to hear all blend.
This place of endearment! How it is clear! And how they cast
their spells upon, the fronds that thereup float, the bookstaff
branchings! The druggeted stems, the leaves incut on trees!
Do you can their tantrist spellings? I can lese, skillmistress
aiding. Elm, bay, this way, cull dare, take a message, tawny
runes ilex sallow, meet me at the pine. Yes, they shall have
brought us to the water trysting, by hedjes of maiden ferm"
(571.1-10).

The above passage, spoken in Mark's section of the Four
Old Men's watching over the Earwicker household, like the
Anna Livia Plurabelle chapter, continues the teller and lis-

4. In "babilionias" Joyce combines the two trees—Tree of Truth and Tree of
Life—at the East gate of the Babylonian heaven.

tener pattern. Making the deaf (the stone) to hear throughout the *Wake* is a primary attribute of the creative artist. The listener in this passage asks, "Please say me how sing you them. . . . Do you can [ken] their tantrist [oak sad] spellings?" The teller's "I can lese, skillmistress aiding" returns to the inspirational female, as does the meeting at the pine. The message ("tawny runes") of evergreen ("ilex") combines the early straight-line or stick characters of the runic alphabet, traditionally formed of ash sticks, with the elm as pine tree and with the oak (*tan* in "tantrist" and Kildare, "church of the oak," in "cull dare"). When the watchers in the Earwicker household pass Issy's door, there is an echo of the close of the ALP chapter: "Cant ear! Her dorters ofe? Whofe? Her eskmeno daughters hope? Whope? Ellme, elmme, elskmestoon ["elm" plus "ask me, stone"! and Scandinavian "love me soon"] Soon!" (572.16–17).

As indicated earlier, the elm as the Gaelic letter A (*ailm*) meaning pine or silver fir obviously adopts the role of teller-artist because of associations with Anna and the origin, therefore, of both human life and alphabetic letters. In the introduction to the *Wake,* the intriguing positioning of elm as successor to oak and ash ("The oaks of ald now they lie in peat yet elms leap where askes lay" (4.14–15) just before the statement of theme, "Phall if you but will, rise you must," indicates that Joyce urges the cause of his favorite cosmology through the replacement of the Druidic oak and the Irish or Scandinavian ash[5] by the Joycean elm; "askes" as combined *ashes* and *ask us* (also *ask* is Danish or Swedish for *ash*) posits an ash tree asking and listening as well as the recumbent ashes of the past ("askes lay").[6] The rainbow girls survey

5. Margaret Solomon approaches this statement when she writes, "The legend of the world-ash is supposed to antedate the Biblical fall-myth." See Solomon, p. 74.
6. Bayley writes, "According to the author of the *Bogs and Ancient Forests,* when

the world's revered trees to confirm this impression of replacement by the elm; "Luccombe oaks, Turkish hazels, Greek fire, incense palm edcedras. The hypsometers of Mount Anville is held to be dying out of arthataxis but, praise send Larix U'Thule, the wych elm of Manelagh is still flourishing in the open, because its native of our nature and the seeds was sent by Fortune" (235.16–21). Of the "native" trees the Branching Tree (a T tree) as one of the Five Magic Trees of Ireland was, according to Graves, the ash, as was another, the Tree of Tortu; and the fall of these trees established precedence for the accession to prominence of the Joycean elm. According to Graves, "in mediaeval poetry [the fall of those trees] symbolized the triumph of Christianity over paganism."[7]

Joyce's lists of seven or so trees (264.26–265.4, 361.6–10, 460.22–24, 542.5–546.1, 588.29–34) most frequently have in common the oak, elm, ash, and some variant of evergreen. The oak, sacred to the Druids as a symbol of Jupiter, was "topped and trained" by them, according to Bayley, "until it had acquired the holy form" of the T or "Tau" (a variant of *Thau*, meaning God).[8] The oak in the *Wake* appropriately represents paternity, as in "daddyoak" (446.13), in "keeping

the Bog of Allen in Kildare was cut through, oak, fir, yew, and other trees were found buried 20 or 30 feet below the surface, and these trees generally lie prostrated in a horizontal position, and *have the appearance of being burned at the bottom of their trunks and roots*, fire having been found far more powerful in prostrating those forests than cutting them down with an axe; and the great depth at which these trees are found in bogs, shows that they must have lain there for many ages." See Bayley, *Archaic England* (Philadelphia: J. B. Lippincott, 1920), p. 21.

7. Graves confuses these trees, saying the Tree of Tortu and the Branching Tree of Usnech were the two ashes (p. 140) and then later naming the Tree of Tortu and the Branching Tree of Dathi for the same purpose (p. 386). According to Rees and Rees, the five trees stand for the four provinces plus a center; they are "the Ash of Tortu, the Bole of Ross (a comely yew), the Oak of Mugna, the Bough of Dathi (an ash), and the Ash of populous Uisnech." See Alwyn Rees and Brinley Rees, *Celtic Heritage* (London: Thames and Hudson, 1961), p. 120.

8. Bayley, *Archaic England*, p. 393.

the father of curls from the sport of oak" (448.24–25) and in
the "hegoak" on Earwicker's crest (5.7). The oak receives
acclaim for its mistletoe—a convenient vehicle for the love
and war occupational interests when punned into ammuni-
tion ("Once you are balladproof you are unperceable to
haily, icy and missilethroes"—616.31–32)[9] and for the acorns
that adorn the World Tree ("acorns and pinecorns"—505.4–
5). The elm conveys the Joycean message, as in "roaring
mighty shouts, through my longertubes of elm" (542.6–7);
and Joyce models his "Big Elm" (507.36), a bisexual cosmic
tree, on Yggdrasil. The ash represents the past, as in "dilapidating ashpits" (544.13–14), "leaving clashing ash" (84.28),
"ashtray" (503.07), "gone ashley" (213.14), and "silver ash"
(28.30) for gray hair. The evergreen, like those variants
planted over graves, assures continuing life; the father
sleeps "neath stone pine" (14.32), the grave is "pineshrouded"
(546.1), the yew is the last letter of life's alphabet (553.3).
Another common tree, the sycamore, is most frequently
associated with Issy and means lovesick, as in "sickamours"
(460.23), "the maid . . . under the sycamores" (388.24), and
"they were all sycamore" (397.23–24). Irish lore offers
an additional wealth of imaginative trees; the Tree of Mugna,
one of the Five Magic Trees, successively bore apples,

9. Frazer identifies the mistletoe, which grows on the oak tree, as the golden
bough; Bayley quotes a Druidic chant printed in Wilson Armistead's *Tales and Legends
of the Irish Lakes:*

> Spirit who no birth has known,
> Springing from Thyself alone,
> We thy living emblem show
> In the mystic mistletoe,
> Springs and grows without a root,
> Yields without flowers its fruit;
> Seeks from earth no mother's care,
> Lives and blooms the child of air.

See *Archaic England,* p. 681.

nuts, and edible acorns.[10] The quicken tree of Dermot and
Grania bore bell-shaped youth-restoring berries.[11]

When Yggdrasil, the mythical ash tree of Odin or "Woodin"
(503.28), punned into "eggdrazzles" (504.35), becomes the
cosmic elm, the questioner's phrasing ("overlisting eshtree"
—503.30) already modulates toward elmtree and the teller
confirms the elm as successor to oak and ash; it is "Oakley
Ashe's elm" (503.32). It begins and fosters all life ("For we
are fed of its forest, clad in its wood, burqued by its bark"
—503.36) and letters ("and our lecture is its leave"—504.1).
The activities in the tree are "tunc committed" and observed
and described from the teller's reclining position: "I then
tuk my takenplace lying down" (504.12). The discussion
contains an explanation of the washerwomen-to-brothers
transformation. Early in the description of the tree it has a
feminine "snoodrift" and a masculine "maypole," and
the long passage describing the many kinds of life and activities in its branches[12] alternates "his" and "her" references
to the tree. The listener succinctly summarizes these bisexual
attributes: "The form masculine. The gender feminine" (505.
25) in correspondence with common knowledge that in Latin,
although the gender of the names of trees is feminine, the
endings are masculine. The phallic fall (and since the days
of Denis Breen's postcard message in *Ulysses,* "Up" implies
the phallic erection[13]) is in the teller's assertive "Upfellbowm"
["baum," tree, with "down"] (505.29); but in the *Wake* nothing
ever with certainty concludes, and this answer to the ques-

10. Robert Graves, *The White Goddess* (New York: Vintage, 1958), p. 386.
11. See P. W. Joyce, *Old Celtic Romances* (New York: The Devin-Adair Company,
1962), p. 212.
12. For a summation of the *Wake* world tree (503–5), see Joseph Campbell and
Henry Morton Robinson, *A Skeleton Key to Finnegans Wake* (New York: Viking, 1961),
pp. 312–13. See also MacCulloch, pp. 332–36.
13. Bernard Benstock, *Joyce-again's Wake* (Seattle: Washington University Press,
1965), pp. 280–81.

tion "are you derevatov of it yourself in any way?" (505. 26) implies that the teller, rather than fallen, derives his ancestry from that ever green tree. Representing Edenic creation and fall, that ancestor "had put his own nickelname on every toad, duck and herring before the climber clomb aloft" (506.1–2), but yielded to his better half ("bitter hoolft"— 506.3), occasioned the anger of the Supreme Being, and became low and snaky himself.

Several characteristics of the cosmic tree appear in this and other passages: the animal hierarchy with birds in the top (505.1, 505.17, 504.23, 504.35); four-footed animals running up and down (504.28–30); serpents at its roots (505. 7, 506.6); the fall of the tree denoting the doom of the gods (505.29, 506.7); the wind in the top (331.5) as Odin's steed and poetic expression; stories of a tree reaching to heaven, preserved in "Jack and the Beanstalk" (504.19); a link with the Tree of Life in Paradise, a T-shape with "triliteral" roots (505.4) reaching into the Underworld and the two branches of its top stretching into the heavens (503.30).

The tree-stone relationship in the *Wake* has a common point of origin in that the mythical tree was represented in several tall stone pillars topped with the cross. One of these, the Dearham Cross, showed not a complete tree but the phallic tree—stem only (cf. "Treestam"—104.10, "treestem" —424.28, "treestirm"—621.36).[14] Sophus Bugge, studying the Bewcastle Cross of Cumberland with its elaborate carvings of a tree complete with roots, trunk, branches, foliage, and fruits, and with birds and animals eating the fruit, theorized that the Norse poet saw the design on the stone pillar and from it derived the myth of the Ash Yggdrasil.[15] The winding, serpentine designs of these crosses Joyce could

14. Illustrated in John Arnott MacCulloch, *Eddic: The Mythology of All Races* (New York: Cooper Square, 1964), Plates XLII–XLV.

15. Quoted in MacCulloch, p. 334.

relate to the serpentine T of the *Tunc* page ("tunc committed").
Whether the myth of the tree inspired the carving or the
carving generated the myth of the tree, Joyce places beside
his world tree a stone, now the tricolor flagstone of Ireland,
a "grave" marker since the fall. The stone is there before the
discussion of the tree (503.26) and after it (505.21), where the
questioner inquires what its name is ("But that steyne
of law indead what stiles its neming?"); the reply confirms what the questioner "indead" suggests—that it
means, and its name is, "Tod." The stone comes to life only
when the artist-Mercius waves his "lifewand" (195.5).

To determine general characteristics of the trees in the
Wake, a few other passages pertinent to the living-tree and
elm-succession may be observed. One such occurs in the
II.1 recitation of the alphabet, where the central letter, *M*,
names the mimosa tree. Bayley in his discussion of the symbol
M of the Great Deep theorizes that the mimosa is derived
from "Mem, the waters" and has associations with Mare and
Mary as Mother.[16] The children in the grammar lesson approach some understanding of this: "lead us seek, lote us
see, light us find, let us missnot Maidadate, Mimosa Multi-
mimetica, the maymeaminning of maimoomeining!"
(267.1–3).

HCE's family tree, when he begs a "dear lady" at a trial
to "judge on my tree by our fruits" (535.31–32), includes
"two smells, three eats" (535.32)—the two impregnations
resulting in three children. Added, these represent the five
"fruits" of the Tree of Knowledge—the five senses through
which knowledge is obtained. Further, Jones makes of the
"genus Inexhaustible" numerous possibilities for sexuality
as he includes some twenty trees by name, suggestively

16. Bayley adds that "the *Mimosa* has been adopted as the symbol of South
Africa." See *Lost Language*, 2: 278.

associating a "lodgepole" with a "pure stand" and a habit ("habitat") of "selfsownseedling" (159.34–160.16).

On another occasion, HCE in his self-defense addresses the court, "Big Seat," asking of the enthroned judge, "you did hear?" (361.6). The Brehon Law classification of seven chieftain trees included the ash, because its timber supported the King's thigh.[17] But HCE next recites a conundrum of seven trees, reminiscent of Ophelia's flowers: "And teach him twisters in tongue irish. Pat lad may goh too. Quicken [the rowan], aspen; ash and yew; willow, broom with oak for you. And move your tellabout. Not nice is that, limpet lady! Spose we try it promissly. Love all. Naytellmeknot tennis! Taunt me treattening!" (361.6–10). The giving of a piece of birch or hazel traditionally meant encouragement or discouragement. Here, as elsewhere, the important issue is Earwicker's guilt or the girls' or men's compliance. In the same way "Does he love me or does he not?" as daisy petals are plucked in the child's flower game, or alternates chosen in "Eeny Meeny Miny Mo" ("pat lad may goh too"), "Taunt treattening" is the promise of a treat or of threat, as the giving of birch meant "you may begin" or the giving of hazel meant "be wise and desist."[18] This confusion of male ("pat lad") and female ("limpet lady") existed with the same symbol earlier, when "Mr Whitlock gave him a piece of wood" (98.25–26). In that instance "baton" and "hod" may suggest male-female union, while "cup and ball" and "heer prefers a punsil shapner" (98.30–31) are sexually ambivalent. As indicated in the counting rhyme, moving the "tellabout"—the point of beginning the counting—alters the results.

Like the conflicting stories, or the many voices of the *Wake* who inconclusively "tellabout" a single subject a

17. Graves, p. 169.
18. *Ibid.*, p. 160.

number of stories, tree symbolism in world cultures is so complex, with remarkable similarities, that to some extent one may choose his tree and his interpretation. In Ireland the Five Magical Trees[19] differed from those five representing the vowels of the Beth-Luis-Nion, whose arrangement of vowels are yet unlike the sequence of another stick alphabet, the Boibel-Loth. Also Druidic signals, arranged on the five fingers of the hand, designated letters of the alphabet denoting names of trees, a total of twenty letters or sounds. Brehon Law in medieval Ireland provided four categories of trees—chieftain, peasant, shrub, and bramble—for a total of twenty-nine trees.[20] The interpretations from Irish folklore alone are sufficiently "inexhaustible" without recourse to other cultures which, of course, Joyce had. No wonder then that rumors of Earwicker's indiscretion would include the statement, "The war is in words and the wood is the world. Maply me, willowy we, hickory he and yew yourselves" (98.34–36). The Pythagorean term "the wood" was a quincunx of five trees representing the world—understood by the five senses—and included earth, air, fire, water, and the soul, and with the elements corresponding to the seasons.[21] Trees for Joyce become another means, in regard to time (the changing seasons), space (the elements), and spirit, to present the creation of the cosmos.[22]

Another naming of seven trees, from Luke's position, combines a possible seven chieftains with seven trees and the power of the word: "Only trees such as these such were those, waving there, the barketree, the o'briertree, the rowantree, the o'corneltree, the behanshrub near windy arbour, the magill o'dendron more. Trem! All the trees in the wood

19. The Trees of Mugna, Tortu, Dathi, Ross, and Usnech.
20. Graves, pp. 168–70.
21. Quoted in *ibid.*, p. 156.
22. For another discussion of this passage, see Solomon, pp. 71–72.

they trembold, humbild, when they heard the stoppress from domday's erewold" (588.29–34). Suggesting Berkeley, O'Brien, Rowan O'Connell, Behan, Magill, and Moore, this passage names bark (possibly the holly, whose bark was used for tanning), the briar tree, the rowan (or quicken) tree, the cornel (dogwood), shrub, the gill or ground ivy (used for flavoring ale), and *dendron* as the Greek word for tree plus an implication of endless variety ("magill o'dendron more" may be read as "many trees more"). The passage, expressing pride in a variety of Irishmen of two generations, contrasts with the egoism of Simon Dedalus in the *Portrait,* where in a Cork pub he claims he will be "the best man for it" in any contest with his son.

This tree symbolism stresses several passages, since Joyce interweaves pagan customs with their Christian successors and represents, in the manner of the "Saint Patrick and the Archdruid" stories, the fall of an old faith with the arrival of a new at the same time Christian liturgy augments a metaphor for the fall of his hero (Earwicker). Luke speaks of all these when he says, "Hollymerry, ivysad, whicher and whoer, Mr Black Atkins and you tanapanny troopertwos, were you there?" (588.17–19). The holly-ivy contention was that of the declining ivy of the old year (pertinent in the *Wake* to the wren song because the wren nested in ivy and was killed with a birch rod the day after Christmas), with the evergreen holly welcoming the new year. The passage then becomes a marriage vow—happy and sad, in sickness and in health, for richer and poorer, with the Druidic oak (*tan*) questioned by Christian ritual (cf. "Were you there when they lagged um through the coombe?"—506.11–12). The seven old Irish men of the previous passage, indicated by seven trees and suggesting tree worship, "trembold," like Earwicker today, "humbild, when they heard the stoppress from domday's erewold" (588.33–34). The holly symbolizes Earwicker's reign and the ivy his death in "As hollyday in his house so was he priest and king to that: ulvy came, envy saw, ivy conquered" (58.5–6) and in "how it is triste to death, all his dark ivytod" (571.14). With ivy and holly representing the old and new, Joyce continues the fidelity theme with "where I cling true 'tis there I climb tree and where Innocent looks best (pick!) there's holly in his ives" (152.2–3).

When parodying Psalm 137, which begins "By the rivers of Babylon, there we sat down, yea, we wept, when we remembered Zion. We hanged our harps upon the willows in the midst thereof," Joyce allows the Jordan to assume Anna's musical characteristics: "we have taken our sheet upon her stones where we have hanged our hearts in her trees; and we list, as she bibs us, by the waters of babalong" (103.9–11). Another echo of Scripture occurs in the Butt and Taff episode, in which the "blasted" tree of Christianity appears in connection with the stick (ogham) alphabet: "The field of karhags and that bloasted tree. Forget not the felled! For the lomondations of Oghrem" (340.7–9).

As concepts echo and re-echo throughout the *Wake*, another application of the oak has interesting vibrations. Graves comments, "When Gwion writes in the *Cad Goddeu*, 'Stout Guardian of the door, His name in every tongue,' he is saying that doors are customarily made of oak as the strongest and toughest wood and that 'Duir,' the Beth-Luis-Nion name for 'Oak,' means 'door' in many European languages, including Old Goidelic *dorus* [cf. "Roman Godhelic faix"—91.35–36], Latin *foris*, Greek *thur*, and German *tur,* all derived from the Sanskrit *Dwr,* and that *Daleth,* the Hebrew letter D, means 'Door'—the 'l' being originally an 'r' "[23] The oak is the tree of "endurance and triumph,"

23. Graves, p. 147.

and we have seen Jarl von Hoother as a stout guardian of his "dour" withstanding the approach of the Prankquean. In the conclusion of Book III, the demise of Earwicker is counted backward from seven ("seven days license," "six junelooking flamefaces," "his fives' court," "four hurrigan gales," "three boy buglehorners," "two hussites"—589.20–34) to himself alone, with the comment "That's his last tryon to march through the grand tryomphal arch. His reignbolt's shot" (590.9–10). Constable Sackerson evidently enters the pub through an oak doorway: "What soresen's head subrises thus tous out of rumpumplikun oak with, well, we cannot say whom we are looking like through his nowface?" (370. 23–26). The tavern is called "Big Elm and the Arch" (507.36–508.1); the oak's hardness explains "Hearts of Oak, may ye root to piece" (545.36). Just as Shem is *oak sad* when he is a *Tristan,* so also Issy's lack of love is explained as a "sere Sahara of sad oakleaves" (336.15).

Joyce's concern with durational time emerges in the many uses of the number seven, whose most obvious application in time is the seven days of the week; but also his preference for lunar time becomes apparent in his extension of the alphabet so that its twenty-eight letters (248.2) comprise a lunar month. His characterization of twenty-nine leap year girls (as in 159.16) shows a concern with that attempt to reconcile lunar and solar time. The astronomical connection with the physiological is in Bertha, who is married to a tree (Richard Rowan);[24] in the notes to *Exiles,* Joyce wrote, "Her age is 28. Robert likens her to the moon because of her dress. Her age is the completion of a lunar rhythm. Cf. Oriani on menstrual flow." To Leopold Bloom, Molly is like the moon; and the washerwomen link HCE in his sun-god role with

---

24. Richard Rowan as a tree has been remarked by Robert Scholes in "James Joyce, Irish Poet," *James Joyce Quarterly,* 2, no. 4 (1965): 264, and by Bernard Benstock in *"Exiles:* 'Paradox Lust' and 'Lost Paladays,'" *English Literary History* 36 (December 1969): 754.

ALP as moon: "She was just a young thin pale soft shy slim slip of a thing then, sauntering, by silvamoonlake and he was a heavy trudging lurching lieabroad of a Curraghman, making his hay for whose sun to shine on" (202.26–30). Joyce's lunar time, then, expresses the feminine principle of continuing creation, as does the succession of trees telling the tale of old faiths replaced by Joyce's A-Anna-*ailm*. The tree as the symbol of new and inexhaustible life is "aplantad" by the river of time "in her liveside" to represent continuous growth. Bergson wrote "to exist is to change, to change is to mature, to mature is to go on creating oneself endlessly"; but Earwicker's time has run out when his created world of seven days winds down. Counter-clockwise, the repeated "death do us part" (626.31) or "Till Breath us depart" (167.30–31) and "till deltas twoport" (318.13) concept runs throughout the *Wake*. Like Yeats, who placed the stone ("The stone's in the midst of all") in the center of a poem with the theme "All changed, changed utterly," Joyce presents the opposite of inexhaustible life (which means continuous change) in the durability and immutability of stone.

When the creator is spirit, word, primal matter, tree, artist, teller, and inexhaustible life, a correspondingly broad scope of treatment reveals the world he created; in other words, a succession of images and concepts discloses the cessation of life, although, by implication, such cessation is temporary. The close of any story, even though implying that no story ever really ends, must give the feeling of completion as well as of anticipation; and Ellmann relates that Joyce had Nora read " 'Mildred Lawson,' the first story in Moore's *Celibates*, which ends with a woman ruminating in bed . . . and she complained, 'That man doesn't know how to finish a story.' "[25] Anna Livia at the close of *Finnegans Wake* expresses completion through a pathetic weariness with all of life:

25. Ellmann, p. 195.

"All me life I have been lived among them but now they are becoming lothed to me. And I am lothing their little warm tricks. And lothing their mean cosy turns. And all the greedy gushes out through their small souls. And all the lazy leaks down over their brash bodies" (627.16–20). At the same time the monologue's most beautiful passages express regret that there will be no more such experiences: "To hide away the tear, the parted. It's thinking of all. The brave that gave their. The fair that wore. All them that's gunne" (625.30–32). "Loth" assumes a tone of loss as Anna passes out: "But I'm loothing them that's here and all I lothe. Loonely in my loneness. For all their faults" (627.33 –34). All in all the whole vast past engenders, in retrospect, a feeling of sadness and ennui—except during those remarkably lucid moments when the outgoing Anna, forgetting that for her there will be no tomorrow, remembers the past with pleasure and makes plans for the future. Her attitude of weariness completes the image of river as sense of loss and passage of time into oblivion; and this dramatization, in the ricorso, of the river's eternal movement therefore completes the entire cycle of existence by reversing the process of the washerwomen in their transformation into tree and stone.

Tree and stone transformations abound in the book dedicated to transformations, Ovid's *Metamorphoses*, and most frequently the transformations into trees occur to the innocent or the good; for the good they offer the desirable assurance of continuing life. Among others, Daphne implored such a change to protect her chastity (Book I); Baucis and Philemon were rewarded for enduring love and hospitality with transformation into an oak and a linden (Book VIII); Cyparissus asked to mourn forever the death of his deer and was transformed into the cypress (Book X); and Myrrha, begging a transformation because of her commission of incest, became the myrrh tree (Book X), with its bitter resin an appropriate expression of her remorse. Book VIII offers not only the epigraph for the *Portrait* but also the characteristics of the partridge, a Shaun-type (cf. "I am perdrix and upon my pet ridge"—447.28) who approved the death of Icarus. Book VIII includes Mopsus (cf. 614.1) who helped to kill the Calydonian boar, and the sacred oak so large that twelve dryads were needed to circle its trunk (cf. "you could fell an elmstree twelve urchins couldn't ring round"—25.30–31) but that was felled by the axe of Erysichthon. Book IX includes a cunning serpent that took refuge in a tree, as does the pursued Earwicker, and the lotus flower, which bleeds.

Although Book II of the *Metamorphoses* includes the bleeding of the tree-daughters of Clymene, and Book VIII the bleeding of the sacred oak that Erysichthon felled, the story of Dryope in Book IX best serves as background for the late revision of Joyce's poem "Tilly." There the crimson lotus blooms near water and drops blood from its flowers when Dryope tears a branch for her small son. Dryope, punished for an act committed in innocence, becomes a lotus tree and speaks when only her face remains uncovered by bark (cf. "the face in the treebark feigns afear"—279.1); but the lesson she asks be taught her son is that all bushes may be bodies of goddesses. The concept of a human spirit trapped in living tree suggests not so much transformation as it does a benign spirit that imbues all nature. Indeed, the introduction of the poem suggests such because the gods "made the changes"; and, as we have seen, Joyce as poet identifies himself with that creative spirit. In this sense the cattleman of Joyce's poem "Tilly" "drives them with a flowering branch before him," but the poet writes "I bleed by the black stream/ For my torn bough" (*CP* 47). Robert Scholes, in discussing this poem in connection with the tree transformations in the *Metamorphoses,* Dante's "Inferno," Vergil's *Aeneid,* and Spenser's *Faerie Queene,* theorizes that the final version in which the image of the torn bough first appears "probably dates from shortly before its first publication in 1927."[26] John T. Shawcross, writing about the same poem, offers a tantalizing suggestion of additional significance about the initial position of "Tilly" in *Pomes Penyeach*;[27] and, since Robert Scholes's suggested date is approximately three years after Joyce wrote to Miss Weaver the letter explaining chapter 8 of *Finnegans Wake,* I believe that the late revision of the poem, as Joyce progressed with his writing of the *Wake,* represents his growing awareness of the significance of tree as artist-creator.

Only in the instance of Earwicker's fall do the negative reasons for tree transformations—exile, banishment, or suicide—occur in the *Wake.* Earwicker's emergence from hiding is "aslike as asnake comes sliduant down that oaktree onto the duke of beavers, (you may have seen some liquidamber exude exotic from a balsam poplar at Parteen-a-lax Limestone" (100.11–13). In another example, the "bleeding" of a tree in the *Wake,* though still that common and natural exudation of resin or "gum," sticks rather than cleaves and implies procreation: "By gum, but you have resin! Of these tallworts are yielded out juices for jointoils and pappasses for paynims" (564.19–20). Elsewhere "Sweet gum" (160.4) is a tree among many trees, as is "achewing of his maple gum" (587.31–32) a common activity for a Jimmy. "I will stick to you, by gum, no matter what" (253.12–13) is an assertion of undying devotion. The Dodds, of course, have "nogumtree-umption" (191.13). For Joyce's purpose, the tree-Shem transformation promises to continue the inexhaustible-life

26. Scholes, 263.
27. John J. Shawcross, "Tilly and Dante," *James Joyce Quarterly* 7, no. 1 (1969): 61–64.

theme of the *Wake* and contrasts directly with the stone-
Shaun transformation, which is a process of petrifaction.
As a means of punishment in tales ranging from biblical
myth to fairy tale (and, again, many appear in the *Metamorphoses*), the victim of petrifaction, transformed into stone
or statue (or sometimes cast into eternal slumber), was made
to suffer awareness of other's happiness, as in the example
of the wicked sisters of Apuleius's Cupid and Psyche story.
As Anna Livia in the monologue seeks a reason for "no
peace at all" with her two sons, her reflection on the washerwomen implies that they deserve their transformations for
talking too much: "Maybe it's those two old crony aunts
held them out to the water front. Queer Mrs Quickenough
[the tree and the widow] and odd Miss Doddpebble [the
stone and the listener]. And when them two has a good few
there isn't much more dirty clothes to publish" (620.18–21).
Allegorically, because of sin, petrifaction means the arrest
of the soul on its journey to bliss, as in the example of Lot's
wife; and, though Earwicker is not *transformed* (like the listening washerwoman-Shaun), the *Wake's* most obvious parallel is in the hump of Howth containing the demiurge of the
fallen Finn. As a cycle of existence, however, the process of
petrifaction is involution, the reverse of evolution.

With the construction of the ALP chapter and the closing
monologue, Joyce presents at once polaric version and
reversion in the sense that, while stationary, the washerwomen paradoxically claim to be moving (rowing comprises
four passages as they talk: 202.15–16; 202.22–23; 205.5–6;
206.21–26) and Anna Livia in the monologue, while moving,
imagines herself stationary. As they plan to go home by
land (Moyvalley and Rathmine) Mrs. Quickenough exclaims
in impatience, "If you don't like my story get out of the
punt" (206.21); and Miss Doddpebble makes amends with
"Here, sit down and do as you're bid. Take my stroke and

bend to your bow. Forward in and pull your overthepoise!
Lisp it slaney and crisp it quiet. Deel me longsome. Tongue
your time now. Breathe thet deep. Thouat's the fairway.
Hurry slow and scheldt you go. . . . Flow now. Ower more.
And pooleypooley'' (206.22–28). In bed beside her husband,
Anna exclaims as she begins the monologue, "Rise up, man
of the hooths, you have slept so long!" (619.25–26). Later,
forgetfully planning a new beginning, she adds, "How glad
you'll be I waked you!" (623.33); and later still she signals
her resignation to death with "I'll slip away before they're
up. They'll never see. Nor know. Nor miss me" (627.35–36).
As witness to the need for the human artist to unite himself
with primal matter in the interaction of material and artistic
creation, the artist son as Mercius (forgiveness) can quicken
the washerwomen to temporary life (195.5), while the river
as nature itself survives art and begins a new cycle. The
transformation of these women into alternate tree (a "living"
petrifaction) and stone represents the artist-creator's span
over all life—over the living and the dead.

Deafness is, appropriately, the chief sense-failure of the
listener and a chief characteristic of the stone. Not only is
the sleeping or dead stone deaf (cf. "liamstone deaf do his
part"—331.4, "drop down dead and deaf"—323.19,
"deafadumped"—590.1), but also problems with being heard
epitomize the frustration of the father. The Jarl von Hoother
shouts futilely at the Prankquean, "Stop deef stop" (21.23)
and "come back with my earring stop" (22.10). In his
disgrace Earwicker is "herd of hoarding" (331.03) and
"deff as Adder" (535.31). At the same time, while Anna Livia
ripples while he sleeps, he will awake because "Impalpabunt,
he abhears" (23.25–26); or, as Ellmann writes, Joyce believed
that "in sleep our senses are dormant, except the sense of
hearing, which is always awake, since you can't close your

ears."[28] An excellent passage setting forth the possibility of resurrection, when the deaf-dead hear, is one that
describes the father-mountain: "Suffering trumpet! He
thought he want. Whath? Hear, O hear, living of the land!
Hungreb, dead era, hark! He hea, eyes ravenous on her
lippling lills. He hear her voi of day gon by. He hears!
Zay, zay, zay! But, by the beer of his profit, he cannot
answer. Upterputty till rise and shine!" (68.24–28). The
"disincarnated spirit" is explained: "he is not all hear" (536.1).
Gutteral speech, as in the Mutt and Jute episode (16.10–
18.16), represents the Stone Age's earliest form of communication and marks the beginning of an era; conversely
the lapse into silence, accompanied by deafness, marks
the close of an era. Mutt exclaims to Jute at the close of
their conversation, "Ore you astoneaged, jute you?" [i.e.,
astonished, turned to stone] (18.15). The power to make the
deaf to hear ("the daft to hear all blend"—571.3), which may
be likened to the *Portrait's* power of the priest "to bind and
to loose," is the power and the responsibility of the "priest
of the eternal imagination."

Such power makes the artist both reviled and feared. One
such experience confirmed the mental "paralysis" of
Dubliners and provided for Joyce the metaphor of the "dead"
stones in the land where Dodd lives. Ellmann gives the
backgrounds of the Reuben J. Dodd story in *Ulysses,* the
ludicrous and pathetic incident of the son who, while his
father indifferently walked the quay, leaped into the Liffey
to commit suicide and was saved from drowning by a poor
man whose pulmonary ailment was aggravated by the
incident. The newspaper exposé of the impoverished wife's
attempt to seek aid from Dodd's father sarcastically refer-

28. Ellmann, p. 560.

red to Dodd's tempting "the recuperative benefits of Anna Liffey" and the trifling sum the hero's wife received—two shillings, six pence—for the life of Dodd, Jr. This incident provided an aborted display of wit and laughter for Bloom and his fellow-mourners in the funeral-bound carriage of the Hades episode. Later the real Dodd, Jr., sued the B.B.C. for defamation after a reading of the passage in *Ulysses*.[29] The artist figure, therefore, in the land where Dodd lives, becomes a Cain; and Shaun-Justius jealously as a Dodd himself typically inverts this incident. Lapsing into the "inspired form of the third person singular" (187.29–30) which he declares he has abandoned, Shaun evokes the "brother's keeper" and describes Shem "on his keeping and in yours" as "our handsome young spiritual physician that was to be" (191.16), being babied and smothered with pharasaic kindness in the garden of Eire when they let the exile return for Abel's edification: "let him tome to Tindertarten, pease, and bing his scooter 'long and 'tend they were all real brothers in the big justright home where Dodd lives, just to teddyfy the life out of him" (191.21–23). Justius describes Shem-Cain as a tree, "the most winning counterfeuille on our incomeshare lotetree" (191.17–18), and excuses the person who seems dead or "plays possum" in "I pose you know why possum hides is cause he haint the nogumtreeumption" (191.12–13). But, according to Shaun-Justius, one small offense of his countrymen incurs Shem's poisonpen wrath (as Joyce exposed the Dodds and their like in *Ulysses*): "but him you laid low with one hand one fine May morning in the Meddle of your Might, your bosom foe, because he mussed your speller on you or because he cut a pretty figure in the focus of your frontispecs (not one did you slay, no, but a continent!) to find out how his innards

29. *Ibid.*, pp. 38–39 n.

worked!" (191.28–33). The superior edification of the artist as revealed in the mathematics lesson postulates another psychological (or mathematical) reduction. The "dodd-hunters" cannot appreciate Dolph's "bringing alliving stone allaughing down to grave cloth nails" (283.17–19)[30] and "bate him up jerrybly!" (283.27–28).

In the Dodd world of appearances, like self-destruction in the garden and the Cain-Abel fratricide, the perfect Porter family lives. According to the narrator, they are "very nice people" (560.23) of Catholic harmony ("A so united family pateramater is not more existing on papel or off of it"—560. 28–29) and exclusive self-righteousness ("They care for nothing except everything that is allporterous"—560.30–31). Since mother and father shared the fruit of the fall and Cain was believed to have stoned his brother to death (cf. "stud stoned before a racecourseful" in the Justius-Mercius section —194.26), the listener quickly perceives the outcome of this idyllic family relationship: "I think I begin to divine so much. Only snakkest me truesome!" (560.35). And the narrator implies the continuation of the story, "I stone us I'm hable" (560.36).

Since guilt embellishes the term *stone* as center of fruit and the fall, it lends emphasis to the "stone's throw away" expression. When HCE in self-defense attempts to employ this common expression for recollection of near-past events, he stammers about "a stone his throw's fruit's fall" (357. 26–27). Throwing stones to knock down fruit from the world tree means the sexual fall (504.31–33), just as Pegger Festy, claiming that "he did not fire a stone either before or after he was born down and up to that time" (91.11–12), denies both inherited and merited guilt. He goes on to claim innocence of both materialism and sexualism and to disclaim

30. Campbell and Robinson refer to Livingstone and British imperialism. See p. 179.

a right to Tir-na-nOg or Valhalla "if ever in all his exchequered career he up or lave a chancery hand to take or throw the sign of a·mortal stick or stone at man" (91.30–32). As Benstock observed, the stones rest heavily on earth,[31] and this has double significance when Shaun the stone is known for his feet (cf. "dearest Haun of all, you of the boots"—472.20–21) and when the fallen father is represented in the Welling*ton* monument (while living he is a "Wellingtonia Sequoia"—126.12; he "weighed a new ton when there felled his first lapapple"—126.16–17). The stone as a measure of weight (usually fourteen pounds) plus the family plurality gives "Noah Beery weighed stone thousand one when Hazel was a hen" (64.33–34) and the stoneroot as a plant returns to the destruction theme ("they're raised on bruised stone root ginger"—65.1). Where the needed beverage is a purgative, the process of petrifaction, as a result of Earwicker's fall (of becoming "stone dead") then, can be predicted as a fruit's fall: "You ought to tak a dos of frut. Jik. Sauss. You're getting hoovier, a twelve stone hoovier, fullends a twelve stone hoovier, in your corpus entis and it scurves you right, demnye!" (376.13–16). The well-wishers-mourners arrive, "afeerd he was a gunner but affaird to stay away" (497.16–17), to pay their respects, "for to contemplate in manifest and pay their firstrate duties before the both of him, twelve stone a side" (497.20–22).

The stone as a mark of bourn offered permanence; the London stone, for example, was the place where "oaths were sworn and proclamations posted."[32] Not to be outdone by the English, Joyce offers "so many miles from bank and Dublin stone" (84.31), "at Parteen-a-lax Limestone" (100.13), "millestones" (322.33), "out collecting milestones" (375.31), "mailstanes" (462.25), "at broadstone

31. Benstock, *"Exiles,"* pp. 739–56.
32. *Archaic England*, p. 513.

barrow" (568.23–24). Soon such enduring marks acquire veneration, and in the Joycean universe his stone marks the father city. Veneration modulates to sacred use, and a theory of sun-worship has been logically derived from the Celtic placement of twelve stones in a circle to mark the progress of the year. The Old Testament alludes to altars of twelve stones; there were twelve writers for the *Exagmination*, twelve customers in Earwicker's pub, and twelve apostles of Christ.[33] The stone, then, becomes a symbol for the life process, the fall and the death. But because the place of the venerated dead is also the abode of the gods, the stone enters the next stage of veneration and symbolizes the resurrection (stones form "the reverend and allaverred cromlecks"—343.30–31).[34] Joyce's stone, by the tree in Phoenix Park, becomes an omphalos for the Joycean universe.

The particular stone in the park has a classification. It is limestone; its color is white, as was the omphalos at Delphi. The concept of sacred stone was suggested in *Ulysses* where the tower as omphalos represents a "new paganism" (*U* 7). In the past stone rituals in various gradations of sincerity have linked the profoundest ceremonies of many world cultures. The Greek omphalos as center of the world achieved, through the emanation of subterranean vapors, the intercommunication of man, the dead, and the gods. Among the Greeks in general, white stones were honored as symbols of the gods, and the Irish customarily placed white stones on graves.

The large standing stones, "idols of isthmians" (594.25), both menhir and ovoid in the "macroliths" and "cairns

33. See Ellmann, p. 626.

34. Evans-Wentz finds in *The Book of Ballymote* evidence that the tomb of a divine personage (such as Finn MacCool) "came to be regarded as the actual dwelling of the once incarnate god." Such a place was Ireland's Newgrange. See Walter Y. Evans-Wentz, *The Fairy Faith in Celtic Countries* (London: University Books, 1966), p. 410.

stanserstanded" (594.22–24), suggest cosmic sexual principles and can be found in Ireland, France, and England. Such is the arrangement of stones forming the Giant's Grave at St. Andrew's, Penrith, a picture of which Miss Weaver sent to Joyce with the whimsical request that he incorporate it in his new novel.[35] In 1924 Joyce viewed the stones at Carnac and preferred that their embarrassing shapes not be discussed with the women present;[36] but in the *Wake* he could turn embarrassment to humor and relate it to HCE's fall by placing an obelisk (like the monument in Phoenix Park) in a merry greenwood: "And it was the lang in the shirt in the green of the wood, where obelisk rises when odalisks fall, major threft on the make and jollyjackques spindthrift on the merry" (335.32–34).

Similarities among stone monuments could be observed; and, while theorizing that large pyramids and tumuli, both having low entrance passageways, were originally intended for the mystic burial of initiation rather than sepulchres, Evans-Wentz concludes that "in view of all the definite provable relations between Gavrinis and New Grange, we are strongly inclined to regard them both as having the same origin and purpose, Gavrinis being for Armorica what New Grange was for Ireland, the royal or principal spirit-temple."[37] The Knowth burial passage, opened in 1967 in the Boyne country near Tara, is said to resemble no other than a tomb in Brittany.[38] When Joyce wrote "topsawyer's rocks" (3.7) and "North Armorica on this side the scraggy isthmus of Europe Minor" (3.5–6), he could connect not only

---

35 Ellmann, p. 594 and Plate XIV.
36. *Ibid.*, p. 578.
37. Evans-Wentz, p. 426.
38. Katherine Kuh, "The Circuitous Odyssey of Irish Art," *Saturday Review*, 23 March 1968, p. 26.

North America's Tom Sawyer with topsawyer as a sexual term but also, acting on Miss Weaver's inspiration, link by implication the monoliths and "tablestoane" monuments of England's Stonehenge and Ireland's Boyne with those of France's Armorica. Joyce visited Stonehenge in 1932[39] and was probably aware of the theory that the stones had been brought from Ireland. The ancient Celts constructed the stone circles of thirty stones possibly to mark the progress of a month's time, as in the Grand Circle of Stonehenge; and, for the Druids, thirty years comprised an age or a generation.[40]

Corresponding with the design of cromlechs formed by a tabled stone upon A-shaped supports, the construction of the A and T (first and last letters of the Hebrew alphabet) is discussed by Bayley: "The syllables *a* and *tau* occur significantly in various directions. The words *auteur* and *author* may be compared with *athir*, the Celtic for *father*, and with *ether*, the All-Pervading and All-Embracing. . . . *A-tau*, the symbol of the First and Last, is presumably the root of the words *eternitas*, *eternal*, and *eternity*. The Latin for *author* is *auctor*, i.e., *actor*, the Great Tor, the Eternal Author of the Universe."[41] Bayley counted 163 cromlechs in Sligo alone,[42] and these are fitting monuments to Joyce's desire to unite material and artistic creation and to make his author the author of the universe. At the same time, the stone provides a continuing witness to that creation in its most enduring form.

Remarkable examples of such enduring forms, both crude and carved, could be observed in Ireland as forms of nature and of intellect, based on concepts ranging from myth

39. Ellmann, p. 652.
40. *Lost Language*, 2: 190.
41. Bayley, pp. 184–85.
42. *Ibid.*, p. 186. Published in 1912; doubtless more have been unearthed since.

through history. The stone outcropping in the Liffey called "Standfast Dick" (210.28) gets its due; and, no doubt, it constitutes one of the "stone hairpins" (312.21) of Anna Liffey. On the Customs House in Dublin, carved heads represent the rivers of Ireland with the produce of the area through which the river flows, and all appear in the ALP chapter: the Lee (210.7), the Liffey (215.33), the Shannon (211.9), the Suir (203.9), the Lagan (212.1), the Blackwater (196.12), the Barrow (198.33, 210.7), the Nore (203.10), the Bann (210.7), the Foyle (212.13), the Slaney (206.24), and the Boyne (198.05), with Lough Erne (207.21) and the Atlantic Ocean (197.29) added.[43] As Robert Sage remarked in the *Exagmination*, only one—the Liffey—is represented with feminine features.[44] After its destruction by fire in 1921, limestone rather than Portland (from England, oolite, a variety of limestone) was used to replace part of the Customs dome. Joyce could have written of his choice of limestone as he did of the elm tree: "it's native of our nature." The name of the basalt Giant's Causeway, which Joyce places in Dublin and puns into "giant's holes in Grafton's causeway" (198.32), derives from the Latin word for a passage paved with limestone. Limestone forms the peat-covered central plain of Ireland, as well as many monuments, of which one is the Four Evangelists of St. Finbarr's in Cork.[45] Of Ireland's thirty-one stone quarries listed by Seamus Murphy, eleven are in Joyce's ancestral County Cork, where journeymen enlivened the work with the telling of many tales of stone and where, for reverence of the

43. For pictures and comment, see Ann Crookshank, "The River Gods," *Ireland of the Welcomes* 19, no. 3 (1970): 23–26.

44. Sage gives sixteen as the number of rivers. See "Before *Ulysses*—and After," *Our Exagmination Round His Factification for Incamination of Work In Progress* (New York: New Directions, 1939), p. 159. *The Shell Guide* (p. 250) gives thirteen, probably omitting the Atlantic Ocean.

45. *Stone Mad* (London: Routledge & Kegan Paul, 1966), p. 206.

trade, one journeyman whom Murphy quotes credited the stonecarvers with assisting God Himself: "Didn't we cut the Ten Commandments on the slabs for Moses?"[46]

In the natural trend of veneration from marker to bourn to sacred stone, Ireland had also the tradition of the *Lia Fail*, the witness-stone or "stone of destiny" (40.19). On the *Lia Fail*, the Irish chiefs and kings took their solemn oaths; and Evans-Wentz mentions its magical properties as recorded in the *Book of Lismore*: "it is said that ever when Ireland's monarch stepped upon it the stone would cry out under him, but that if any other person stepped upon it, there was only silence."[47] Joyce's limestone is the *Lia Fail* in "the stone that Liam failed" (25.31), "Liam Fail" (131.10), and "liam-stone" (331.4). It is part of the tradition of the bull-roarer, a piece of wood that makes a singing noise and that, as Atherton observed, was "believed to have been used by the Druids to produce the effect of a singing stone when a king stood on a sacred stone such as the famous Lia Fail."[48] Shaun identifies himself with many gods and replies to interrogation, "with my tongue through my toecap on the headlong stone of kismet if so 'tis the will of Whose B. Dunn" (518.9–10). The bullroarer mentioned by the washerwoman is the sound of Anna's eagerness for Earwicker's love during their courting and of the sea breaking against the Bull Wall: "her bulls they were ruhring, surfed with spree" (198.4–5). Only through some supernatural agency can the usually silent stone become "the stone that moans when stricken" (94.5). Although Shaun likes to brag about his "voicical lilt too true," (450.24) he fails to convince; and as Shaun-Mookse, when he sits on a stone "pompifically" (153.23–24), he does not sing. Singing stones have appeared in mythology

46. Murphy, p. 19.
47. Evans-Wentz, p. 401.
48. Atherton, p. 228.

(and in the *Metamorphoses*) and explain the apparent reversal of tree-stone roles in "Tholedoth, treetrene! Zokrahsing, stone!" (230.26).

In Ireland one might be told that stone monuments are the beds of Dermot and Grania, and Joyce's transformation of one washerwoman into a stone had precedent in the legends of the Fenians. When Dermot died, so the story goes, Aengus carried his body to the Boyne, where he breathed into it a soul so that he might speak to it each day.[49] The implication is, of course, that one of the stones, perhaps at Newgrange, is Dermot. Several stones bear Finn's name or fame: the Mottha Stone (his hurling stone); the Six Fingers, which he threw; the tomb of his son Oisin in County Limerick, his Finger Stone in County Cavan, another called Finn MacCool's Stone. Finn's greatest competitor for such honors is Saint Patrick, of whose "stones" may be cited Patrick's Stone and Saint Patrick's Chair, both in County Mayo near Finn MacCool's Grave. Joyce discloses this tradition when he describes the multitude of placed stones, as if browsing "up hill and down coombe" in parts of Ireland, that tell the history of its past and in that way serve as evaluation and evolution of society and await the time when Finn shall awake. Stones as "a cloudletlitter silent" may engage the Kentish term "Perrydancers" for the light clouds of summer, and these Bayley associates with the peri-stones mentioned by Pausanias.[50] The bitterness of Oliver Cromwell's rampage through Ireland intrudes in the description of the many stones called "Oliver's lambs":

> Yed he med leave to many a door beside of Oxmanswold for so witness his chambered cairns a cloudletlitter silent that are at browse up hill and down coombe and on eolithostroton, at Howth

49. P. W. Joyce, p. 236; MacCulloch, p. 178.
50. *Archaic England*, p. 873.

or at Coolock or even at Enniskerry, a theory none too rectiline
of the evoluation of human society and a testament of the rocks
from all the dead unto some the living. Olivers lambs we do call
them, skatterlings of a stone, and they shall be gathered unto him,
their herd and paladin, as nubilettes to cumule, in that day hwen,
same the lightning lancer of Azava Arthurhonoured (some Finn,
some Finn avant!), he skall wake from earthsleep, haught crested
elmer, in his valle of briers of Greenman's Rise O, (lost leaders
live! the heroes return!) and o'er dun and dale the Wulverulverlord
(protect us!) his mighty horn skall roll, orland, roll" (73.28–74.5).

The tree means present life, the stone past life; or the stone
embodies the past. At the beginning of Ireland, in the Mutt and
Jute episode, the father figure sleeps: "Lean neath stone pine
the pastor lies with his crook" (14.32). As Finn MacCool, who
had a magical mask with three faces, "his threefaced stonehead
was found on a whitehorse hill and the print of his costellous
feet is seen in the goat's grasscircle" (132.12–14). During his
burial rites he will be presented with "a stone slab with the
usual Mac Pelah address of velediction, a very fairworded
instance of falsemeaning adamelegy: We have done ours gohellt
with you, Heer Herewhippit, overgiven it, skidoo!" (77.24–27).
But residence in either the flippant go-to-hell underworld
("gohellt") or the serious Norse "Helway" (for which passage
a horse was buried with the deceased person) is not permanent,
as indicated by a similar expression, "Hell's bells," in a passage
that marks the Joycean dawn of creation: "The spearspid of
dawnfire totouches ain the tablestoane ath the centre of the
great circle of the macroliths of Helusbelus in the boshiman
brush on this our peneplain by Fangaluvu Bight whence the
horned cairns erge, stanserstanded, to floran frohn, idols of
isthmians" (594.21–25).
   Of the Tom and Tim motif that permeates the *Wake*, one
may turn to the stone circles for an additional explanation.
Bayley writes of Stonehenge, "This word *temenos* [enclosed

circle] must be allied to *tommen*, the Welsh for *barrow*, and, as has already been suggested, *tem* or *tom* is the root of *temps* and *time*. *Tommen* may thus be resolved into Sole Time or Stone Time, and *temenos* into the light of sole, stable, and abiding Time."[51] Mrs. Quickenough remarks oracularly, "But toms will till. I know he well. Temp untamed will hist for no man" (196.22–23). Atherton in discussing Tom and Tim as representative of time in the *Wake* adds that the name Tom-Tim "mutates into Atem and so on, for Time is a sort of God in that it puts a period to our lives"[52] and Epstein has included time in his study of the applications of the Tom-Tim motif.[53] The Joycean concept of stone time, however, is not so much the "period to our lives" as it is "stable and abiding Time," such as the stone time in "Tal the tem of the tumulum" (56.34); typical of Joyce's "rise you must" theme, Earwicker will awake, and the stone at the close of I.8 is also Shaun, subject to resurrection.

Joyce's "whitehorse hill" recalls the annual "scouring of the white horse of Berkshire," a spring festival custom of cleaning a prehistoric stone figure of a horse on the chalk downs of England. Bayley believes that the ceremony, now preserved in spring horse races, was initiated to mark the progress of the sun in its course; analogy with the sun explains the veneration of white horses. When one washerwoman believes she sights the ghostly "Finnleader" on his white horse, the other replies, "You're thinking of Astley's Amphitheayter where the bobby restrained you making sugarstuck pouts to the ghostwhite horse of the Peppers" (214.13–16). Ellmann relates this to a passage in Robertson's play *Caste*,[54] but Bayley describes a similar place at Berkshire, where there is "a huge scoop in

51. *Lost Language*, 2: 192.
52. Atherton, p. 55.
53. Epstein, "Tom and Tim," *James Joyce Quarterly* 6, no. 2 (1969): 158–62.
54. Ellmann, p. 97 n.

the downs forming a natural amphitheatre, and at the base of this so-called 'manger' are the clear traces of artificial banks or tiers."[55] Joyce, of course, moves his "whitehorse hill" to Dublin, where the Celtic stones circumscribe Earwicker's lechery as a "goat's grass circle."

Much folklore, too much in fact to summarize, is suggested by Joyce's descriptions of stones in Ireland; but two other echoes of messages to be read from stone, in the Jarl von Hoother story and in the Saint Kevin story, will serve as examples.

Where the jeminies of the Jarl von Hoother story recall the Gemini, MacCulloch relates how the Cuchulain myth may be associated with Castor and Pollux:

> Diodorus says that the Dioscruri, i.e. Castor and Pollux, were the gods most worshipped by the Celts in the west of Gaul, and M. d'Arbois finds these in Cuchulainn and Conall Cernach, the former being foster-brother of the latter, having been suckled by Findchoém, Conall's mother. He bases this identification on an altar found at Paris, on the four sides of which are represented the Roman Castor and Pollux and two Gaulish divinities—Smertullos, attacking a serpent with a club, and an unnamed horned god, perhaps the god Cernunnos (cernu-, "horn"). Smertullos is, therefore, the native equivalent of Pollux, Cernunnos of Castor; and at the same time Smertullos is Cuchulainn, and Cernunnos is Conall Cernach. In the Tain Cuchulainn vanquished Morrigan as an eel—the serpent of the monument—and, again, to hide his youthfulness, he smeared (smérthain, hence Smertullos) his chin with a false beard.[56]

MacCulloch theorizes that the Celtic Lug was the god equated by Caesar with Mercury; according to MacCulloch, M. d'Arbois in his comment on Caesar cites a standing-stone of Gaul that pictures Mercury with a child, "and M. d'Arbois as-

55. Archaic England, p. 416.
56. MacCulloch, p. 158.

sumes that this represents the god Lug with his son Cuchulainn."[57]

The not-so-unique story of Saint Kevin's bathtub altar echoes a strange prehistoric ritual described by W.C. Borlase in his *Dolmens of Ireland*. Attempting to find the exact nature of the *Sidhepalace* of legend, he believes it to be the *sanctum sanctorum* of a spirit temple for fasting and sacrificing. Such exists at Lough Crew, New Grange, and Dowth; and, using pre-Christian structures, both saints and Christian pilgrims lay in stone troughs while at their devotions. Because of the shortened tublike shapes, writes Borlase, "they must have sat in them in Eastern fashion."[58] Evans-Wentz adds that "a good example of a saint's stone bed can be seen now at Glendalough, the stone bed of Saint Kevin, high above a rocky shore of the lake."[59] When Joyce relates "holy Kevin bided till the third morn hour" (605.22–23) in his "bath *propter* altar," he alludes to a ritual described in the "Colloquy with the Ancients" in the *Book of Lismore*, a biding three days and three nights in unbroken fast in a spirit-temple northwest of Tara.[60] The stone basin in Newgrange resembles one in the Great Pyramid in Egypt and to some scholars suggests initiation rather than burial.[61]

The stone's chief function, when one of the "living," is asking and listening; when sleeping or "stone dead" he functions as a repository for the culture of his people, because the culture of the past may be read from both the carvings of prehistoric peoples and the monuments of civilization. When Joyce described the world's need for writing letters ("All the world's in want and is writing a letters"—278.13–14), he added the other half of the duality: "And all the world's

57. *Ibid.*, p. 159.
58. Quoted in Evans-Wentz, p. 414.
59. *Ibid.*, p. 414 n.
60. *Ibid.*, pp. 412–13.
61. *Ibid.*, pp. 418–19.

on wish to be carrying a letters" (278.15–16). Shaun's carrying the letter means the distribution-perpetuation of that
information. The preservation of the past in stone has a
champion in the *Wake* in the important Wellington monument; a "museyroom" presided over by Kate the cleaner (an
aspect of the cleaning washerwomen), it is both museum and
musing-room. The vital record of the past is preserved there
and in the *Book of Kells*, in the Tuami brooch, in Hammurabi's Code, in all the obelisks and stone crosses and
buildings and books (especially the old manuscripts) of the
world, and Shaun's finding the letter is compared with
the finding of the Ardagh chalice. Earwicker's fall amounts to
the news reported after the event, a staggering "stoppréss
from domday's erewold" (588.34). A living process stopped
becomes stone, or a stone marks the presence of those who
for one reason or another do not really live. The ideas or
the life are the artist's; the preservation is the craftsman's.
Shaun or Miss Doddpebble will not create but will provide
an imperfect ear for hearing; and, as stone, Shaun will
persevere—and preserve.

The extent of tree and stone symbolism marks the fall, the
death, and the resurrection—the life cycle of man. So HCE,
who engendered the opposites Shem-tree and Shaun-stone
in his prime, is described as a living tree, the center of the
Dublin world, and the promise of inexhaustible life, while
his roots in the ashes of the past (or ash-tree of the past about
to be replaced by the elm) indicate his fall and the phoenix
his rise: "their convoy wheeled encirculingly abound the
gigantig's lifetree, our fireleaved loverlucky blomsterbohm,
phoenix in our woodlessness, haughty, cacuminal, erubescent
(repetition!) whose roots they be asches with lustres of peins"
(55.26–30). Then, in this "review of Earwicker's fall," as
Benstock titled it, after the fall there is a pause, a natural
result of a fall from a tree of life ("high chief evervirens and

only abfalltree in auld the land"—88.2). Joyce presents the gap in time in "timesported acorss the yawning (abyss)" (56.3–4). The phallic-tree-father is transformed into the phallic-stone-father symbol of the Wellington monument, "that overgrown leadpencil which was soon, monumentally at least, to rise as Molyvdokondylon to, to be, to be his mausoleum" (56.12–14). The sons engendered by and united in the father figure mark that transition from death to life; the father lives as tree, falls as stone, exists as stone monument. The continual process of Joyce's cycles requires that the tree live while the stone stands silent and the river flows past both tree and stone: "Before he fell hill he filled the heaven: a stream, alplapping streamlet, coyly coiled um, cool of her curls" (57.10–12).

The tree and the stone are one method by which Joyce carried out his intention to write a universal history, using Anna and Earwicker to show the simultaneous and continuous process of the fall and the resurrection with the tree and the stone on opposite sides of the cycle. The second old man, Mark Lyons, declares, "Talkingtree and sinningstone stay on either hand" (564.30–31). And Anna's song title confirms that distinction, "As Tree is Quick and Stone is White So is My Washing Done by Night" (106.36–107.1). But the artist's prayer as he prepares the Ballad of Persse O'Reilly recognizes the necessity of the living-tree and preserving-stone tension: "may the treeth we tale of live in stoney" (44.9).

4

"From the Laundersdale Minssions" (620.21)

The present discussion began with the ALP chapter of *Finnegans Wake,* where two washerwomen materialize from nothingness—one to tell the tale of Anna Livia and one to listen. As night falls and the telling ends, they merge into tree and stone, or the brothers Shem and Shaun; but in the meantime they have established a basic characterization and a basic contention for the entire novel.

In an article entitled "The Quiddity of Shem and the Whatness of Shaun," Bernard Benstock in 1963 set forth the problems of following the *Wake's* merging and blending and deviously separating identities, centered in the indistinguishable twins who, by their mother's testimony, are admittedly "as doffered as nors in soun" (620.16). As Benstock writes,

> The Brunoesque opposites that appear and re-appear throughout the *Wake* are usually identified with the antagonistic sons of H. C. Earwicker; the range of their diversity can be seen in a listing of the most important variations: Shem and Shaun, Caddy and Primas, Jerry and Kevin, Dolph and Kev, Mick and Nick, Glugg and Chuff, Butt and Taff, Mutt and Jute, Muta and Juva, St. Patrick and the Archdruid, Tristopher and Hilary, Festy King and Pegger Festy, the Mookse and the Gripes, the Ondt and the Gracehopper, Burrus and Caseous, Justius and Mercius, time and space, a tree and a stone, etc.[1]

1. Bernard Benstock, "The Quiddity of Shem and the Whatness of Shaun," *James Joyce Quarterly* 1, no. 1 (1963): 26–33, and *Joyce-again's Wake* (Seattle: Washington University Press, 1965), pp. 11–19.

There are several other less familiar pairs; and because these sometimes appear indistinguishable or purposely interchangeable, Benstock voices a common scholarly opinion when he warns against a "single-minded view of Shem and Shaun exclusively as antagonists."[2] It is possible, however, throughout the ALP chapter, to distinguish the asking-listening woman from the telling-answering woman and, knowing they become tree and stone, to derive distinguishing characteristics of the twin brothers.

The brother-contention, in its most obvious form, is an artist-audience problem. As contention, it has been variously and metaphorically set forth, in such works as Morris Beja's "The Wooden Sword: Threatener and Threatened in the Fiction of James Joyce,"[3] and Robert Scholes's explication of the torn bough and the tearing hand in "James Joyce, Irish Poet."[4] Where such table-turning as the threatened himself becoming threatener exists, it complicates a problem developing from the nature of the rebellious artist and his unappreciative public. Such an interchange occurs when Shaun-Muta borrows Shem-Juva's gun, his pen, the symbol of his art:

> *Muta:* May I borrow that hordwanderbaffle from you, old rubberskin?
> *Juva:* Here it is and I hope it's your worminpen, Erinmonker! Shoot. (610.30–33)

Certainly Stephen, as Morris Beja shows he does in the *Portrait,* can sneer at the "Wooden sword" of his antagonist; but the reason is that the artist, if he cares to, can flourish his

2. Benstock, p. 33.
3. Morris Beja, "The Wooden Sword: Threatener and Threatened in the Fiction of James Joyce," *James Joyce Quarterly* 2, no. 1 (1964): 33–41.
4. Robert Scholes, "James Joyce, Irish Poet," *James Joyce Quarterly* 2, no. 4 (1965): 255–70.

poison pen, and no one—even Shaun, as this example shows—need smile at its comparative might. Shem by Shaun's accusation commits not mere fratricide but genocide ("not one did you slay, no, but a continent!"—191.32–33). Shem as Cain, however, is intentionally erroneous for the purpose of presenting the misunderstood artist; idealistically he purposes to create, to strike off the shackles of "paralysis" among the "living dead" in the land where Dodd lives. At the same time Shaun has public merits of durability and stability, which as Kevin make him suitable for sainthood. Early in the novel his finding of the letter provides him "a motive for future saintity" (110.34).

Opposite the concept of artist as creator of the material universe, a theme that Joyce carried through the *Portrait, Exiles, Ulysses,* and *Finnegans Wake,* the necessity for the artist to have an audience and to preserve his creation in some permanent form explains the attention to written records and lost letters in the *Wake* and finds expression in Joyce's serio-comic and oft-quoted need for "that ideal reader suffering from an ideal insomnia" (120.13–14). Through the multiple identities of the *Wake,* this artist-audience duality appears, for example, in Shem and Shaun, who as Tristan and Mark have one common love, Isolde; even the single letter with "a multiplicity of personalities inflicted on the documents or document" (107.24–25) is in one analysis claimed to be "the tale of a Treestone with one Ysold" (113.18–19).

Where opposing characteristics of the sons blend in the father, the creating artist and preserved record blend when the record contains the secrets of creation. As we have seen, in the one respect the problem of merging and diverging identities developed historically from the example of the tree and the stone: the Scandinavian world tree, by some analyses, began not with the sight of or reverence for a live, heaven-arching tree, but was derived from a dead stone—a huge stone pillar intricately carved with a tree sheltering a hierarchy of animals, flowers, and fruit. Further, Joyce's tree and stone are not any tree and stone. The tree is an ever-green elm, with talking its function and with life and love in its leaves. The stone is a white standing limestone, with listening its function and with the "evolu-ation" of human life preserved in its placement. Chapter 8, where the tale begins, provides the "key" to these mysteries and also establishes in the characters of Mrs. Quickenough and Miss Doddpebble the characteristics of Shem and Shaun that will determine their respective identities in many confused roles: the artist-teller's arrogant use of language and the au-dience's resentful response, the application of trees and stones in their conversation, and the artist's problems with physical sight and the audience's problems with hearing. These, com-bined with Miss Doddpebble's major physical defect, will provide clues for fathoming the Shem-Shaun aspects of many of the *Wake's* characters.

The superior vocabulary of the artist is indeed a mighty in-tellectual weapon, and it engenders much jealousy and frus-tration on the part of the listener. Nor does the teller have any patience with the undiscerning mind:

> (*after Mrs. Quickenough has described the chase and capture of ALP*)
>
> Miss D: "Pilcomayo! Suchcaughtawan! And the whale's away with the grayling!"
>
> Mrs. Q: "Tune your pipes and fall ahumming, you born ijypt, and you're nothing short of one!"
>
> Miss D: "Well, ptellomey soon and curb your escumo."
>
> (197.35–198.02)
>
> (*after Mrs. Quickenough describes ALP's pandering for HCE*)
>
> Miss D: "Proxenete and phwhat is phthat? Emme for your re-ussischer Honddu jarkon! Tell us in franca langua. And call a spate a spate."
>
> Mrs. Q: "Did they never sharee you ebro at skol, you antiabece-darian?
>
> (198.17–20)

(That Mrs. Quickenough uses even bigger words in the explanation—as does Samuel Johnson's dictionary—and Miss Doddpebble then purports to understand probably is a Joycean joke on several levels.)

> (*when giving instructions on synchronising washing, breathing, and telling*)
>
> Miss D: "Tongue your time now." (206.25)
>
> (*complaining of available literature*)
>
> Miss D: "Foul strips of his chinook's bible I do be reading, dodwell disgustered but chickled with chuckles at the tittles is drawn on the tattlepage" (212.32–34)

(The examples she gives make sport of all art.)

> (*a humorous exchange on the building of a city through* HCE's *known lechery*)
>
> Miss D: "Northmen's thing made southfolk's place but howmulty plurators made eachone in person? Latin me that, my trinity scholard, out of eure sanscreed into oure eryan!"
>
> Mrs. Q: "*Hircus Civis Eblanensis* [goat of Eblana city]!"
>
> (215.24–27)

It is no accident that Miss Doddpebble describes herself as "dodwell disgustered"; she can describe sex with stone characteristics, as in "a swamp for Altmuehler [German *old mill*] and a stone for his flossies! I know how racy they move his wheel" (213.2–4). Mrs. Quickenough recalls the runic inscriptions on stones with her description of Anna's necklace as "rhunerhinerstones" (207.7), and Anna's garment has "alpheubett buttons" (208.20). The stone characteristic of deafness mentioned previously for the inactive state describes HCE in his "winter's doze"; according to Mrs. Quickenough he is "deaf as a yawn" (200.15) and completely impervious to Anna's musical attempts to arouse him. Miss Doddpebble sympathizes, "Poor deef old deary!" (200.15–16). Earwicker in his prime while courting Anna was "as tough as the oak-trees" (202.30); he was a tree when he "forstfellfoss with a plash across her" (202.32), but a parenthetical "peats be with them!" (202.30) signals his own fall. For her part, back in her youth Anna displayed remarkable precociousness in tempt-ing "a birch canoedler" (204.09) and once the music of her waters seduced the young hermit, Michael Arklow, "in the silence, of the sycomores, all listening" (203.21–22). Would that she had the power now to make the usually talking trees silent! But now, as Miss Doddpebble remarks, those trees of the past have turned to stone; she wishes that "Letty Lerck's lafing light [could] throw those laurals now on her daphdaph teasesong petrock" (203.29–31). The gifts include a "stone-cold shoulder" (211.32), "scrub-oak beads" (210.29), "a Con-goswood cross on the back for Sunny Twimjim" (211.5–6), with the latter bit of Joyce's autobiography alluding to the donkey (the cross on the back); and receivers of gifts include the stones "Standfast Dick" and "Stumblestone Davy" (210. 28–29).

Several remarks hint at Miss Doddpebble's gradual petri-faction. At the very beginning Mrs. Quickenough answers the "tell me" plea with "You'll die when you hear" (196.5–6), while Miss Doddpebble herself unwittingly forecasts her fu-ture and indicates Shaun's problems with feet: "I'm dying down off my iodine feet until I lerryn Anna Livia's cushingloo" (200.35–36). Mrs. Quickenough shows awareness of Miss Doddpebble's deficient hearing as she insists, "Listen now. Are you listening?" (201.3), and although Miss Doddpebble answers, "Yes, yes! Idneed I am," Mrs. Quickenough repeats "Tarn your ore ouse! Essone inne!" (201.3–4). Miss Dodd-pebble, nevertheless, typically fails to hear; she *hears nothing* of Anna's message, and when Anna stops speaking, having presented her story, Miss Doddpebble asks for more story of Anna ("Onon! Onon! tell me more"—201.21).

Their dualistic natures as revealed in pairs of terms such as *forgive* and *forget*, befitting their identities as alternate aspects of the twin sons, do not emerge clearly until the end of the chapter. As they represent the quick and the dead, the "sinningstone" calls "Forgivemequick [forgive me, quick], I'm going! Bubye!" (215.7), and the "Talkingtree" appropriately replies to that symbol of endurance, "And you, pluck your watch, forgetmenot. Your evenlods" (215.7-8), with the last term combining lodestone, lodestar (after her own mention of the Milky Way in "My chart shines high where the blue milk's upset"—215.6-7), and *lode* as a reach of water. In the last two pages of the chapter the transformation into tree and stone is clearly stated, as the listening woman ("as deaf as a stone") consistently misrepresents her companion's remarks. Earlier, in the gathering darkness, both gave over finding the "pattern chayney" said to be "lying beside the sedge" (213.6), but the teller's answer indicated she could no longer discern where land ("the sedge") meets water: "With that turbary water who could see?" (213.7). When Mrs. Quickenough asserts "I can see that, I see you are!" (201.2), she intends understanding, not sight. Soon ("as blind as a bat") she complains, "My sights are swimming thicker on me by the shadows to this place" (215.9-10).

Their conversation, read as follows, determines the described characterizations and foreshadows the transformations:

Mrs. Q: "Well, you know or don't you kennet or haven't I told you every telling has a taling and that's the he and the she of it."
Miss D: "Look, look, the dusk is growing!"
Mrs. Q: "My branches lofty are taking root. And my cold cher's gone ashley."
Miss D: "Fieluhr?"
Mrs. Q: "Filou!"
Miss D: "What age is at?"

Mrs. Q: "It soan is late. 'Tis endless now senne eye or erewone last saw Waterhouse's clogh. They took it asunder, I hurd thum sigh."

Miss D: "When will they reassemble it?"

Mrs. Q: "O, my back, my back, my bach! I'd want to go to Aches-les-Pains. . . ."

Miss D: "Will we spread them here now?"

Mrs. Q: "Ay we will. Flip! Spread on your bank and I'll spread on mine on mine.

Miss D: "Flep! It's what I'm doing."

Mrs. Q: "Spread! It's churning chill. Der went is rising. I'll lay a few stones on the hostel sheets. A man and his bride embraced between them. Else I'd have sprinkled and folded them only."

Miss D: "And I'll tie my butcher's apron here. It's suety yet. The strollers will pass it by."

Mrs. Q: "Six shifts, ten kerchiefs. . . . Good mother Jossiph knows, she said."

Miss D: "Whose head? Mutter snores?"

Mrs. Q: "Deataceas!"

Miss D: "Wharnow are alle her childer, say? In kingdome gone or power to come or gloria be to them farther?"

Mrs. Q: "Allalivial, allalluvial! Some here . . . ." (213.11–213.32)

The closing lines, with Miss Doddpebble continuing her questions, should be read as follows:

Mrs. Q: "Lord save us! And ho!"

Miss D: "Hey?"

Mrs. Q: "What all men."

Miss D: "Hot?"

Mrs. Q: "His tittering daughters of."

Miss D: "Whawk?" [paragraph]

Miss D: "Can't hear with the waters of. The chittering waters of. Flittering bats, fieldmice bawk talk."

Mrs. Q: "Ho! Are you not gone ahome?"

Miss D: "What Thom Malone? Can't hear with bawk of bats, all thim liffeying waters of."

Mrs. Q: "Ho, talk save us!"
Miss D: "My foos won't moos."
Mrs. Q: "I feel as old as yonder elm."
Miss D: "A tale told of Shaun (or) Shem?"
Mrs. Q: "All Livia's daughter-sons. Dark hawks hear us. Night!"
Miss D: "Night! My ho head halls. I feel as heavy as yonder
    stone. Tell me of John or Shaun? Who were Shem and
    Shaun the living sons or daughters of?"
Mrs. Q: "Night now!"
Miss D: "Tell me, tell me, tell me, elm!"
Mrs. Q: "Night night!"
Miss D: "Telmetale of stem or stone. Beside the rivering waters
    of, hitherandthithering waters of."
Mrs. Q: "Night!"   (215.28–216.5)

Mrs. Quickenough's "Ho" gives, appropriately, the
Chinese word for river; and when Miss Doddpebble asks for
the tale of Shem and Shaun, she demonstrates that no story
ever ends, because she alters her original request for the tale
of Anna Livia. Miss Doddpebble's concern for bats may derive from folklore belief that bats sleep by day and fly by
night; folklore includes also a tale of the bat testing its
strength by lifting a stone. The hawk in the Eddic earth tree
was common knowledge and here, remembering Biddy the
Hen, tempts speculation regarding the ancient enmity between hawk and hen, especially because of Shaun's affinity
with the hen as in "that hen of Kaven's (382.n). In passing
also, Miss Doddpebble has been identified with a butcher
(213.26).

Miss Doddpebble's name as derived from a hip injury that
occurred during a sexual misadventure (214.28–30) provides
some humor. At the beginning of the tale she expresses concern for her "butt": "And don't butt me—hike!—when you
bend" (196.9). Joyce continues the joke with permitting
Mrs.Quickenough to call her "hobbledyhips" (214.21) and

to point out that her "rear gate" creaks: "Your rere gait's creakorheuman bitt your butts disagrees" (214.21–22). Graves associates the partridge, known for lechery, with the bull-footed god whose dislocation of a thigh forced him to walk on his toes and to wear the high-heeled boots called buskins.[5] As Miss "Hobbleedyhips" is a Butt, Taff in the Butt and Taff episode exclaims "Take the cawraidd's blow! Yia! Your partridge's last!" (344.7).

As indicated in the ALP chapter, certain characteristics delineating the separate identities of Shem and Shaun are unfolded as the novel develops.

Shem	Shaun
artist	the public
partially blind	partially deaf
tree	stone
fond of words	fond of food
the hawk or eagle	the hen or partridge
head (high as a tree)	feet (low as a stone)
condemned as obscene	exonerated as saint

Chapter 1 presents Sir Tristram with his "penisolate war" (3.6), suggesting both the phallic tree and the isolation of the artist, and the punctuation separates the next image of rock and stream (3.6–9) from the third, Saint Patrick himself (3.9–10), who learns his vocation when "avoice from afire" bellows. Of the four basic elements, fire cannot destroy earth, air, or water; but as a force in contention it can destroy the stick, associated with Shem. In the Phoenix Park, the setting of the novel, the fabulous obelisk to the Duke of Wellington rises as a "Wallinstone national museum" (8.1–2) housing a pictorial synopsis of the novel as the visitor passes in review. It includes the Earwicker type, "the big Straughter Willingdone" with

5. Robert Graves, *The White Goddess* (New York: Vintage, 1958), p. 356.

white horse and three-cornered hat. Wounderworker and Belchum appear to be the antagonistic brothers, the first a creator and the later having "thin red lines cross the shortfront" (9.3–4) designating his religious orientation. Elsewhere in the novel Shaun's affinity with the hen will appear in another such crusader image: "the hen and crusader everintermutuomergent" (55.12). Outside "heelgills and collines" play "at a treepurty on the planko in the park" (12.24) and the tree, already associated with romance, next bears its message, "the leaves of the living in the boke of the deeds" (13.30–31), the foliage of "follyages" (8.4) now "fassilwise" (13.32) when committed to writing. Caddy is Shem "who wrote o peace a farce" (14.14) to designate the artist and Shem's fear of battle; Primas is Shaun, who "drilled all decent people" (14.13), just as later Shaun as Butt shoots the Russian General and Shaun typically rails against his acquaintances.

The first clear tree-and-stone identities emerge in the Mutt and Jute dialogue, where Jute, a primitive Shaun, begins asking the questions, confesses that he has problems hearing, which he confuses with eating ("You that side your voise are almost inedible to me"—16.23), offers Jute a symbol of the Druidic ancestors ("have sylvan coyne, a piece of oak"—16.31), blasts Mutt's explanation as Shaun will do with Shem later ("Onheard of and umscene!"—17.15–16). For his part, Mutt-Shem is observed by Jute to have a Joycean "One eyegonblack" (16.29). He acts the role of the teller-artist in recounting the history of life in the park, recommends reading ("He who runes may rede it on all fours"—18.5–6), and observes the stone-aspects of Jute's appearance ("Ore you astoneaged, jute you?"—18.15) while Jute admits to being struck into silence ("Oye am thonthorstrok"—18.16). In the same dialogue Jute unctuously recommends similarity of appearance: "Become a bitskin more wiseable, as if I were you" (16.24–25).

Also in chapter 1, the Prankquean kidnaps the "jiminy Tristopher" (21.21), or Shem, as an accumulation of details indicates *Trist* with its various endings to be Shem. She may work her influence while she has the jiminies away from home, and alter their characters, but while the Pranquean is away with the second jiminy, the first reverts to type; he is Shem the tree, now called "the jiminy Toughertrees" (22.24). This and the previous Mutt-Jute accounts are related in that Mutt cited the "Mearmerge two races" (17.24), and the father-city suffers two attacks by the Prankquean before as a city the Earl defends his "three shuttoned castles" (22.34), and all races—Danish, English, Irish—live in peace.

Where the mourned father figure merits high praise because there was never another like him, it is said that he "could fell an elmstree twelve urchins couldn't ring round and hoist high the stone that Liam failed" (25.30–31); and he evokes not only classical oak of the *Metamorphoses* but also the legends of the twelve stones in the circle around a central monolith, which bowed toward Tara (the seat of Saint Patrick and site of the present *Lia Fail*) with the coming of Saint Patrick. Felling the tree of inexhaustible life and raising high the stone that rests solidly on earth epitomizes human and political-historical strength.

Tree and stone in chapters 2 and 3 illustrate the father figure. Chapter 2 recounts Earwicker's rise and demise told in the terms of tree and stone: "One still hears that pebble crusted laughta; japijap cheerycherrily, among the roadside tree the lady Holmpatrick planted and still one feels the amossive silence of the cladstone allegibelling: Ive mies outs ide [outside] Bourn" (31.29–33). For the living, stone qualities mean despair: age ("fossilyears"—40.10), poverty ("stonybroke"—40.15), and homelessness ("pillowed upon the stone of destiny colder than man's knee or woman's breast"—40.19–20). At the same time, for the dead Gladstone of the monument, an evocation of a tree cult marks all desirability: "under the shadow of the monument of shouldhavebeen legislator (Eleutheriodendron! Spare, woodmann, spare!)" (42.19–20). "The rann that Hosty made" (44.7–8) will be preserved in stone ("piersified") as the ballad tells the story of the father's fall and death.

The third chapter's review of the crime contains a now-familiar consolation for "the humphriad of that fall and rise" (53.9). The viewer is told to dry his tears because "paradigm maymay rererise in eren" (53.13), and then there is an exclamation on sighting the tree and stone: "Lo behold! *La arboro, lo petrusu.* The augustan peacebetothem oaks, the monolith rising stark from the moonlit pinebarren" (53.14–16). One passage clearly explains why the tree has been universally a symbol of inexhaustible life as it passes through the apparent death state (*frore,* German *frozen*) to "cladagain"; on an Irish jaunting car (suggesting the movement of life within a still environment) one might behold "the clad pursue the bare, the bare the green, the green the frore, the frore the cladagain" (55.25–26) and the giant tree (Earwicker) around which all life whirls becomes a symbol of the phoenix and of Vico's cycles. Also in chapter 3 a bit of editorializing about the artist-audience problem recognizes that life turned to stone needs no exotic examples from folklore (as in the example of the stones of the circle, which "sunk" with the coming of Saint Patrick). Here Joyce puns the "obscene" of the fall with the obelisk monument ("obseen") and the Shem-type expression and, on a further level, the "obseen" is the position of the artist who will make the deaf to hear or raise the dead. At the same time Shaun's need to carry the mail, which lurks "dormant in the paunch of a herm, a pillarbox" (66.26–27), combines with his threats and indignation in the term "black mail."

Nor needs none shaft ne stele from Phenicia or Little Asia to obelise on the spout, neither pobaclock neither folksstone, nor sunkenness in Tomar's Wood to bewray how erpressgangs score off the rued. The mouth that tells not will ever attract the unthinking tongue and so long as the obseen draws theirs which hear not [the Shaun-stone type] so long till allearth's dumbnation shall the blind lead the deaf [the artist lead the public]. Tatcho, tawney yeeklings! The column of lumps lends the pattrin of the leaves behind us. If violence to life, limb and chattels, often as not, has been the expression, direct or through an agent male [the role of the artist-Shem], of womanhid offended, (ah! ah!), has not levy of black mail [Shaun and his disapproval] from the times the fairies were in it, and fain or wilde erthe blothoms followed an impressive private reputation for whispered sins? (68.28–69.4).

Those who hear not have not acquired the Joycean view of art's embracing all life, and, refusing to be instructed, continue in ignorance, leaving the blind artist to lead the deaf.

The derivation of the tree-stone from the legends of Finn MacCool emerges as a natural development from an awareness of Irish myth-history. Seumas MacManus writes that the Fenians are known today because "they hung rare tales of themselves on every rowan-tree, and ten thousand great grey rocks that stud the island's face are monuments immortal, proclaiming to the wondering generations, 'Here passed Fionn and his Fian.' "[6] These stones, "a testament of the rocks from all the dead unto some living," (73.32–33) offer the message of the past as well as hope for resurrection as tree: the "skatterlings of a stone . . . shall be gathered unto him . . . in that day hewen . . . he skall wake from earth-sleep, haught crested elmer [elmtree]" (73.34–74.2). The chapter closes with a reassertion of the falling of green leaves to mean "Humph in his doge": "Silence was in thy faustive halls, O Truiga, when thy green woods went dry but there will be sounds of manymirth on the night's ear ringing when our pantriarch of Comestowntonobble gets the pullover on his boots" (74.9–12), and the reawakening will occur with the falling of the rain.

The characteristics of the tree and stone as Shem and Shaun unravel the deceptions of chapter 4 in the trial of Festy King (Earwicker). Prior to that trial Earwicker as a tree fortresses himself, when his powers begin to fail him, with bricks: "He afterwards whaanever his blaether began to fail off him and his rough bark was wholly husky and, stopp by stoop, he neared it (wouldmanspare!) carefully lined the ferroconcrete result with rotproof bricks and mortar, fassed to fossed, and retired beneath the heptarchy of his towerettes" (77.14–19). This is another way of saying he will arise, though the people go through the routine of erecting a grave marker for him. In his burial place in Lough Neagh "portrifaction" (78.21) sets in. Meanwhile Kate Strong of the famous stone monument demonstrates herself a Shaun type through her living in a cottage of "elvanstone" (79.29), carrying the letter and dumping it in the park (80.4–6), and keeping the hen that finds the letter (79.30). The saintly Shaun-Kevin who will observe the hen is "some hastyswasty timberman torchpriest" (80.26–27), that is, he cuts down or burns down trees; "here where race began" and now, at the dropping of the letter, the new god is born of "the ward of the wind that lightened the fire that lay in the wood that Jove bolt, at his rude word" (80.27–28)/(just as, in the ricorso, religious terms and Saint Kevin mark the dawn of the new era). Venturesome children on the "filthdump" are warned to leave things as they are: "Lave that bloody stone as it is! What are you doing your dirty minx and his big treeblock way up your path?" (80.29–30).

At Festy King's trial appears the Wet Pinter, a type "suspected of being a plain clothes priest W.P." (86.33–34) who needs to be "cautioned against yawning" (86.36) and, further signaling his transformation to stone, "was going . . . to decembs within the ephemerides of profane history, all one with Tournay, Yetstoslay and Temorah" (87.6–8) and "he was patrified" (87.11). Other Shaun characteristics are in his edible clothing, his determination to sleep (88.9–9), and his saintliness in his awareness of Saint Patrick's bell (88.10–11). When the interrogation veers to its proper subject—Earwicker (an Yggdrasselmann—88.23)—the fall is described as a "renting of his rocks" (88.26) by "three wicked Vuncouverers Forests bent down awhits" (88.27–28) as Shaun in his affinity for stone defends stone and disparages trees. The questions vary between Shaun (as in "Are you not danzzling on the age of a vulcano? Siar, I am deed—89.28), who again demonstrates his alliance with the "dead" stone, and Earwicker ("And how olld of him?—89.29) who as "up Finn" has a "threehatted ladder" (89.31).

When Pegger Festy steps forward to testify, he has definitely the Shem characteristics as he speaks "through his Brythonic interpreter" (91.3-4) the special language of the poets "in a loudburst of poesy" (91.3), denies that he is Cain ("he did not fire a stone"—91.11–12), suffers a handicap of speaking to a deaf audience ("his lipreaders"—91.17) who want to know why he left Dublin (91.21–22), identifies himself with the Scandinavian hawks ("the moving way of the hawks with his heroes in Warhorror"—91.29–30), and hastily scrambles his Catholic background with the more recently acquired knowledge of the writer; while attempting to "make the sign of the Roman Godhelic faix . . . the laddo had broken exthro Castilian" (91.35–92.1) and he angers his listeners.

I believe the clearest statement on the confused identities of the twins through the similarity of their appearance follows this testimony. "The hilariohoot of Pegger's Windup" (92.6) makes Shem sound like the Hilary-Shaun of the Prankquean episode while "the tristitone of the Wet Pinter's" (92.7) makes Shaun sound like Shem-Tristan "as were they *isce et ille* equals of opposites, evolved by onesame power of nature or of spirit, *iste*, as the sole condition and means of its himundher manifestation and polaraised for reunion by the symphysis of their antipathies" (92.7–11); that is, parents, "himundher" polarities by sex and by temperament, manifest their union in the birth of the sons, who are similar in appearance but opposite by nature. Only the twenty-ninth leapyear girl, Issy herself, who later as a cloud hovers over the brothers' verbal battles, realizes the artist-identity of the last witness and exposes him so that the other "twofromthirty" girls cry "Shun the Punman" (93.13) and protest his "gift of gaft."

At the close of the chapter the disputes and searches end with turning to ALP; she mothers both the stones in her stream and the trees beside her stream: "we have taken our sheet upon her stones where we have hanged our hearts in her trees" (103.9–10).

Chapter 5 deals exclusively with the letter found by Shaun-Kevin's observing the hen Biddy Doran. A bit of tree symbolism ("how palmy date in waste's oasis"—112.26) parenthetically acknowledges that the finding should begin a new era, while being lost in the woods is a jungle of words ("jungle of woods"—112.4). The brothers' characteristics explain the reaction to the letter, with Shaun represented in "I am a worker, a tombstone mason, anxious to pleace averyburies" (113.34–35), and Shaun's denunciation of Shem in "You are a poorjoist, unctuous to polise nopebobbies" (113.35–36).

Chapter 6 begins with Finn MacCool, now of the past, with the height of a tree suggested in the monument: "the first to rise taller through his beanstale than the bluegum buaboababbaun or the giganteous Wellingtonia Sequoia" (126.11–12), and moves through the many characteristics of standing tree and fallen stone. Like the tales told around a camp fire or the tales whispered by the rustling leaves of the tree, the tree itself becomes a symbol of walking the way of life; the placement of a stone monument leaves a record of the paths already covered: "to all his foretellers [varying *forebears*] he [Finn] reared a stone and for all his comethers [co-methers from *meth* meaning *way*, the Fiana or those who made the stories with him] he planted a tree" (135.4–5). His marvelous accomplishments are told in that he "put a matchhead on an aspenstalk and set the living a fire" (131.13–14). The falling of a tree would mean Finn's fall, while his rebirth would come through the awakening of the stone: "he crashed in the hollow of the park, trees down, as he soared in the vaguum of the phoenix, stones up" (136.33–35). Thence Earwicker during the wake exemplifies the same process, "phoenix in our woodlessness," especially with the coincidence of a stone monument of the phoenix in Phoenix Park.

This background unravels a deceptively-simple sentence which on the surface looks like an unauthenticated statement that Finn MacCool was killed by someone named William in West Munster, although "Finn's Grave" is near Westport in County Mayo and West Munster was once a province: "his Tiara of scones was held unfillable till one Liam Fail felled him in Westmunster" (131.9–11). But in the stone context of the *Wake*, the sentence compresses much history and myth. Finn's fall means the fall of Ireland, the loss of the old faith in the *Lia Fail*, the replacement of the kings of Tara in the Boyne valley of provocative stones by the government at Westminster (where British sovereigns are crowned); and, of course, William of Orange fought the battle of the Boyne.

The prospect of the living tree's anticipating new life, as represented in the sleeping-dead-stone, makes the tree and stone a proper meeting place for paramours, as in the seductive tenth-question love letter, where Issy writes, "Hear, pippy, under the limes. You know bigtree are all against gravestone" (146.33–34).

The Gripes as a Shem sits in a tree (153.10–11); the Mookse

as a Shaun on a stone (153.23–24), filling it "quote poposter-
ously." The Gripes hails him with a wish for "Good appetite"
(153.35), claiming to be "blessed" to see him and, teasing him,
asks him to tell "all about aulne and lithial and allsall allinall
about awn and liseias" (154.4–5). Still teasing the Mookse
about his own weakness, the Gripes-Shem asks the time (a
Shaun concern) and receives Shaun's reply of indignation
(154.21–23). Nuvoletta, fluttering over their heads and trying
to appeal to the antagonists' strong points, cannot catch the
gaze of the Mookse-Shaun's far-seeing eyes (157.20–21) nor
make herself heard to the Gripes-Shem (157.22–23); and at the
close of the tale, the Shem-Gripes "had light ears left yet he
could but ill see" (158.13) and the Shaun-Mookse "had a
sound eyes right but he could not all hear" (158.12–13). A
weird woman "with chills at her feet" (158.26) gathers up the
"holy sacred solem" Mookse, and a weird woman with "the
cold in her heed" (158.33) gathers down the "hawker's hank"
Gripes. At their departure there is left "an only elmtree and
but a stone" (159.4).

Professor Jones digresses to a seductive passage on trees
(159.34–160.16) before proceeding to the story of Burrus and
Caseous, in which Burrus, like the Mookse who was "broady
oval" (152.20), has "the reachly roundered head that goes
best with thofthinking defensive fideism" (162.22–3). A Shaun
type, he is famous for his "seeingscraft" (162.30) and as
food he is a "genuine prime" (161.15). Caseous, a Shem-tree
type, is "highstinks aforefelt" (163.9) and "not an ideal
choose by any meals" (161.18–19). As writer, Caseous is identified by "the pawnbreaking pathos of the first of these shod-
dy pieces" (164.23), while the next chapter confirms this
picture of Shem, who "lives on loans" (173.7).

Chapter 7 develops several autobigraphical elements of
Joyce and Shem: his isolation, his exile, his having a brother
"jonathan" similar to "Johns" the butcher. The list of games

played by the children includes "Appletree Bearstone" (176. 8) and "I know a Washerwoman" (176.8–9). The apple as sexual fall, and bear as a sexual term denoting the superior position, offer with "tree and "stone" the rivalry of the two brothers. When the brother Shaun scolds Shem he includes in the castigation the insinuation that the artist spans deathlike winter months (cf. "whistlewhirling your crazy elegies around Templetombmount"—192.34–35) in "Perpending that Putterick O'Purcell [according to Adaline Glasheen, a nineteenth-century mail-coach owner[7] or a Shaun surrogate] pulls the coald stoane out of Winterwater's and Silder Seas sing for Harreng our Keng, sept okt nov dez John Phibbs march!" (187.18–20). Shaun has so far sublimated his stone identity and, as indicated in the earlier discussions of this passage, further disguises it in discussing himself in the third person, using the imagery of the tree: "There grew up beside you (191.9) . . . that other, Immaculatus" (191.13), meaning himself. He incriminates himself with his fury as he attempts to conclude with the final withering blast. "Just a little judas tonic, my ghem of all jokes, to make you go green in the gazer" (193.9–10), and concentrates on their respective skills, "Do you hear what I'm seeing" (193.10), concluding with a prayer that he may "rock anchor through the ages" (193. 25–26).

Because Shaun-Justius has drawn the analogy of the tree, Shem-Mercius, who has patiently listened to this address to "himother" (187.24), subtly alludes to the Two Trees by mentioning one (the one associated with Shaun), and omits himself, who would fit the analogy of the Tree of Life. Shem promises that to Shaun, "firstborn and firstfruit of woe" (194.12), and to himself, "branded sheep" (194.13), and again to Shaun, "winblasted tree of the knowledge of beautiful and-

7. Adaline Glasheen, *A Second Census of Finnegans Wake* (Evanston: Northwestern University Press, 1963), p. 216.

evil" (194.14–15) will come Anna Livia, the "turfbrown mummy" (194.22). Thus he introduces Anna Livia of chapter 8.

Book II develops the characteristics of tree and stone important on all levels: the life and fall of the father figure, the opposing characteristics of the two sons, the union between them of the "sick amour" Issy. Chapter 9 sets the stage with the credits as the Mime opens with Shem-Glugg of the storybooks and Shaun-Chuff of the mails, including "Tree taken for grafted. Rock rent" (221.31–32), the problem with hearing in "Phenician blends and Sourdanian doofpoosts by Shauvesourishe and Wohntbedarft" (221.32–33), trees in "The Oakmulberryeke with silktrick twomesh from Shop-Sowry, seedsmanchap" (221.33–34); and the stone with political implications is "Grabstone" (a pun on Gladstone), while the omphalos appears in "the crack (that's Cork!) by a smoker from the gods" (221.35–36). The three questions addressed to Glugg must be answered negatively because all concern his opposite, the stone (225.22–26). Tree and rock become the opposites of desirability and reality, the extent of the geographic range of possibility and responsibility when Glugg-Shem's failure, with connotations of Earwicker's fall, is felt as "vicereversing thereout from those palms of perfection to anger arbour" (227.19–20); the artist is the "treerack monatan, scroucely out of scout of ocean, virid with woad" (227.20-21); and the girls' reaction of outrage shakes him profoundly: "what tornaments of complementary rages rocked the divlun from his punchpoll to his tummy's shentre as he displaid all the oathword science of his visible disgrace" (227. 21–23). The exclamation "Tholedoth, treetrene!" (*treen* the plural of trees) urges endurance for the disgraced and discouraged Glugg-tree, and celebrates the triumph of the antagonistic Chuff-stone in "Zokrahsing, stone!" (230.26). Shem's next defeat, rather than the triumph of Birnam Wood, is called "a burning would is come to dance inane" (250.16), and the magical "fork of hazel" is predicted as a weapon of Shaun, a "blasting rod" (250.25). Tree and stone are not only the bourns of two places, or of space and time, in "on the hike from Elmstree to Stene and back" (247.4–5), but also an exhibition of Shem-Jeremy-Glugg's rhetorical talents:

> Jeremy, the chastenot coulter, the flowing taal that brooks no brooking runs on to say how, as it was mutualiter foretold of him by a timekiller to his spacemaker, velos ambos and arubyat knychts, with their tales within wheels and stucks between spokes; on the hike from Elmstree to Stene and back, how, running awage with the use of reason (sics) and ramming amok at the brake of his voice (secs), his lasterhalft [Shaun-Chuff-stone] was set for getting the besterwhole of his yougentougend, for control number thrice [in Morton Prince's *Dissociation of a Personality*] was operating the subliminal of his invaded personality." (246.36–247. 1–9)

The chapter closes with two kinds of time; tree time for the living reads "from generation unto generation" and stone time for the past remains a memorial for ever, but never do the two exist in time as one. The children's prayer begins "Till tree from tree, tree among trees, tree over tree become stone to stone, stone between stones, stone under stone for ever" (259.1–2).

Chapter 10, with its children's concern with growth and with Issy's undeniable presence, develops trees at the expense of stones, but tree and stone together represent the going and coming of continual existence: "Ever a-going, ever a-coming. Between a stare and a sough [sight and sound]. Fossilisation, all branches. Wherefore Petra [stone] sware unto Ulma [elm tree]: By the mortals' frost! And Ulma sware unto Petra: On my veiny life!" (264.10–14). The Irish landscape offers orchards of laurels, ash, chestnut, thorn, mulberry, elm, and hedges of ivy and holly, and a bower of mistletoe, while stone work appears in the "king's house," the mill, and the tombshape" (264.25-265.17). "Una Unica," a "one of charmers," marks the beginning of life, but the stone foreshadows its end in "under the branches of the elms, in shoes as yet unshent by stoniness" (267.25–27). The children's history lesson includes "Eat early earthapples" (271.24); and the familiar "House That Jack Built" rhyme as a cosmic metaphor includes the delightful temptation of Eve in the beautiful garden: "This is the glider that gladdened the girl that list to the wind that lifted the leaves that folded the fruit that hung on the tree that grew in the garden Gough gave" (271.25–29). The "datetree," which "leafeth earlier than every growth" (274.16–17), bears the date 1132. Through tree and stone, in varied phrasings, the children learn that "in the midst of life we are in death," so that the thought intrudes like a third personality (Morton Prince) on their lives, and awareness of death descends like hail: "We have wounded our way on foe tris prince till that force in the gill is faint afarred and the face in the treebark feigns afear. This is rainstones ringing. Strangely cult for this ceasing of the yore. But Erigureen is ever" (278.25–279.3). Since *gill* was anciently the ground-ivy but also in Icelandic meant a woody glen with a rivulet running through it, and gill associates with the salmonfilled Liffey, the "force in the gill" also suggests creativity on at least three levels. Through the divisiveness of the present age ("this ceasing of the yore") and out of the rituals of the past ("strangely cult"), Erin continues green ("Erigureen is ever"). At home Anna Livia, "our lavy in waving" (275.12) with "birchleaves her jointure," honors the birch as the Beth-Luis-Nion first month. She and Earwicker, called by the children "Airyanna and Blowyhart," inhabit the "palace of quicken boughs" of Irish myth,[8] while the trees as

8. Patrick Weston Joyce, *Old Celtic Romance* (New York: Devin-Adair, 1962), pp. 123–53.

poetry or message sing "tomorrows gone and yesters outcome" (208.6–7).

Chapter 10 distinguishes Dolph as Shem, for his relationship with the stone is "meager suckling of gert stoan," and this compares with a similarly degrading use of "suck" when Shaun in turn swigs a "slug of Jon Jacobsen from his treestem sucker cane" (424.27–28). Shem is "druider" (288.5), a "twicedhecame time" (288.14), representing not only the exile's return but also the two—Danish and English—invasions of Ireland. All Irish history is therefore seen through the narrator's description, including the arrival of Saint Patrick (288. 22), whose "cultous is very prevailend" up to the present time "in spite of all the bloot, all the braim, all the brawn, all the brile, that was shod" (288.25–27), so that "the prence di Propagandi" remains "the pillar of the perished and the rock o'ralereality" (289.2–4). Tree and stone together surround the diagram in the "lapis" (293.11), who is the Father City marked by "the Turnpike under the Great Elm" (293.13–14), which has the famous "Mearingstone in Foreground" (293. 14–15). Shem's revelation of the sexual universe leaves him "floored on his plankraft of shittim wood" (301.23–24), where the knowledge of the artist (touch wood) becomes a warning, "Sink deep or touch not the Cartesian spring!"; for Shem's revelations threaten the dignity of both country ("laying siege to goblin castle"—301.27) and religion, with the devout climb up stony Croagh Patrick ("lying sack to croakpartridge"—301.29–30), a method of ridiculing Shaun as Saint Patrick and partridge.

Chapter 11 in its long tale of the Norwegian Captain elaborates in a convoluted fashion, on the personal level, the story of Earwicker's arrival by boat in his courting of Anna Livia, that which the washerwoman phrased "In a gabbard he barqued it, the boat of life, from the harbourless Ivernikan Okean" (197.28–29), with the garment fashioned over the hump, "his

cameleer's burnous" (197.34), as loosely flowing as the "peer
of trouders under the pattern of a cassack" (311.29). On a
national level the story details the development of the city or
country, with Earwicker's fall representing the fall of the
realm to England and his "hiberniating after seven oak ages"
(316.14–15)—the seven centuries of British rule. The number
three frequently describes Earwicker, as in Finn's three hats
or three-faced stone head, and may refer to the three races—
Firbolgs, Fomorians, and Tuatha de Danaan—of the past,
or the Irish, Danish, and English backgrounds of the nation
as in "And three's here's for repeat of the unium" (317.29).
"Three climbs threequickenthrees in the garb of nine" (377.
11–12) alludes to the national identity of Earwicker and to Dermot's escape in the quicken tree as well as to the continuing
nationalism in the mystical nine.

The demise of Earwicker, a petrification process signaled
by deficient hearing, engenders a corresponding disappointment for Anna Livia. The existence of the tree, however, always reassures those who have lost hope. At the close of the
Norwegian Captain story, "He's herd of hoarding [hard of
hearing] and her faiths is altared. Becoming ungoing, their
seeming sames for though that liamstone deaf do his part
there's a windtreetop whipples the damp off the mourning"
(331.3–6). The tree-stone coexistence shows the continual process of being-becoming, coming-going, fall-rise.

Taff can be distinguished as Shem with the vegetation and
free-thinking of "peat freers," his tree-top orientation in
"looking through the roof towards a relevution" (338.5–6) and
his use of an "umberolum" for the "rhyttel in his hedd" (338.
7–8). Taff, like Mutt with his one-eye-gone-black, is a "blackseer" (340.13). Taff addresses Shaun-Butt in terms of the
butcher and the hen Biddy Moriarty, "All was flashing and
krashning blurty moriartsky blutcherudd?" (338.8–9); and
Butt as a "pied friar" claims the foot and stone identity of

Shaun, especially as he later acts the part of "dodewodedook" (340.20). Taff addresses Butt as "scattering giant's hail over the curseway" (343.6–7), or creating the Giant's Causeway, and Butt speaks of himself as saint and stone monument in imagining the Russian General's defecation in terms of "perished popes, the reverend and allaverred cromlecks" (343.30–31). Butt as the mail carrier gestures "by mailbag mundaynism" (350.11–12). Butt's statement, "I shuttm, missus, like a wide sleever!" (352.14), places squarely on him the blame for shooting the Russian General and identifies him with the clergy, whose garments have wide sleeves. At the close of the drama, Butt and Taff take their bows together, with the stage direction "now one and the same person" indicating the calm at the end of the play's strife; but their likeness to the samurai, who wore two swords each (as in "samuraised twimbs," 354.23–24), indicates perpetual strife. The stage-direction interlude offers life itself, symbolized by the genitals, in "testies touchwood and shenstone" (332.12–13);[9] and this concept is repeated in the "tree of livings in the middenst of the garerden" (350.2), or the Phoenix Park's midden and "the lepers inhabit in the place of the stones" (350.4).

Chapter 12, while it develops the Tristan-Mark-Isolde love story, most frequently describes the sycamores on the landscape (384.1,388.24), for "they were all sycamore" (397.23), while Isolde is "deaf with love" (395.29), and the sturdiness of the oak appropriately suggests a proper staff for that emotion: "whiteboys and oakboys, peep of tim boys and piping tom boys, raising hell while the sin was shining" (385.9–11).

9. For a discussion of this passage as wood for heterosexual and stone for homosexual activity, see Solomon, p. 70. Touching wood in folklore may mean knocking to scare off evil spirits or to summon aid of Druidic wood nymphs; after boasting, knocking counteracts the envy of the spirit, abiding in wood, who should have been honored; and touching wood may date from a religious habit of touching a wooden crucifix while taking an oath. One would shun stone because of its associations with death.

Although Shem does not die in the novel, Shaun does in chapters 13 and 15, and, in regard to the tree-stone controversy, this is the major significance of book III. In chapter 13 the descriptions, some of them representing Joyce's best humor, support Shaun's role as saint; in general the conditions are now familiar, with his "handpalm lifted" (407.23) as in blessing, his final sleep suggested in "Shaun yawned" (407.28), his residence in his houseful of deadheads" (407.35–36), his exhaustion as total "as winded hare, utterly spent" (408.4). Like the proverbial reaching for floating straws, his declarations of continuing life, based on tree imagery ("I am awful good, I believe, so I am, at the root of me"—411.13), only emphasize the hopelessness of his case. He readily admits having painted the town a "wearing greenridinghued" (411.24), and to say he was wrong to do so would be a "freudful mistake" (411.35–36), because he bases his thinking on the "prophecies" and his purpose was to demonstrate "new worlds for all!" (412.2). In his scorn of the sinful letter and its provocative subject he asserts "there were treefellers in the shrubrubs" (420.08) to spy on the crime, and he acknowledges the continuing life in tree marked by stone: "Their livetree (may it flourish!) by their ecotaph (let it stayne!)" (420.11–12). In denouncing Shem he calls attention to the head and the lack of the solid footing (since feet are Shaun's strong point): "The alum that winters on his top is the stale of the staun that will soar when he stambles till that hag of the coombe rapes the pad off his lock" (423.23–35), and he adds "Never mind his falls feet and his tanbark complexion" (423.28–29). One of his means of denigrating Shem is his announcement, "'Tis pebils before Sweeney's" (424.26–27) as he swigs "a slug of Jon Jacobsen from his treestem sucker cane" (424.27–28).

The first page of chapter 14, describing the newly risen Jaunty Jaun, contains four references to feet, which are the last part of him to return to life, "for far and wide, as large as he was lively, was he noted for his humane treatment of any kind of abused footgear" (429.6–8). Also, one of the best examples of tree-stone antinomies occurs in chapter 14 where Shaun meets the "twentynine hedge daughters" (430.1) who are "learning their antemeridian lesson of life, under its tree, against its warning" (430.4–5) when they spy the risen Shaun (Jaun), "the first human yellowstone landmark" (430.6). In his attempts to disparage love and trees, he cannot avoid linking them. He recites a history of sinful sequence intended to frighten Issy away from the love; the fallen ever-green tree under the auspices of "the stardaft journalwriter" (439.10) then becomes a barrel (he "fellhim the firtree out"—439.11) on which two lovers sit, and (like Mark and Isolde) they are uncle and niece: "my grandydad's lustiest sat his seat of unwisdom with my tante's petted sister for the cause of his joy!" (439.13–14). The use of his "best pair of galloper's heels" (457. 13–14) he intends for punishment of his enemies, and the girls acknowledge the importance of his footwear in saying farewell to "dearest Haun of all, you of the boots" (472.20–21). Issy in her letter asserts the unfixed boundaries of her love, "Till the ulmost of all elmoes shall stele our harts asthone!" (460.16–17). Shaun imagines himself hearing stones—as mail carrier and stone in "Do mailstanes mumble?" (462.25). His tirade against Shem, an undeniable Eire-man (Mr. R. E. Meehan), includes insinuations of his leaving the country ("there's not so much green in his Ireland's eye—466.34–35) at the same time his nationality cannot be overlooked when he wears "the schamlooking leaf" which he has disgraced, the "national umbloom!" (467.10–11). Ridiculing Shem's voice (the gracehoper), Shaun claims the brother "stones out of stune" (466.35–36); but the autobiographical elements of exile and missing teeth appear when Shem is "lost Dave the Dancekerl, a squamous runaway" (462.17–18) and when the "bark is still there but the molars are gone" (467.1). Shaun lent Shem the "misery billyboots" (467.1) that leaked, Shaun's Irish ancestor who went "stomebathred" (467.15), as Shaun will do later when he is Saint Kevin, used to scotch Shem's tongue, but "it's all deafman's duff" to Shaun (467.17), who wishes to "cannonise his dead feet" (467.21–22); but the cannon Shaun would choose for Shem would blast him into outer space, "by thinking himself into the fourth dimension and place the ocean between his and ours" (467.22–23). With his deficient hearing he of course hears through his feet, and even the middle toe encourages his fabulous appetite: "I hereby hear by ear from by seeless socks 'tis time to be up and ambling. Mymiddle toe's mitching, so mizzle I must else 't will sarve me out" (468.24–27). Tree imagery, in the form of Earwicker as the hump of Howth, his sleeping stage, signals Shaun's departure, by way of sea, where the whale's spout is a tree: "I feel like that hill of a whaler . . . with his tree full of seaweeds" (469.15–17).

Chapter 15, in its presentation of the cosmic tree (503–6) with the flagstone beside it, summarizes all the characteristics here set forth. Its standing "foreninst us" (504.5) offers at the present time the same pattern as that of Finn MacCool who, to all his foretellers, reared a tree; the birds "sweenyswinging" recalls Sweeny, who lived in trees; the apples continually fall as "epples playing hopptociel bommptaterre" (504.24); the Kilmainham pensioners become "killmaimthem" to throw "milestones" up at the fruit; there is both holly and ivy ("hollow mid ivy") while the woman in slithering satin dress becomes identified with the snake (505.7–8). Even the Ondt is there (505.12). At the same time, one remembers the flagstone that Oisin tried to lift on his return to Ireland from the Land-of-Youth, and this flagstone, "too hard parted" (505.23), laments the dead Ireland of the past. The passage that questions the "extraoldandairy" qualities of the tree finds for answer its distinction "amengst menlike trees walking [Shem] or trees like angels weeping [a modulation toward Shaun's saintliness]" (505.16–17) and, as a world tree embracing all types, moves into Shaunish threats with "rocked of agues, cliffed for aye!" (505.17–18). Is that the "treeth"? The answer "Mushe, mushe of a mixness (505.20) alludes to Saint Patrick (cf. "mishe mishe to tauftauf thuartpeatrick"—3.9–10), who offers a mixed truth, for certainly the Archdruid who opposes him has much of truth on his side also. The falling of the trees "remounts to the sense arrest" (505.31). Adam's fall makes him "the foerst of our treefellers" (506.15–16).

Earwicker's seven trees as he tells about his "Seven ills" (541.1) mark the story of his life, beginning with his "bathtub of roundwood" (542.5) and his shouting through "longertubes of elm" (542.6–7). His threat to "feshest cheoilboys" in the rod of chastisement is the birch, because their "feshness" calls for "the song of a birtch" (543.9–10). His undesirable activities, represented in the ash, consist of taking advantage of "unfortunates against dilapidating ashpits" (544.13–14). The rowan berries, expected to restore youth, provide him nourishment ("Rowntrees and dumplings"—544.35); his enemies have "hearts of Oak" (545.36); and his demise in "clayed sheets" is "pineshrouded" (546.1). Seeming to close his tale, since he has lived as tree, he can point to the stone, "upon the altarstane. May all have mossyhonours!"(552.30); but after cheers from the Four he begins boasting about his dominance of Anna Livia, and this becomes a metaphor for the building of Dublin City. As "her chastener" (553.1) he whipped her into shape; he taught her the alphabet (government) "from alderbirk to tannenyou [alder, birch, to oak and yew]" (553.3), planted for her " a quickset vineyard" fenced with "huge Chesterfield elms," and so on until his family life becomes a metaphor for the founding of the city, including the park and the streets ("my stony battered waggonways"—553.29–30); and Anna's rippling laughter continues through his rule of the city—a dramatizing of the motto "The obedience of the citizens is the good of the town," for always "for her pleashadure: and she lalaughed in her diddydid domino to the switcheries of the whip" (554.7–8). Chapter 16 develops those many images of trees appropriate for the young persons of the Earwicker household. As a meeting place and record the phallic stone ("effigy of standard royal"—567.10) marks Dublin, the Phoenix Park, and the place where Anna Liffey meets the tide (Sara's Bridge): "I show because I must see before my misfortune so a stark pointing pole. Lord of ladders, what for lungitube! Can you read the verst legend hereon? I am hather of the missed. Areed! To the dunleary obelisk via the rock vhat myles knox furlongs; to the general's postoffice howsands of patience; to the Wellington memorial half a league wrongwards; to Sara's bridge good hunter and nine to meet her: to the point, one yeoman's yard" (566.33–567.4). The Watcher's trip to a leaf-embowered outhouse combines with love-making, religion, and watching the children sleep, so that "you become quite crimstone in the face" (570.34), offers several possible meanings other than the most obvious of exertion with defecation.

In Chapter 17 Saint Kevin is certainly Shaun, the gastronome saint. Kevin is "increate God the servant" (604.27), "fond of stones, friend of gnewgnawns bones" (605.1). The romantic qualities of leaves appear, appropriately, with Victoria and Albert at Glendalough, the place of Saint Kevin's hermitage, where "an alomdree begins to green, soreen seen for loveseat" (600.20–21). But Shaun-Kevin encloses himself in stone to contemplate "the regeneration of all man by affusion of water" (606.11–12). Actually it is a place of many gravestones and stone crosses ("slab slobs, immermemorial," and "so boulder"—600.26–27), and the juxtaposition of stone with tree at Glendalough acts as a sobering religious influence on the forward thrust of romantic green: "But, while gleam with gloom swan here and there, this shame rock and that whispy planter tell Paudheen Steel-the Poghue and his perty Molly Vardant, in goodbroomirish, arrah, this place is a propper and his feist a ferial for communial" (600.30–34). The tree being grown here, "the poplarest wood in the entire district . . . eminently adapted for the requirements of pacnincstricken humanity" (599.26–28) Cambell and Robinson interpret as a World Tree.[10] Abiding through the Viconian ricorso, tree and stone mean the dawn of a new era, which to Saint Kevin "begins in feint to light his legend" (603.35–36). In the same way that whatever is sealed in stone remains to be revealed (or, as Anna says, "the lausafire has lost and the book of the depth is. Closed"—621.2–3), the anticipated fullness of life in the new era rises out of recognition that the secrets of the past are yet unrevealed: "The vinebranch of Heremonheber on Bregia's plane where Teffia lies is leaved invert and fructed proper but the cublic hatches endnot open yet for hourly rincers' mess. Read Higgins, Cairns and Egen. Malthus is yet lukked in close" (604.3–7).

To switch to Earwicker himself, the scene "bevels to rock's rite" (606.13), where that family tree was socerdatal" (607. 6), befitting the liturgical dawn-of-creation tone of the ricorso. The introduction to the Earwicker twins Shem and Shaun includes the tree, a "house with heaven roof" (609.13) and the stone, "staneglass on stonegloss" (609.15). Muta is clearly Shaun when he expresses typically unctuous disapproval of Shem-Juva: "He odda be thorly well ashamed of himself for smoking before the high host" (609.26–27). He exclaims in Latin-stony fashion "Petrificationibus!"(610.3), and borrows a pen-weapon from Juva (610.30–31). Shem-Juva

10. Joseph Campbell and Henry Morton Robinson, *A Skeleton Key to Finnegans Wake* (New York: Viking, 1961), p. 342, n. 10.

responds with tree-orientation to the Latin form of petrification: "Beleave filmly, beleave!" (610.5). Shaun as Saint Patrick has deficient hearing ("comprehendurient"—611.30–31) as a part of his stony nature (enduring) in the discussion with the Archdruid-Shem; Shaun typically imagines Leary as something edible and having a tree with a "verdant readyrainroof belongahim" (612.3) and "plenty laurel leaves" (612.5). Shaun-Saint Patrick addresses Shem as the poet seer, "Bigseer" (612.16), which may be compared with Taff as "*a blackseer*" (340.13) in the Butt-Taff episode. Saint Patrick exposes his identity while expostulating his and God's virtues and while closing his speech with a very heathenish kind of sunworship-praise of the Father, Son, and the Holy Ghost, whom he calls "firethere the sun in his halo cast" (612.30); but Shaun-Patrick is frequently associated with fire.

Anna Livia's final soliloquy acknowledges the artist-Shem's tree affiliations in "the birds start their treestirm shindy" (621.35–36). For her the mystical hazel as continuing life acquires sexual connotations when she remembers her romance with Earwicker: "With you drawing out great aims to hazel me from the hummock with your sling" (622.18–19). Earwicker is her tree: "One time you'd stand fornenst me, fairly laughing, in your bark and tan billows of branches for to fan me cooly" (626.21–23). She wants to be called "Leafiest" (624.22); first she loves her "loveleavest dress" and later cherishes the last leaf that floats upon her outgoing waters. The years of the past, those lifelong, lovelong years, are "allbeleaved" (625.30).

5

"Treely and rurally" (90.31)

The artist's romantic longings, like treetop sighings and the freedom of the fabulous artificer, Joyce phrased as "fain for wilde erthe blothoms" (69.4), and the washerwomen's "later Lammas" necessarily includes "a field of faery blithe as this flowing wild" (281.3). Joyce, choosing to soar beyond the limited vision of the Dodds, but not too far to have his wings scorched by the fire of the sun, builds the labyrinth of *Finnegans Wake* from such common associations as the hawklike man and the hawk in the world tree. Opposing the hawk and confined to earth, the hen scratches in the midden, the foundation level of the Shaun-stone parabola, which arches in the saints Kevin and Patrick. The latter's native name in Wales (*Maenwyn*) meant "Sacred Stone,"[1] and the name's Latin and Greek origins formed the rock of the Catholic church. Bayley notes "The French for rock is *pierre*, Father Fire"[2] and adds "In *peuhen*, a Breton name for *menhir*, one may recognise the Celtic *hen*, meaning *ancient*; the remaining syllable *peu* may no doubt be equated with *pa.*"[3] Earwicker as father city suffers "his X ray picture turned out in wealthy red in the sabbath sheets"

1. Harold Bayley, *The Lost Language of Symbolism* (New York: Barnes and Noble, 1912), 2: 176.
2. *Ibid.*, p. 175.
3. *Ibid.*, p. 176.

(530.8–9) to mark both the red of the church and crusades against sin. Of his proper, stonelike, crusading son, not only does Kevin's finding the literary-litter-letter provide him with "a motive for future saintity" (110.34) but also as mail carrier he belongs with Patrick; he is "a litterydistributer in Saint Patrick's Lavatory" (530.10–11). Yawn in the chapter 15 inquiry is addressed as "Mr Trickpat" (487.23), a syllabic transposition of Patrick. The children's lessons offer a related sequence of topics: "How to Understand the Deaf, Should Ladies learn Music or Mathematics? Glory be to Saint Patrick! What is to be found in a Dustheap" (307.20–23). Shaun typically would fondle "one of his cowheel cuffs" (410.31–32) so that, between Shem's urge to travel and Shaun's maledicted feet, by the time Anna Livia in the ricorso's new beginning remarks "Heel trouble and heal travel" (620.13), she foresees the dual identities of the sons.

A famous traveler of Ireland, Tristan, that "sad hero" (398.29), fled "Muster Mark," who "hasn't got much of a bark" (383.2), either of sound or tree. A syllabically transposed Tristan in the "tantrist spellings" (571.7) of tree messages derives from Tristan's having adopted the name Tantrist to disguise himself while seeking Isolde's help without revealing his identity as her brother's murderer; the term also associates Tristan with trees, as does "triste to death, all his dark ivytod." Shem, with delicate preferences "via foodstuff" (170.26), has a "bladder tristended" (169.20). But the variants of "trist" confuse several dialogues. The suspicious Four who conduct the chapter 15 inquiry of Shaun have their doubts about his name (at one point one remarks "That's never the postal cleric"—485.36—to which Shaun eventually answers "I never dramped of prebeing a postman but I mean in ostralian someplace"—488.19–20), and once they address him as "my tristy minstrel" (521.22), to which Shaun capably replies with metaphors of gastric disturbances. When Luke inquires, "Are you roman cawthrick 432?" (486.1–2), Shaun answers

> Quadrigue my yoke.
> Triple my tryst.
> Tandem my sire.   (486.3–5)

thereby spelling out the geography of four provinces, three nationalities (or three nets of city, church, and state against which Stephen Dedalus rebelled), and the tandem father figures of church and state or the druidic faith being replaced by that of Patrick. When the inquirer responds, he agrees with this summary of the history of Ireland: "History as her is harped. Too the toone your owldfrow lied of. Tantris, hattrick, tryst and parting, by vowelglide!" (486.6–7). Here "Tantris" in the context just examined reveals the "oak sad" fall of Finn, and "hattrick" in apposition to "Tantris" refers to the three hats—like Finn's three hats— the nation wears: English, Danish, Irish. Applied to Saint Patrick and the Archdruid (if "hattrick" is to be read as a variant of Patrick), "Tantris" relates to the oak of the druid displaced by Patrick. In the same away "tryst and parting," with its linguistic analogy ("by vowelglide"), marks the national English-Irish meeting and parting or the religious druid-Catholic meeting and parting.

To summarize, I believe the common associations on which Joyce based this novel include items as familiar as the first Psalm's description of the godlike man: "And he shall be like a tree planted by the rivers of water." In tree and stone Joyce could embody the philosophy of the young Stephen of the *Portrait* ("The past is consumed in the present and the present is living only because it brings forth the future"—*AP* 251) and thereby present a view of imminent creation, a process "patrified" at the precise instant when "follyages" (8.4) become "fassilwise" (13.32), or the message assumes completed form, the "stoppress from domday's erewold" (588.33–34). Joyce, consequently, chooses for his hero not Cuchulain of the *Tain* but Finn MacCool, of whom an ancient authentic manuscript prior to *The Colloquy of the Old Men* has never been found and whose exploits, therefore, have not been "patrified." Regarding the twin sons, the eternal mother of the past has known them to be "as doffered as nors in soun" (620.16), but north is certainly distinguishable from south and noise is connotatively distinguishable from sound. Most important, I believe Joyce would not close a central chapter developed carefully with "baith our washwives," and with a transformation into life-and-death opposites of tree and stone, without fully intending that they have distinguishing characteristics that bear on the entirety of the novel. The washerwoman who is Miss Doddpebble is also deaf-dead-stone-Shaun-Justius, who "points the deathbone and the quick are still" (193.29). The washerwoman who is Mrs. Quickenough is also blind seer-quick-tree-Shem-Mercius, who "lifts the lifewand and the dumb speak" (195.5).

Bibliography to Part Two

Atherton, James S. *The Books at the Wake*. London: Faber and Faber, 1959.

Bayley, Harold. *Archaic England*. Philadelphia: J. B. Lippincott, 1920.

———. *The Lost Language of Symbolism*. New York: Barnes and Noble, 1912.

Beckett, Samuel, et al. *Our Exagmination Round His Factification for Incamination of Work in Progress*. New York: New Directions, 1939.

Benstock, Bernard. "A Covey of Clerics in Joyce and O'Casey." *James Joyce Quarterly* 2, no. 1 (1964): 18–32.

———. "*Exiles:* 'Paradox Lust' and Lost Paladays.'" *English Literary History* 36 (December 1969): 739–56.

———. *Joyce-again's Wake*. Seattle: Washington University Press, 1965.

———. "The Quiddity of Shem and the Whatness of Shaun." *James Joyce Quarterly* 1, no. 1 (1963): 26–33.

Beja, Morris. "The Wooden Sword: Threatener and Threatened in the Fiction of James Joyce." *James Joyce Quarterly* 2, no. 1 (1964): 33–41.

Bonheim, Helmut. *A Lexicon of the German in Finnegans Wake*. Berkeley: University of California Press, 1967.

Campbell, Joseph, and Robinson, Henry Morton. *A Skeleton Key to Finnegans Wake*. New York: Viking Press, 1961.

Crookshank, Ann. "The River Gods." *Ireland of the Welcomes* 19, no. 3 (1970): 23–26.

Ellmann, Richard. *James Joyce*. New York: Oxford University Press, 1965.

236

Epstein, Edmund L. "Interpreting *Finnegans Wake:* A Half-Way House." *James Joyce Quarterly* 3, no. 4 (1966): 252–71.

———. "Tom and Tim." *James Joyce Quarterly* 6, no. 2 (1969): 158–62.

Evans-Wentz, Walter Y. *The Fairy Faith in Celtic Countries.* London: University Books, 1966.

Gilbert, Stuart, ed. *The Letters of James Joyce.* New York: Viking Press, 1957.

Glasheen, Adaline. *A Second Census of Finnegans Wake.* Evanston: Northwestern University Press, 1963.

Graves, Robert. *The Greek Myths.* Baltimore: Penguin Books, 1955.

———. *The White Goddess.* New York: Vintage, 1958.

———. and Patai, Raphael. *Hebrew Myths: The Book of Genesis.* New York: McGraw Hill, 1963.

Halley, Harry H. *Bible Handbook.* Chicago: Henry H. Halley, 1957.

Hart, Clive, ed. *James Joyce's Dubliners.* New York: Viking Press, 1969.

———. *Structure and Motif in Finnegans Wake.* Evanston: Northwestern University Press, 1962.

Higginson, Fred. *Anna Livia Plurabelle: The Making of a Chapter.* Minneapolis: University of Minnesota Press, 1960.

Joyce, Patrick Weston. *Old Celtic Romance.* New York: The Devin-Adair Company, 1962.

Kelleher, John V. "Notes on *Finnegans Wake* and *Ulysses.*" *The Analyst* 10 (March 1956): 2.

Killanin, Lord, and Duignan, Michael V. *The Shell Guide to Ireland.* New York: Norton, 1967.

Kuh, Katherine, "The Circuitous Odyssey of Irish Art." *Saturday Review* 23 (March 1968): 26–33.

Litz, A. Walton. *The Art of James Joyce: Method and Design in Ulysses and Finnegans Wake.* New York: Oxford University Press, 1961.

MacCulloch, John Arnott. *Eddic: The Mythology of All Races.* New York: Cooper Square, 1964.

McManus, Seumas. *The Story of the Irish Race.* New York: The Devin-Adair Company, 1964.

Morse, J. Mitchell. "HCE's Chaste Ecstasy." *Yale Review* 56 (March 1967): 397–405.

Mould, D. D. C. Pochin. *Ireland of the Saints.* London: B. T. Batsford, 1953.

Murphy, Seamus. *Stone Mad*. London: Routledge & Kegan Paul, 1966.

O Hehir, Brendan. *A Gaelic Lexicon for Finnegans Wake*. Berkeley: University of California Press, 1967.

Rees, Alwyn, and Rees, Brinley. *Celtic Heritage*. London: Thames and Hudson, 1961.

Scholes, Robert. "James Joyce, Irish Poet." *James Joyce Quarterly* 2, no. 4 (1965): 255–70.

Shawcross, John T. "'Tilly' and Dante." *James Joyce Quarterly* 7, no. 1 (1969): 61–64.

Solomon, Margaret. *Eternal Geomater*. Carbondale: Southern Illinois University Press, 1969.

Torchiana, Donald T. "Joyce's 'Eveline' and the Blessed Margaret Mary Alacoque." *James Joyce Quarterly* 6, no. 1 (1968): 22–28.

Index

239